Presented to ....

....

From ....

Date ....

Goodword Books

Tell Me About the Prophet Muhammad (HB)

Tell Me About the Prophet Muhammad (PB)

Tell Me About the Prophet Musa (HB)

Tell Me About Hajj (HB)

Tell Me About Hajj (PB)

Honeybees that Build Perfect Combs

The World of Our Little Friends, the Ants

Life Begins (PB)

The First Man (HB)

The First Man (PB)

The Two Brothers (HB)

The Two Brothers (PB)

The Ark of Nuh (HB)

The Ark of Nuh (PB)

The Brave Boy (PB)

Allah's Best Friend (PB)

The Travels of the Prophet Ibrahim

The Origin of Life (Colouring Book)

The First Man on the Earth (Colouring Book)

The Two Sons of Adam (Colouring Book)

The Ark of Nuh and the Animals (Colouring Book)

The Brave Boy (Colouring Book)

Allah's Best Friend (Colouring Book)

The Travels of the Prophet Ibrahim (Colouring Book)

The Ark of Nuh and the Great Flood (Sticker Book)

The Story of the Prophet Nuh (HB)

The Story of the Prophet Nuh (PB)

The Blessings of Ramadan (PB)

The Story of Prophet Yusuf

Stories from the Quran

The Holy Mosques

The Holy Quran (PB)

The Holy Quran (Laminated Board)

The Holy Quran (HB)

A Dictionary of Muslim Names

The Most Beautiful Names of Allah (HB)

The Most Beautiful Names of Allah (PB)

The Pilgrimage to Makkah

One Religion

Islamic Economics

The Story of Islamic Spain (PB)

The Travels of Ibn Battuta

Humayun Nama

Islamic Sciences

Islamic Thought...

The Qur'an for Astronomy

Arabic-English Dictionary for Advanced Learners

The Spread of Islam in the World

A Handbook of Muslim Belief

The Muslims in Spain

The Moriscos of Spain

Spanish Islam (A History of the Muslims in Spain)

A Simple Guide to Muslim Prayer

A Simple Guide to Islam

A Simple Guide to Islam's Contribution to Science

The Quran, Bible and Science

Islamic Medicine

Islam and the Divine Comedy

The Travels of Ibn Jubayr

The Arabs in History

Decisive Moments in the History of Islam

My Discovery of Islam

Islam At the Crossroads

The Spread of Islam in France

The Islamic Art and Architecture

The Islamic Art of Persia

The Hadith for Beginners

How Greek Science Passed to Arabs

Islamic Thought and its Place in History

Muhammad: The Hero As Prophet

A History of Arabian Music

A History of Arabic Literature

The Quran

Selections from the Noble Reading

The Koran

Allah is Known Through Reason

The Miracle in the Ant

The Miracle in the Immune System

The Miracle of Creation in Plants

The Miracle in the Spider

Eternity Has Already Begun

Timelessness and the Reality of Fate

Ever Thought About the Truth?

Crude Understanding of Disbelief

Quick Grasp of Faith

Death Resurrection Hell

The Basic Concepts in the Quran

The Moral Values of the Quran

Heart of the Koran

Muhammad: A Mercy to All the Nations

The Sayings of Muhammad

The Beautiful Commands of Allah

The Beautiful Promises of Allah

The Muslim Prayer Encyclopaedia

After Death, Life!

Living Islam: Treading the Path of Ideal

A Basic Dictionary of Islam

The Muslim Marriage Guide

GCSE Islam—The Do-It-Yourself Guide

The Soul of the Quran

Presenting the Quran

The Wonderful Universe of Allah

The Life of the Prophet Muhammad

History of the Prophet Muhammad

A-Z Steps to Leadership

The Essential Arabic

A Case of Discovery

A HANDBOOK OF
MUSLIM
BELIEF

DR. AHMAD A. GALWASH

Goodword
B·O·O·K·S

First published in 2001
© Goodword Books 2002
Reprinted 2001 (twice), 2002

Goodword Books Pvt. Ltd.
1, Nizamuddin West Market
New Delhi 110 013
Tel. 435 5454, 435 6666
Fax 435 7333, 435 7980
e-mail: info@goodwordbooks.com
www.goodwordbooks.com

Contents

PART ONE

PRACTICAL DEVOTIONS

1

Prayers to God

Pronouncing the Formula of the Faith

After whole-heartedly believing that Allah is one, having no partner, or son, and that Muhammad was chosen as His Prophet and Messenger to announce God's word to mankind, it is the religious duty of every believer embracing Islam to perfom the practical devotions of the religion.

1. The first and foremost of these is to pronounce publicly the formula of the faith as follows:

> "I bear witness that there is no deity save Allah, and that Muhammad is His servant and His Messanger."

2. Next comes the duty of repeating the specified prayers, as given in detail, though only summarized hereinafter.

Praying to God, according to Islam, is the essence of man's duty to God. It is an outpouring of the heart's sentiments, a devout supplication to God, and a reverential expression of the soul's utmost sincerity towards its Maker.

In Islam the idea of prayer, like all other religious duties, finds its highest development. According to the Quran, prayer is the only way to communion with God. The word of God in the Quran teaches thus:

> "Rehearse that which has been revealed to you of
> the Book (the Quran) and be constant at prayer, for
> prayer restrains man from that which is evil and
> wrongful, while constant remembrance of God is
> the spirit's most supreme enjoyment." (29:45)

Islam, therefore, enjoins prayers as a means of the moral elevation of man. But if a prayer is said carelessly, or with an absent heart, it degenerates into mere ritual, into a lifeless and vapid ceremony gone through with insincerity of heart. This is not the sort of prayer accepted by Islam. Such a prayer is denounced by the Quran, which gives the warning:-

> "Woe to those who mouth their prayers without
> putting their hearts into it, just to make a show".

Whilst the rite of salat, i.e. saying the enjoined prayers, is being performed, one concentrates inwardly on God, while reflections on the meaning and reason of the verses one reads, stir and exalt one's soul to everything that is supreme, lofty and good. This salat is, so to say, a form of exercise and training. But it is not enough merely to practise its various movements of standing, bending, prostrating oneself and sitting. (These movements will be fully described later.) The real spirit of salat is to be in constant communion with and veneration of God.

The Fatiha—the opening Chapter of the Quran—forms an essential part of every prayer, so that no prayer, according to a teaching of the Prophet of Islam, is complete without the Fatiha, which is really a wonder in sense and meaning. Its translation is as follows:

> "All praise is due to Allah the Lord of all Worlds,
> the Beneficent, the Merciful, the King of the day
> of reckoning. You alone we worship, and from You

alone we seek help. Guide us to the right path, the
path of those to whom You have been gracious, not
of those who are condemned, nor of those who are
misguided".

The *Fatiha* is rightly described as a wonder in sense and
meaning. In a way, it has greater importance for a Muslim than
the Lord's prayer for a Christian. The latter was taught to pray
for the coming of God's Kingdom, whereas a Muslim is instructed
to seek his right place in that Kingdom which has already come;
the implication, no doubt, being that the coming of the Prophet
Muhammad was really the advent of the Kingdom of God, about
which Jesus Christ had preached to his followers (St.Mark, I-15)[1].

Some hostile critics have suggested that the form of the
Muslim prayer is fit only for blind and sinful men groping to find
the way out of their darkness. Surely it is a very distorted view
of the sublime words, which express the natural yearning of the
sincere soul to be kept on the right path and to be saved from
stumbling.

Honestly speaking, the prayer contained in the *Fatiha* is the
most sublime of all prayers that exist in any religion. It is
composed of seven verses, the first three of which speak of the
Divine attributes of Providence, Beneficence, Mercy and Requital;
the last three verses lay before the Creator of the Universe the
earnest desire of man to be entirely dependent on God (Allah).
The attributes referred to are those which proclaim God's
encompassing beneficence and care, and His unbounded love for
all His creatures; the ideal to which a human soul is made to aspire
is the highest to which man can rise, namely the path of
righteousness, the path of grace on which there is no stumbling.

On the one hand, the narrow views which addressed the
Divine being as the Lord of a particular nation (the "Lord of
Israel", for instance) are swept away by the reference to His equal
providence and equal love for all human beings, nay, for all the
creatures that exist in the world; the narrow idea of paternal care
contained in the appellation "Father" gives way before the all-
embracing beneficence and love of the "Great Author" of all

existence, which was responsible for the nourishment and perfection of all creatures long before they came into existence. On the other hand, there is the high aspiration of the soul for an unbounded spiritual rise without the least consideration of care of the body which craves for its "daily bread."' The Muslim prayer, as contained in the *Fatiha*, sets before the eye that high goal of Divine Grace wherein is known no displeasure, and which is beyond the reach of error.

With all its beauty, even the "Lord's Prayer" pales into insignificance before the majestic glory of the *Fatiha*, and one would in vain turn over the pages of Sacred Books to find anything approaching to the grand and sublime ideas contained in this Opening Chapter of the Quran.

The Prophet of Islam attached great importance to the human body as well as to the soul, and to the preservation of its cleanliness and purity, the well-spring of cleanliness being faith.

Islam considers the human body as something entrusted to man by God, and, therefore, obliges him to take care of it. Islam enjoins upon its followers to keep it clean and pure, morally as well as materially.

Prayer — A Principle of Action

We now take the practical side of the faith of Islam. As already said, actions in Islam are no less essential a component of the religion than belief. In this respect, Islam occupies a middle position between religions which have ignored practicalities altogether and those which bind their followers to the minutiae of ritual. Islam sees the necessity of developing the faculties of man by giving him general directions, and then leaving ample scope for him to exercise his will in his individual, practical life.

The precepts of Islam which inculcate duties towards God and duties towards man are based on that deep knowledge of human nature, which cannot be possessed but by the Author of that nature. They cover the whole range of the different grades of man's development and are thus wonderfully adapted to the requirements of different peoples. In the Scripture of Islam—the

11

Quran—guiding rules will be found for the ordinary man of the world as well as the philosopher, and for communities in the lowest grade of civilization as well as the highly civilized nations of the world. Practicality is the keynote of its precepts, and thus the same universality which marks its principles of faith is met with in its practical ordinances, suiting as they do the requirements of all ages and nations.

Prayer is the second of the five fundamental principles, or pillars, of practical devotion in Islam. It is a devotional exercise which every Muslim is required to render to God five times a day, namely in the early morning before sunrise, at midday, in the afternoon, in the evening after sunset, and fifthly at night.

Prayer as a general duty, or service, is frequently enjoined in the Quran, while the appointed times as well as the mode of saying prayers were clearly prescribed by the Prophet as a matter of personal practice and also in his teachings.

The hints and orders met with in the Quran as regards the enjoinment of *salat* are rendered as follows:

"Attend to your prayers in the early morning, at the close of the day, and at the approach of the night. Prayers are good deeds which drive away sin." (11:114.)

"Glorify God (by offering prayers to Him) when it is evening and in the morning. Praise be to Him in the heavens and the earth, in the afternoon and at noontime." (17-18)

"Put up then with what they say; and celebrate the praise of your Lord before sunrise, and before sunset, and during the night, and in the extreme of the day, so that you may find comfort." (20:130)

"Say prayers at sunset until the first darkening of the night and read the Quran at daybreak. Lo! the recital of the Quran (that is the offering of prayers) is ever witnessed. Pray during the night as well;

an additional duty, for the fulfilment of which your Lord may exalt you to an honourable station." (17:78-79)

"Fortify yourselves by patience and prayers" (2:45). "When your prayers are ended, remember God, standing and sitting and lying on your sides. And when you are safe, be steadfast in prayer. Truly, prayer is a duty incumbent on believers to be conducted at appointed times." (4:103).

It is absolutely necessary that the service of *salat* should be performed in Arabic as far as possible, the clothes and body of the worshipper must be clean, and the place of worship free of all impurity. Prayers may be said either privately or in company, or in a mosque, although services in a mosque are more meritorious.

The obligatory prayers are always preceded by the ablution of the face, hands, and feet, as will be fully described later.

The *salat*, or liturgical service, is thus one of the most prominent features of the Islamic religion, and very numerous are the injunctions regarding it, which have been handed down in the Traditions of the Prophet. These are alluded to in the following quotations:

"That which leads man to infidelity is neglect of prayers."

"None of you must say his prayers in a garment which does not cover the whole body."

"God does not accept the prayers of a woman who has arrived at the age of puberty unless she covers her head as well as the whole body."

"The prescribed prayers erase the sins which have been committed during the intervals between them, if they have not been mortal sins."

"The prayers of a person who has sullied himself

13

after performing his ablutions will not be accepted, until he has once again cleansed himself".

"Order your children to say the prescribed prayers when they are seven years of age, and beat them if they do not do so when they are ten years old."

"Tell me if any of you had a rivulet before his doors, and bathed five times a day therein, whether any dirt would remain on his body?" The companions said, "Nothing would remain." The Prophet said, "In this manner the five daily prayers as ordered by God will erase all minor sins."

Times of the Five Prescribed Prayers

The Prophet taught that "the time for the *zuhr* (noon) prayer begins from the inclination of the sun to the west and ends when the shadow of a person shall be the length of his own stature, which time marks the beginning of the 'asr (afternoon) prayer. The time of the 'asr prayer is from that point till the sun assumes a yellow appearance. The time of the *maghrib* (sunset) prayer is from sunset for so long as the red appearance in the horizon remains. The time of the *'isha* (night) prayer is from that point till near daybreak. And the time for the *fajr* (daybreak or morning) prayer is from the break of day till the sun rises." At the first light of dawn, a Muslim must wait to recite his morning prayers (if not already recited) until the sun has fully risen.

Aim of the Prayers

The aim of the prayers enjoined upon Muslims is to think of God, to have a pure heart, to take care of the body and clothes, to overcome evil desires, and to be a good-natured, decent person in all respects. The prayers recited by an immoral person are not acceptable. Good character comes before everything else.

Considering that modern life obliges us to be constantly busy, one might imagine that there would be no time to perform *salat* five times a day. But the case is quite the contrary; by performing the prescribed prayers, the body will be kept clean and at ease by virtue of the repeated ablution, or washing, which is a preparatory practice to reciting prayers. With *salat*, the stiffness of the organs will be enlivened and will regain their natural briskness. Thus no better means than the two rites of ablution and *salat* can be suggested to remove the languor and fatigue caused by the tiresome occupations of the day.

In other words, the practice of *salat* ensures us moral, spiritual and material advantages.

Muslim Prayer — A Spiritual Diet

To the Muslim, prayer is his spiritual diet, of which he partakes five times a day. Those who think that prayer is over-prescribed should remember how many times a day they require food for their physical bodies. Is not spiritual growth much more essential than physical growth? If to minister to the needs of the inner man, we need breakfast, lunch, afternoon tea, supper and late tea, do we not badly need spiritual refreshment at the same time? A Muslim says his prayers simultaneously with his meals.

Jesus Christ was quoted as having said, "Man shall not live by bread alone, but by every word that proceeds from the mouth of God." The word "shall" is too emphatic, and we are left wishing that the Church could make Christ's words a reality.

"The people of England", says General Gordon[2], "care more for their dinner than they do for anything else." What Gordon said of England seems true of the rest of the Christian World. But the flock cannot be blamed so much as the shepherd who neglects to give proper guidance. To save us from the demon of Epicureanism (devotion to earthly desires and lust), Jesus Christ laid down the above-mentioned maxim. Unfortunately his short ministry left him neither the time nor the occasion to enlighten us on the practical aspect of this noble pronouncement.

Jesus was also quoted as having said to the disciples. "I have yet many things to say to you but you cannot bear them now."

The time for full manifestation of the Divine Will had not yet arrived. Christ promised the disciples the coming of the "Comforter" after him to guide people "into all truth" and that "the spirit of truth had to come" to "show things"[3] and make up the deficiency. "The Spirit of Truth" descended on Prophet Muhammad, the "Comforter", who brought the teachings of Christ to the stage of practical reality. Five times we think of our bread, and five times a *muezzin*[4] from the mosque calls us to prayer and reminds us of the words that proceed "from the lips of God." The Muslim *azan* (call to prayer) is literally as well as formally a reminder that man shall not live by bread alone, but by every word that proceeds from the lips of One Who is the greatest of all. The following is the translation of the *azan*:

> "God is Great, God is Great. I testify that there is no deity save God. I testify that Muhammad brought the message from God. Come to prayer. Come to prayer. Come to prosperity. Come to prosperity. God is Great. God is Great. There is no deity save God."

This is what a Muslim hears from the mosque five times a day, when the inner man craves sustenance. The call from the mosque reminds him that he shall not serve the inner man by living by bread alone, but that God is the Greatest, and that all other concerns are small by comparision. God alone is to be served first. And if a man is poverty-stricken, true prosperity shall come to him through prayer, which is to live on the words that proceed from the lips of God.

Description of the Muslim Prayers

There are certain minor differences amongst the various schools of Islam regarding the formula, but its main features are alike in all Muslim countries.

We shall describe prayer according to the Hanafi School of Sunni, or Orthodox, Muslims.

The prescribed prayers are always preceded by the cleansing of the face, hands and feet.

Ablution

Ablution (Arabic: *wudu*, Persian *abdas*) is described by the Prophet as the key of prayer, and is founded on the authority of the Quran:

> "O believers. When you prepare yourselves for prayer, wash your faces and hands up to the elbows and wipe your heads and wash your feet to the ankles (5-6)".

Ablutions are absolutely necessary as a preparation for the recital of the liturgical form of prayer, and are performed as follows:

The worshipper washes his hands first, then he rinses his mouth, throwing the water into it with the right hand. He then throws water up his nostrils, sniffing it up at the same time, and then blows it out, compressing his nostrils with the thumb of the left hand. He then washes his face with both hands. He next washes his right hand and arm, as high as the elbow, causing the water to run along the arm from the palm of the hand to the elbow, and in the same manner he washes the left. Afterwards he draws his wetted right hand over the upper part of his head. If he has a beard, he then combs it with the wetted fingers of his right hand. After that he puts the tips of his forefingers wetted with water into his ears and twists them round, passing his thumbs at the same time round the back of the ears from the bottom upwards. Next, he wipes his neck with the fingers of both hands, making the ends of his fingers meet behind his neck, and then drawing them forward. Lastly, he washes his feet, as high as the ankles, and passes his fingers between the toes, thereby ensuring their cleanness.

During this ceremony, which is generally performed in a few minutes, the intending worshipper usually recites some pious utterances or prayers before commencing the *wudu* (ablution), e.g. "In the name of God, the Merciful and Beneficent, I perform my

17

wudu. Praise be to God Who caused water to purify our uncleanliness, and Islam to be our light to the right guidance."

The ablution need not be performed before each of the five appointed periods of prayer, when the person is conscious, since the last performance of the ablution, of not having been asleep or having avoided every kind of impurity, particularly urination, defecation or breaking wind. The private parts of the body must also be purified when answering a call of nature.

When water cannot be procured, or would be injurious to health, the ablution may be performed with pure dust or sand. This ceremony is called *tayammum*. The permission to use sand for this purpose, when water cannot be obtained,is granted in the Quran:

> "If you cannot find water, then take fine surface
> pure sand and wipe your faces and your hands
> with it. God does not wish to burden you, but He
> wishes to purify you and complete His favour to
> you, so that you may be grateful (5-6)."

It is related in the traditions (hadith) that the Prophet said:

> "The whole earth is fit to serve as a mosque for
> Muslims to worship on; and the very dust of the
> earth is fit for purification when water cannot be
> obtained."

Tayammum, or purification by sand or clean dust, is allowable under the following circumstances: (a) when water cannot be procured except at a great distance (about two miles); (b) in case of sickness; (c) when the use of water is infeasible because of incurring danger from the enemy, a beast or a reptile; and (d) when, on the occasion of the prayers of a feast day or at a funeral, the worshipper is late and has no time to perform the *wudu*. On ordinary days or under normal conditions, this substitution of *tayammum* is not allowable.

The washing of the whole body to rid it of uncleanliness and to prepare it for the recitatoin of prayer, is absolutely necessary after the following: nocturnal emission, menses, coitus, puerperium.

Washing of the whole body is highly recommended (by *sunna*, or practice and precept of the Prophet) on Friday before going to the mosque for the Friday prayer, on festivals and after washing the dead.

Purification

Water which may be used for Purification. The following kinds of water are lawful for purification: rain, sea, river, fountain, well, and snow water. All kinds of water are fit for purification, provided always that the normal colour, smell and taste are not changed, and when the water has not been used before.

Rubbing the socks with water in substitution for washing the feet in ceremonial ablution is legally allowed, provided that the socks have been put on after performing a regular ablution, including washing the feet. This legality is sound for twenty-four hours from the time of the regular ablution, after which period the feet must be washed as well as the face and hands.

How The Prayer Service Is Performed

At the time of public prayer, as stated before, the muezzin or crier ascends the minaret or stands at the side of the mosque nearest to the public thoroughfare, and gives the *azan*, or the call to prayer, as follows:-

1. God is Great (*twice*).
2. I bear witness the there is no deity but Allah (*twice*).
3. I bear witness that Muhammad is the Apostle of God (*twice*).
4. Come to prayer (O Muslims)(*twice*).
5. Come to salvation and prosperity (*twice*).
6. God is Great (*twice*).
7. There is no deity but Allah.

In the early morning, the following "verse" is added: "Really, prayers are better than sleep (*twice*).

When the prayers are said privately, in a congregation or in the mosque, they begin with the *iqama*, which is the second call to the *salat*, with the addition of the sentence "Prayers are now ready *(twice)*". The regular form of prayer then begins with the *niyya*, i.e. the worshipper's intention, expressed (better by heart) that he purposes to offer up to God such *rak'ats*[5] as the case may be, while standing up with the face qibla-wards, i.e. towards Makkah. The Arabic expression is as follows:-

Nawayto osalli rak'atyn fardes-sobhi" (*or* thalatha *or* arba'a rak'ats *if the* maghrib *or* 'asr *or* 'isha *is concerned*) (Transliteration)

1. Then follow the words of "*takbirat-el-ihram:*" *Allahu Akbar*, "God is Great," uttered with the thumbs touching the lobes of the ears and the open hands on each side of the face.
2. Then comes the *qiyam* position: The right hand is placed upon the left over the breast while the standing position is maintained, the eyes looking to the ground in self-abasement.
During this posture, the worshipper recites the following:—

"Subhanaka Allahumma wa bi hamdika wa tabaraka ismuka wa ta'ala judduka wa la llaha ghayruk. A'ozu billahi minash-shaytanir-rajim"

"Glory to You O Allah (God) and Your is the praise, and blessed is Your name and exalted is Your Majesty; there is no deity to be worshiped but You. I seek Allah's protection against the cursed Satan." (temptation).

After this, the *Fatiha* (the Opening Chapter of the Quran) is recited in the same position. It runs as follows:-

"Bismillahir-rahmanir-rahim, al hamdu lillahi-rabbil alamin, ar-rahm anir-rahim, maliki-yawmid-din, iyyaka na'bodu wa iyyaka nasta'in, ihdinas-siratal-mustaqim siratal-lazina an'am-ta'alayhim ghayril-maghdubi 'alayhim walad-dallin. Amen."

"In the name of Allah the Beneficent, the Merciful. All praise is due to Allah (God), the Lord of all Worlds, the Beneficent, the Merciful, King of the day of reckoning. You only do we worship, and from You only do we seek for help. Guide us to the right path, the path of those to whom You have been gracious, not of those who are condemned nor those who are misguided." Amen. (i.e. so be it!)

Then any portion of the Quran which the devotee may have learnt by heart is recited. Generally one of the shorter chapters of the Quran is repeated. The chapter called *Al-Ikhlas* (sincerity) is recommended for those who are unacquainted further with the Quran. It runs as follows:-

"Qul huwallahu ahad Allahus-samad lam yalid wa lam yulad wa lam yakun lahu kufwan ahad."

"Say: He (Allah) is one, Allah is the Support. He does not beget, nor is He begotten; and none is like Him".

3. Then having said, *Allahu Akbar* (Allah is Great), the devotee says:

"Subhana Rabbiyal-'azim wa bihamidih."

"Glory to my Lord, the Great and Praiseworthy".

4. After this posture the standing position is resumed, but unlike the *qiyam* position, the hands are lowered with the head down, so that the palms of the hands reach the knees. In this position, which is called *ruku*, that is bending, words expressive of the Divine glory and majesty are repeated three times. They are the following:-

"Sami'a-Allahu-liman hamida Allahumma wa lakal-hamd".

"Allah accepts him who praises Him. O our Lord,
Thine is all praise".

5. Then the devotee prostrates himself, the toes of both feet,
both knees, the nose and the forehead should be touching and
resting on the ground, while the following words expressing
Divine greatness are uttered three times:

"Subhana Rabbiyal-a'la wa bi-hamdih".
"Glory and praise be to my Lord, the Highest".

The following words are added:
"Allahumma ighfirli", i.e. O Lord! Grant me Your forgivenes.
This is called the first *sajda* (first prostration).

6. Then, raising his hands and body and sinking backward
upon his heels, and placing his hands upon his thighs, he says the
takbir, i.e. Allahu akbar (God is Great). This is called the first *jalsa*,i.e.
the first sitting.

7. Then the devotee performs another *sajda*, the same as the
first, as described before, with the repetition of the same expression
also three times: *"Subhana Rabbiya-a'la wa bi-hamdih"*(Glory and
praise be to my Lord the Highest).

At the close one of *rak'a*, the worshipper should repeat the
takbir while standing; but at the end of two *rak'ats* and at the close
of the prayer, he repeats it sitting: *"Allahu akbar"* (God is Great).

8. Here ends one *rak'a*. The devotee then rises, and assumes
a standing position for the second *rak'a* which is finished in the
same manner as the first, but instead of assuming a standing
position after the second *rak'a*, he sits down in a reverential
position.

At the close of each two *rak'ats*, the worshipper sits down to
recite the *tahiyyat* or the glorification of the Divine Being, and
utters the *tashah-hud* or bearing witness. Both *tahiyyat* and *tashah-hud*
run as follows:

"At-tahiyatu lillahi, wassala watu wattayyibatu,
Assalamu 'alayka ayyuhan-nabiyyu wa
rahmatullahi wa barakatuh. Assalamu 'alayna

wa'ala'ibadillahis-salihin. Ash-hadu anla llaha-
illallahu wa ash-hadu anna Muhammadan'abduhu
wa Rasuluh".

"All prayer and worship, rendered through words, actions
and good deeds, are due to Allah. Peace be to you, O My Prophet
and may the mercy of Allah and His blessings be showered upon
you. Peace be to us and to the righteous servants of Allah. I confess
that there is no deity but Allah (God) and that Muhammad is His
servant and His Apostle".

9. If the devotee intends to peform more than two rak'ats, he
then stands up, but if he has to say a prayer of only two rak'ats,
he repeats the following prayer of blessing for the Prophet:

"Allahumma salli 'ala Muhammad wa ala ali
Muhammad kama sallayta 'ala Ibrahim, wa 'ala-
ali Ibrahim, innaka hamidon majid. Allahumma
barik 'ala Muhammad wa 'ala ali-Muhammad
kama barakta 'ala Ibrahim wa 'ala ali Ibrahim
innaka hamidon majid."

"O my Lord! Kindly bestow your favour upon
Muhammad and the family[6] of Muhammad as You
bestowed Your blessing upon Abraham and the
family of Abraham. O my Lord! Kindly bless
Muhammad and the family of Muhammad as You
blessed Abraham and the family of Abraham, for
surely You are the most Laudable and Glorious".

It is recommended that the following supplication be added
to the above:-

"Rabbijalni muqim-assalati wa min zur-riyati,
Rabbana wa taqabbal du'a-i; Rabbanagh-firli wa li
wa-lidayya wa lilmu'minina yawma yaquamul-
hisab'.

"O my Lord Make me steadfast in prayer to You
and grant that my offspring be steadfast in prayer,

23

too. O my Lord! Kindlly accept my supplication. O my Lord! Forgive my sins and those of my parents and those of the faithful when the day of reckoning shall come."

10. This closes the two rak'ats' service which ends by the *salam* or the greeting thus: Turning the head round to the right the worshipper says, addressing any visible or invisible creature of God on his right:

"Assaalmu 'alaykum wa rahmatul-lahi wa barakatuh."

"May the peace and mercy of God be upon you."

Then, turning the head round to the left, the devotee repeats the *salam* with the same intention as above.

At the close of the whole set of the prescribed prayers, the worshipper raises his hands and offers up some *munajat* or supplication. This usually consists of prayers selected from the Quran or traditions of the Prophet. If possible they ought to be said in Arabic; or, if not, in the vernacular.[7]

Such supplications were highly commended by the Prophet, who was related to have said; "*Supplication is the marrow of worship*".

And he also said:

"Truly, your Lord will not admit that His servants when they raise their hands in supplication should return with them empty", i.e. without the supplication being accepted from the righteous.

The Prescribed Daily Prayers

The daily prayers are either *fard, sunna, nafil or witr. Fard* prayers are those *rak'ats as are enjoined* by God. *Sunna,*those founded on the practice of the Prophet, although desirable, are not obligatory. *Nafil* prayers are the voluntary performances of two *rak'ats,*or more, which may be omited without sin.*Witr* prayers are an odd number of *rak'ats, either one or three, said after the 'isha* or night service. These divisions of prayer are entirely distinct from each other. They each begin with the *niyya* (intention).

The five prescribed times of prayers are known as *zuhr, 'asr, maghrib, isha* and *fajr.*There are also three voluntary periods called *ishraq, douha* and *tahajjud.* The following table shows the exact number of *rak'ats* to be performed at each service:

TABLE SHOWING NUMBER OF RAK'ATS

No	Prescribed Period	Name of Prayer's Time	Fard	Sunna	Witr	Remarks
			Number of Rakat'ats			
THE FIVE ENJOINED OR OBLIGATORY PRAYERS						
1.	From dawn till sunrise	*Fajr* or morning	2	(0) 2		(0) Before the fard
2.	From inclination of the sun to the west; and closes when the shadow of a person shall be equal in the length to his own stature.	*Zuhr* or noon	4	(0) 2" (0) 2		(0) After the fard
3.	From that time till the sun assumes a yellow appearance.	*Asr* or afternoon	4	(0) 4		(0) Before the fard
4.	From sunset till the above appearance in the horizon disappears	*Maghrib* or sunset	3	(0) 2		(0) After the fard
	From that time till some moment before dawn	*'Isha* or night	4	(0) 2	+3	" (+) After the sunna
THE THREE VOLUNTARY PERIODS						
1	When the sun has well arisen	*ishraq* or sunrise	4			
2	From the time till about midday	*Douha* or sunshine	4			
3	After midnight	*Tahajjud*	8			

General Notes

1. A fresh ablution is necessary only when a man has answered a call of nature or has fallen asleep.

2. If there are socks on, and they have been put on after performing an ablution, it is not necesary to take them off: the wet hands may be passed over them. The same practice may be resorted to in case the boots are on, but it would be more decent to take off the boots when going into a mosque. It is, however, necessary that the socks be taken off and the feet washed about once every twenty four hours.

3. The *takbir, i.e.* the utterance of the expression *Allahu akbar* (God is Great) is to be repeated on assuming every form of the *rak'a* as previously explained. This repetition is deemed necessary to serve as a reminder to the worshipper to keep alive to his prayer by presenting his inner man and consciousness throughout the period of the prayers concerned.

4. *Ghusl,*or washing the whole body, is a religious act of bathing the body after a legal impurity. It is founded upon the express injunction of the Quran (5:6) which may be rendered in English as follows: "If you, i.e. *the faithful and believers, are polluted then purify yourselves."* The traditions and the sayings of the Prophet relate the occasions on which the Prophet performed the ceremony of *ghusl* or bathing. The Muslim teachers of all sects are unanimous in prescribing the washing of the whole body after the following acts, which render the body *junub* or impure: (1) *hayd* (menses) (2) *nifas* (child birth); (3) *jima'* (sexual intercourse);(4) *ihtilam* (pollution nocturna). It is absolutely necessary that every part of the body should be washed, otherwise the *ghusl* ceremony is rendered incomplete.

5. *Ghusl masnun* or washing, is meritorious, though not enjoined as an absolute Islamic necessity. Such washings are founded on the precept and practice of the Prophet, although they are not supposed to be a Divine institution. They are four in number:

26

a) Upon the admission of a convert to Islam.
b) Before going to mosque to perform Friday prayer, and on the two great religious festivals, i.e. the two Bairams, the one occuring after the close of the fasting month of Ramadan, and the other on the day following that on which the pilgrims perform their pilgrimage.
c) After washing the dead.
d) After blood-letting.
6. The Friday prayer service.
7. The *qunut*.

The Friday Prayer Service

The Friday prayer is held at the time of *zuhr* (noon) for it takes the place of the Sabbath of some other religion, and it substitutes for the stated *zuhr*.prayer. The four *rak'ats* said in the *zuhr* are reduced to two *rak'ats* preceded by a *khutba* (sermon), given by the *imam* (chaplain of the *mosque)*, exhorting the Muslims to goodness and to be dutiful to God, and showing them the means of their moral elevation and dwelling upon their national and communal welfare.

Salat al-jum'a, or Friday service, is enjoined on Muslims by Divine command in the Quran, Chapter 62 (9:11), where the believers are required, when the call is made to prayer on Friday: *"to hasten to the remembrance of Allah and leave off commerce for the time being; and when the prayer is ended, they can disperse in the land to resume their material and physical activitites."*

The Friday service must be said in a mosque, if there is one, or in a congregation, but not performed in private. If a Muslim cannot join the public Friday service for any lawful reason, he has to make up for this by saying the normal *zuhr* (noon) prayer of four *rak'ats*.

The reasons freeing a Muslim from attending the public Friday prayer are either sickness or heavy rainfall causing great difficulty in going to the mosque.

The Qunut

The *qunut* is a prayer recited at the close of the *isha* (night) prescribed prayer, while the worshipper is still in the standing position at the third *rak'a* of the *witr* posture. The best known *qunut* is the following:

> Allahumma ih-dina fi-man hadayta, wa a'fina fi-man a'fayta wa tawallana fi-man tawal-layta, wa barik lana fi ma a'tayta wa ghina shar-ra ma qadyta fa-in-naka taqdi wa la yuqda 'aliyka wa in-na-hu la yazillu man wal-layta wa la-ya-'izzu man adayta, nastaghifi-ruka wa natubu ilayka wa sallal-lahu 'ala nabiyina Muhammad wa ; ala alihi wa sahbihi wa sallam.

> "O Allah! Guide us among those whom You have guided aright, and preserve us among those whom You have preserved in good health and befriend us among those You have befriended, and bless us in all You have granted to us; and protect us from the evil of all You have judged as evil; for surely You are the only judge, and none can judge against Your judgement. O Allah! invoke Your increasing blessings and favours upon our Prophet Muhammad and upon his family and upon his disciples."

Another Recommended Style of Qunut.

The following supplication of qunut is also commonly adopted:

> Allahumma inna nasta'inu-ka wa nastagh-firuka wa nu'minu bika wa natawakkalu alayka wa nathini alaykalkhayra wa nashkuruka wa la nakfuruka wa nakhla'u wa natrukku man yafijuruka. Allhumma iyyaka n'abudu wa laka nusalli wa nasjud wa ilayka nas'a wa nahfid wa

28

narju rahmataka wa nakhsha azabaka inna 'azabaka
bil-kuffari mulhiq.

"O Allah! We beseech Your help and Your
forgiveness as we are faithful to You and depend
wholly upon Your Divinity. We laud You in the
highest. We thank You and shall never forget Your
favours. We cast off and forsake him who is
unmindful to You. O Allah! We worship none but
You. To You we pray and make obeisance and to
You do we promptly flee. We hope for Your mercy
and we fear Your punishment for surely Your
punishment, overtakes the infidel."

Special Service

In addition to the prescribed daily prayers and the Friday prayer,
there are special services for special occasions as given below:

1. *Salatul-Musafir* (Prayers for the Traveller). —Two rak'ats
   instead of the usual number of the meridian, afternoon, and
   night prayers; the maghrib (evening prayer) always
   remaining the same, i.e. three rak'ats.

2. *Salatul-Khauf* (Prayers of Fear). —This is said in war-time:
   two *rak'ats* recited first by one regiment or company and
   then by the other.

3. *Salatul-Tarawih.* Eight *rak'ats* are performed every evening
   during Ramadan, the fasting month, immediately after the
   fifth daily prayer, the *'isha,* or before the dawn.

4. *Salatul-Istikhara* (Prayers for Guidance). The person who is
   about to undertake any special business performs two *rak'ats*
   just when he goes to bed. During his sleep, he may expect
   to receive some divine *illham* (inspiration) on that, for which
   he seeks guidance.

5. *Salatul-Janazah* (Prayers at a Funeral for the Dead). This
   liturgical special service is founded upon very detailed
   instructions given by the Prophet, which are recorded in the
   hadith. (traditions). This Muslim funeral service is not recited

in the graveyard, but either in a mosque or in some open space near the dwelling of the deceased person or the graveyard. Whoever is next of kin is the proper person to lead the service, but it is usually conducted by the family *imam,* or by a learned man.

The following is the order of the service:

Someone present calls out:"Here begin the prayers for the dead".

Then those present arrange themselves in one, two or three rows or more, as the case permits, opposite the corpse, with their faces qibla-wards (i.e. towards Makkah). The *imam,* or leader, stands in front of the ranks opposite the head of the corpse.

All of the attendants having taken the standing position, the *imam* opens the service by saying :

"I purpose to perform for this dead person prayers to God consisting of four *takbirs".*

Then placing his hands on the lobes of his ears, he recites the first *takbir:* God is Great.

Afterwards, he folds his hands below his breast, and recites the *tasbih,* an ejaculation extolling the holiness of God:

Subhanakal-lahumma	"O holy God,
Wabi hamdika wa	Praise be to you,' O Allah!
Tabarakas-muka	Blessed is Your name.
Wa ta'ala jadduka	High is Your Greatness.
Wa la ilaha Ghairuk	There is no deity but You."

Next, he reicites the *fatiha,* (the opening Chapter of the Quran). Here ends the first *takbir.*

Then follows the second *takbir:* God is Great.

The *imam* recites thereafter the *salatu-'alan-Nabi* (prayer for the Prophet), thus:

"O Allah, we invoke Your increasing blessing and
peace upon our Prophet Muhammad and upon his
family, as You bestowed your blessings and peace
upon the Prophet Abraham and his family; O

Allah, Praise be to You, for You are Great".

Here ends the second *takbir*.

Then follows the third *takbir*, God is Great, after which the following prayer is recited:

> "O Allah, we beseech You to forgive the sins of this dead person ;and have mercy upon him/her. He/She was faithful to Islam, he/she believed in Your Oneness and in the Message of Your Prophet."

Here ends the third *takbir*. Then follows the fourth *takbir*, "God is Great," after which the following prayer is recited:

> "O Allah, forgive our living and our dead and those of us who are present and those who are absent. O Allah, those whom You keep alive amongst us, keep alive in Islam, and those whom You cause to die, let them die in the Faith of Islam."

Turning the head round to the right, the *imam* says the *salam*: "Peace and mercy be to you."

Turning the head round to the left, he repeats the *salam*: Peace and mercy be to you.

The *takbirs* are recited by him aloud, but the *tasbih*, the *salam*, and the prayers are recited by him and by the people attending the funeral in a low voice.

The attendants then raise their hands in silent prayer reading the *Fatiha* on behalf of the deceased soul, and afterwards, addressing the relatives, they say: "It is the decree of God," to which the chief mourner replies: "I am pleased with the will of God." He then gives permission to the people to retire by saying: "God rewards you for your attendance", and they reply by saying "May God grant you better rewards and give you patience and long life."

Those who wish to return to their own business may do so at that time, and the rest proceed to the grave. Lastly, the corpse is placed on its back in the grave, with the head to the north and feet to south, the face being turned towards the *qibla* (Makkah).

The persons who place the corpse in the grave repeat the following sentence: "We commit you to earth in the name of God and in the religion of the Prophet."

The bands of the shroud having been loosened, the recess, which is called *lahd,* is closed in with unburnt bricks and the grave filled in with earth. In most Muslims countries, it is customary to recite verse 55 of the 20th chapter of the Quran while throwing the clods of earth into the grave. The verse may be rendered as follows: *"From it (the earth) have We (God)created you, and to it will We return you, and out of it will We bring you forth the second time."*

After the burial, the people offer a recital of the *fatiha* in the name of the deceased.

> Note:- If the grave be for the body of a woman, it should be plug to the height of man's chest; if for a man, the height of the waist should be the measure. At the bottom of the grave, a recess is made on the side to receive the corpse.

May the peace and mercy of Allah be showered upon the faithful dead! May Almighty God grant the believers a long life to be spent as it should be in the worship of Him and in the service of humanity!

2

Zakat or Legal Alms

Every religion of the world has preached charity, but, like prayer, there is in Islam some method or regularity given to it, so that it has become an institution, assuming a permanence which is not encountered anywhere else. Islam makes charity obligatory and binding upon all those who have embraced the Muslim faith. Here we have a brotherhood into which the rich man cannot enter unless, and until, he is willing to give part of his possessions for the support of the poor and the needy members of the community.

The injunction to the rich to pay *zakat* to the poor subjects him to a practical test, by which a real brotherhood is established between the rich and the poor.

In its primitive sense, the word *zakat* means purification, whence it is also used to express a portion of the property bestowed in alms, as a sanctification of the remainder to the proprietor. It is an institution of Islam founded upon an express command in the Quran, as one of the five foundations of practical religion.

It is a religious duty incumbent upon any person who is free, sane, adult and a Muslim, provided that he is possessed in full property of such estate or effects as are termed, in the language of the law, *nisab*, i.e. fixed amount of property, and that he has been

33

in possession of the same for the space of one complete year. The *nisab* or fixed amount of property upon which *zakat* is due varies with reference to the different kinds of property in possession, as is detailed in the present article.

The one complete year in which the property is held in possession is legally termed *hawlul-haul*, i.e. return of duration.

Zakat is not incumbent upon a man, against whom there are debts equal or exceeding the amount of his whole property, nor is it due upon the necessaries of life, such as dwelling-houses, articles of clothing, household furniture, cattle kept for immediate use, war prisoners employed as actual servants, armour and weapons designed for present use, or upon books of science or law used by scholars, or upon tools used by craftsmen.

Zakat is incumbent upon the *nisab* of the following possessions:-
(a) Camels. (b) Bulls, cows and buffaloes. (c) Sheep and goats. (d) Horses. (e) Silver. (f) Gold and silver ornaments. (g) Cash, bank notes, etc. (h) Articles of merchandise (i) Mines or buried treasures. (j) Fruits of the earth.

The following is the *nisab* or proportionate property, upon which *zakat* is due under the above headings:

Zakat

(a) Camels

Zakat is not due upon less than five camels; and upon five camels it is one goat or sheep, provided that they subsist upon pasture throughout the year; because *zakat* is due only upon such camels as live on pasture and not upon those which are fed at home on forage. One goat or sheep is due upon any number of camels from five to nine: two goats for any number of camels from ten to fourteen; three goats for any number from twenty to twenty-four. Upon any number of camels from twenty-five to thirty-five, the *zakat* is a *bint-makhad*, or a yearling female camel; from thirty six to forty-five a *bint-labun*, or a two year old female camel, from forty-six to sixty, a *hoqqa*, or a three-year-old female camel; from sixty-one to seventy-four, a *jazu'a* or four-year-old female camel; from seventy-five to ninety-two, female two-year-old colts. When the number of camels exceeds one hundred and twenty, the *zakat* is calculated by the aforesaid rule.

(b) Bulls, Cows, and Buffaloes

No *zakat* is due upon fewer than thirty cattle. Upon thirty cattle which are fed on pasture for the greater part of the year, there is due at the end of the year a *jazu'a,* or one year-old calf; and upon thirty is due a *musinna,* or a calf of two years old; and where the number exceeds forty, the *zakat* is to be calculated according to this rule. For example, upon sixty, the *zakat* is two yearling calves, upon seventy, one *tabi'a* and one *musinna;* upon eighty, two *musinnas;* upon ninety, three *tabi'as* and one *musinna;* and thus upon every ten head of cattle a *musinna* and a *tabi'a* alternately. Upon one hundred and nine, the *zakat* is two *musinnas* and one *tabi'a;* and upon one hundred and twenty, four *tabi'as.* The usual method, however, of calculating the *zakat* upon large herds of cattle is by dividing them into thirties and forties, imposing upon every thirty-one a *tabi'a,*or upon every forty-one a *musinna.*

(c) Sheep and Goats

No *zakat* is due upon less than forty which have fed the greater part of the year on pasture, upon which is due one goat or sheep, until the number reaches one hundred and twenty; for one hundred and twenty-one to two hundred, it is two goats or sheep; and above this, one for every hundred.

(d) Horses

When horses and mares are kept indiscriminately together, feeding for the greater part of the year on pasture, it is the option of the proprietor to give one dinar (a dinar is worth about ten shillings, or fifty Egyptian piastres) per head of the whole, or to estimate the whole and give five per cent upon the total value. No *zakat* is due upon droves of horses consisting entirely of males, or entirely of mares. There is no *zakat* due upon horses or mules, unless they are articles of merchandise, nor it is due upon war horses, or upon beasts of burden, or upon cattle kept for drawing ploughs and so forth.

(e) Silver

It is not due upon silver valued at less than two hundred dirhams (one dirham is equivalent to 3.12 grams), but if one be possessed of this sum for a whole year, the zakat due upon it is five dirhams till such excess amounts to forty, on which the zakat is one dirham, and for every succeeding forty-one dirhams. These dirhams on which silver predominates are to be accounted silver, and the laws respecting silver apply to them, although they should contain some alloy; and the same rule holds with regard to all articles falling under the denomination of plate such as cups and goblets.

(f) Gold and Silver Ornaments

No zakat is due upon gold under the value of twenty misqals[8] and the zakat due upon twenty is half a misqal. When the quality of gold exceeds twenty misqals, on every four misqals above twenty are due two qirats[9] and so on in proportion.

(g) Cash, Bank-notes, etc.

No zakat is due upon notes, etc.,the value of which does not exceed twelve Egyptian pounds or its equivalent of foreign currency. And the zakat due upon a value of twelve pounds and upwards is two and a half per cent of the total money remaining idle in possession for the duration of one year.

(h) Articles of Merchandise

Articles of merchandise should be appraised, and a zakat of two and a half per cent paid upon the value if it exceeds two hundred dirhams of silver in value.

(i) Mines or Buried Treasures

Mines of gold, silver, iron, lead or copper are subject to a zakat of one-fifth, but if the mine is discovered within the precincts of a person's own home, nothing is due. And if a person finds a deposit of buried treasure, one-fifth is due upon it.

No *zakat* is due upon precious stones.

(j) Fruits of the Earth

Upon everything produced from the ground, the tax is one-tenth, whether the soil be watered by the overflow of rivers, or by periodical rains, excepting articles of bamboo, and grass, which are not subject to the tithe. If the soil is watered by means of buckets, machinery, or watering camels, etc., the *zakat* is one - twentieth.

Honey and fruits collected in the wilderness are subject to tithe.

The *zakat* is received by collectors duly appointed by the State, although it is lawful for the possessor to distribute his alms himself.

If a person comes to the collector and makes a declaration upon oath as to the amount of his property or as to his having himself distributed the alms due, his statement is to be credited.

Expenditure of Income from Zakat

As regards the expenditure of income from *zakat*, eight heads are mentioned in the Holy Quran (9:60):

1. The poor.
2. The needy.
3. Those in debt.
4. Ransoming of captives (prisoners of war).
5. The wayfarer.
6. The officials appointed in connection with the collection of *zakat*.
7. Those whose hearts are to be harmonized by material support.
8. The way of God.

A few words may be added to explain the above:

1. The poor are those who are unable physically or otherwise to earn their living.
2. The needy are those who may be able to earn their livelihood but lack the means, such as implements, etc., to do so.
3. By those in debt are meant persons who may be able to support themselves, but if they are in debt, their debts may be paid off from the *zakat* fund.
4. The captives are those who are taken prisoners in war. A portion of the *zakat* must go for their release.
5. The wayfarer is a traveller who, though in well-to-do circumstances, stands in need of help in a strange place or country; hence a part of the *zakat* income must be spent on such a person.
6. The officials who collect *zakat* are members of the staff appointed officially to manage its collection as well as the management of its expenditure; hence their wages are also to be paid out of the *zakat* fund.
7. The last two heads mentioned in the Quran, namely those whose hearts are to be harmonized in the way of God, refer to the propagation of the Faith. With respect to the preaching of a religion, there is always a class of people who are ready to listen and ready to embrace Islam when they are preached to, but who, in the meantime, have to forgo material advantages which it is very difficult for them to relinquish. These persons are spoken of in the Quran as those whose hearts are to be harmonized or united by giving them such a portion of the *zakat* fund as will reassure them. By the way of God is meant the advancement of the cause of Islam or the defence thereof. Under this head, therefore, *zakat* may be spent for the propagation of the religion of Islam and to meet the objections advanced against it.

The above laws, covering the institution of the *zakat* principle in Islam, are detailed according to the Hanafi Schools of Muslim jurisprudence, but the differences amongst the teachings of the rest of the Sunni Schools of Muslims are small, even insignificant.

However, the endorsement of paying the wages of the staff employed in connection with the poor-tax (zakat) from that revenue is clear. This is in order to denote that the institution is meant for raising a public fund, the management of which should be entirely in the hands of a public body, although it is lawful for the possessor to distribute his alms himself: and if he makes a declaration on oath to this effect, his statement is to be credited.

Supplemenary Notes

1. Zakat is not a State Tax

As already mentioned in the foregoing chapter, the scope of zakat is clearly set forth in the Holy Quran, and, therefore, must not be confounded with other forms of compulsory taxes imposed by the State on its Muslim and non-Muslim citizens alike.

In the first place, zakat is not a tax imposed by the State. Nor is zakat a tax destined to the State as such. The very nature of the instituion of zakat requires that the part, which the State is to play in the function thereof, is merely one of "supervision" and not of full control, as is the case where government taxes are concerned.

The difference between supervision and full control is that the latter would imply the right to increase or modify the tax, to extend or limit its scope, to suspend the impostion thereof, or even to abrogate it altogether, whereas, in its role of supervision, the State has the right only to enforce observance of the Divine Law as directed by the precepts of the Quran and the instructions of the Prophet.

2. Practical Application of Zakat

Zakat attaches exclusively to productive wealth, that is wealth represented by:

a) Agricultural produce.
b) Pasturing domestic animals.
c) Things constituting a ready medium of exchange, such

as silver, gold and money invested (in trade capital, in cash and articles of merchandise) or kept as savings.

The law of *zakat* considers the productivity of wealth as either potential or actual, the former, inheriting in such wealth as silver, gold, and money kept as savings, and the latter is actual productivity inheriting in such wealth as agricultural produce, pasturing domestic animals and invested money, i.e. trade capital in cash and articles of trade.

3. Cause and Object of the Zakat Act

The cause of the *zakat* act is the productivity of wealth existing in a quantity, number, value, equal to or above the established minimum taxable limits. The object of *zakat* is the profession of Islam by the legitimate owner of wealth under taxation.

4. Responsibility for Zakat Payment

Zakat is an act of worship; it being an obligatory impost on Muslim-owned wealth, the *zakat* must be discharged regardless of age or state of mind.

Where adult Muslims are concerned, the responsibility devolves directly upon the legitimate owner of the wealth; where minors or insane persons are concerned, it lies with their legal guardians or custodians, as the case may be. Where the *zakat* of wealth belonging to minor children is concerned (as, for example, in the case of wealth inherited from the mother), the responsibility for the payment of dues rests with the persons entrusted with the care and administration thereof (i.e. the child's father, or any other responsible person) until the child comes to full age.

The same ruling applies to Muslim orphaned children or insane Muslim men or women, where the responsibility for payment of *zakat* rests with the legal guardian or custodian, as the case may be.

Trade capital, that is to say, both the reserve and working capital (i.e. money and articles of trade) belonging to individuals or companies, is also subject to the payment of *zakat*, wherever its value is equal to or above the minimum taxable limit.

Where private ownership of business concerns is involved, responsibility for the payment of dues rests with the owner or owners; where endowments are concerned, such responsibility rests with the individual or committee entrusted with the administration of the establishment or concern in question.

5. Exempt from Zakat Dues

It is one of the fundamental doctrines of Islam that the needy and poor citizens of any Muslim community have an inherent right to a share of the wealth of every Muslim of means, and nowhere in the Quranic text is any justification to be found for exempting the wealth owned even by minors, orphans or persons of unsound mind.

However, all establishments privately owned or endowed, which are either totally devoted to charitable purposes (i.e. hospitals, orphanages, homes for the poor, disabled and old people, etc.) or to the service of humanity (i.e. scientific research, free educational institutions), are naturally exempt from the obligation of paying zakat, as by their very nature they fulfil the purpose to which the proceeds of zakat are dedicated. Likewise, wealth which has been purposely set aside to cover the expenses of a first pilgrimage to the Holy Ka'ba is exempt from taxation, regardless of the period of time during which it remains unused. Subsequent pilgrimages being purely optional, wealth set aside to cover expenses of the same is considered as savings, and, is therefore, subject to the taxation of zakat, where the quantity or value is equal to or above the minimum taxable limit.

6. Factors of Responsibility

The person subject to taxation must be:-

a) An avowed Muslim (non-Muslims being exempt from such taxation).

b) Of sound mind.

c) A person enjoying full freedom of action. If, for any reason, he/she be under any kind of duress, his or her responsibility remains suspended until full freedom of action is recovered.

3

Fasting

Fasting is one of those religious institutions which, though universally recognised, have had quite a new meaning introduced into them by the advent of Islam. Fasting was generally resorted to in times of sorrow and affliction, by the heathen, probably to appease any angry "deity!" In Islam, fasting is enjoined for the moral elevation of man and for his spiritual development. The object is made clear in the Holy Quran itself, where fasting is enjoined upon Muslims. Verse 183, Chapter 2 of the Quran is interpreted as follows: *"O you who believe! Fasting is prescribed for you, ...so that you may be more able to guard against evil."* The Holy Quran does not content itself with simply enjoining the doing of good and refraining from evil, but teaches man the ways by walking in which the tendency to evil in him can be suppressed and the tendency to good improved. Fasting is one of those means. Hence, fasting in Islam does not simply mean abstaining only from food, but also from every kind of evil. In fact, abstention from food is but a step to make a man realize — if he can, in obedience to divine injunctions, abstain from food and drink which are otherwise lawful for him—how much more exemplary it is that he should refrain from evil, the consequence of which is no doubt evil. Fasting is actually like a sort of training of man's faculties, for as

42

every faculty of man requires training to attain its full force, the faculty of submission to the Divine will also requires to be trained. Fasting is one of the means by which this is achieved.

In addition to that specified training, fasting has its physical advantages. It not only prepares man to bear hunger and thirst and thus to accustom himself to a life of hardship and frugality, so that he may not be too much given over to ease, but also exercises a very good effect upon health in general. It is a well-known teaching of the Prophet of Islam that hunger is the best cure for many ailments; this is a fact proved and defended nowadays by recent medical authorities.

The injunction of fasting as a religious institution and a devotional practice in Islam is dealt with in the Quran in the second Chapter. Verse 183 teaches that fasting is a religious institution almost as universal as prayer; and in Islam it is one of the four fundamental practical ordinances, the other three being prayer *(salat)*, poor-tax *(zakat)* and pilgrimage *(hajj)*. The Quran teaches that fasting was enjoined on all nations by the Prophets who came before Holy Prophet Muhammad. In the Bible it is stated that fasting has in all ages and among all nations been an exercise much in use in times of mourning and affliction. Fasting has also been in vogue among the Hindus.

Even Christians, who assume that they have no need of any religious exercise on account of Jesus' atonement, are commanded by that Holy Prophet to keep the fasts: "Moreover, when you fast, do not like the hypocrites, be of a sad countenance. But you, when you fast, anoint your head and wash your face." (Matt.,6:16,17) Again when the Pharisees objected to Jesus' disciples not keeping the fast as often as John's, his only answer was that when he was taken away "then shall they fast in those days." (Luke, 5:33-35).

But Islam has introduced quite a new meaning into the institution of fasting. Before Islam, fasting meant the suffering of some privation in times of mourning and sorrow; in Islam it becomes an institution for the improvement of the moral and spiritual character of man. This is plainly stated in the concluding words of the verse of the Quran bearing on the privileges of the enjoinment, *viz. "So that you may guard against evil doings."* The

43

object is that man may learn how he can shun evil. As already stated, all the institutions of Islam are actually practical steps leading to perfect purification of the soul. But along with moral elevation, which is aimed at in fasting, another object is hinted at. In fact, the two-fold object is that Muslims may be able to guard themselves: (a) morally and spiritually, against evil, for he who is able to renounce the lawful satisfaction of his desires in obedience to Divine Commandments, certainly acquires the power to renounce unlawful gratification; and (b) physically against the opponents of the Muslims by habituating themselves to suffer tribulations which they must undergo in defence of the cause of Islam.

The number of days of fasting is definitely stated in verses 184, 185 and 186 of Chapter 2 of the Quran, namely twenty-nine or thirty days of the month of Ramadan, the ninth month of the lunar calendar. But whoever is temporarily sick or on a journey during the month of Ramadan, shall fast for an equal number of days later on. As regards those who cannot keep the fast on account of persistent or long-standing disease, or who are too old or weak, including in this class the woman who is with child or nursing a child, the practice is to give away the equivalent of one man's food to a poor man every day during the whole month. It is pertinent to observe here that doing good to others (charity or otherwise) is enjoined in addition to fasting during the month of Ramadan. We are told that the Holy Prophet, who was universally recognized for his charity, was most charitable during the month of Ramadan.

The number of days of fasting, as already stated, is either 29 or 30 days according to the number of days in the lunar month of Ramadan. Lunar months are not always the same with regard to their number of days. As to the duration of each day of the month of fast, it is from dawn to sunset. Nothing whatsoever may be eaten or drunk within that period. Sexual intercourse is also strictly forbidden. But it has been made lawful to go to the wives during the nights of the fast.

It is meritorious to cut oneself off from worldly connections during the last ten days of the month of Ramadan, passing the days and nights in a mosque. This practice is known as *I'tikaf, i.e.* seclusion. It is, however, voluntary and not obligatory.

An important question arises regarding such countries in which the days are sometimes very long-from dawn to sunset where it would be beyond the ability of ordinary men to abstain from food from the breaking of dawn to sunset. In this case a Muslim is allowed to keep the fast only for such hours of fasting as are kept in ordinary countries. However, in cases of extraordinary difficulties, Muslims may postpone the fast to days of shorter length.

4
Pilgrimage

Pilgrimage as a Fundamental Institution

The pilgrimage to Makkah is performed in the month of Zul Hijja, the twelfth month of the Mohammadan year. It is the fifth pillar of the Muslim practical religion and is a religious duty, incumbent upon believers to be performed once during one's life-time. It is founded upon express injunctions in the Quran. It is a divine institution and has the following interpreted authority in the Quran for its due observation:-

> "And proclaim to the people a pilgrimage. They will ...come to you on foot and on every fleet camel coming from remote defile." (22:27)

> "The rites of pilgrimage are performed in the well-known....months, so whoever determines the performance of the pilgrimage therein, let him not transgress by having any intercourse with women, or by making unlawful dispute or any wrangling, and whatever good you may do, God certainly knows it. And make provision (for your journey);

but the best provision is the fear of God: O men of understanding, be careful of your duty towards God." (2:197)

"It shall be no sin for you to seek bounty[10] from your Lord, so when you hasten on from Arafat, remember God Who has guided you, though, before, you were certainly going astray." (2:198)

"When you have performed your sacred rites, then laud.[11] God as you do your own fathers, or with a yet more intense lauding. But there are some people who say, our Lord, give us (our portion) in this world: but such shall have no portion in the hereafter." (2:200)

"And some other people say, Our Lord, grant us good in this world and good in the next and save us from the chastisement of the fire."

"These shall have the lot of what they have earned; God is swift in reckoning." (3:96)

"The first house (mosque) founded for mankind is that of Makkah. Be it blessed! It is guidance to human beings." (3:94)

"And the pilgrimage to that mosque is a devotional service, due to God, incumbent upon every one (Muslim) who is able to undertake the journey thither".

Certain Rites of the Institution

Preparatory. Pilgrimage is a fundamental ordinance of practical devotion in Islam; and it represents the last stage of spiritual progress in this life. One of the principle requirements of the pilgrimage is what is called *ihram*, which represents the severance of all worldly connections. All costly and fashionable attire, in which the inner self is so often mistaken for the outward appearance, is cast off, and the pilgrim has only two seamless wrappers with which to cover himself, and thus shows that in his love for his Master, he is ready to cast off all lower connections. The other important requirements are *tawaf*, i.e., making circuits round the *Ka'ba* and running between two appointed small hills known as Al-Safa and Al-Marwa. And these are all external manifestations of that fire of divine love which has been kindled within the heart, so that, like the true lover, the pilgrim makes circuits round the house of his beloved.

To call these movements of a true lover "puerile rites and ceremonies" as Christian writers do, is not only to show contempt for the Christ-like appearance of the pilgrim, but also to imply that the love of God is mere talk.

Of the rites to be observed in connection with the institution of pilgrimage there is the kissing of a monumental "Black Stone" when making certain appointed circuits round the *Ka'ba*. A few words must be added in order to clear up serious misunderstandings relating both to the Ka'ba and the Black Stone, which are at the basis of the wrong conclusions drawn by foreign writers.

The Sunni Way of Performing the Pilgrimage

As already stated, the enjoined pilgrimage to Makkah and the Sacred House of God, i.e. the Holy ancient Mosque, is performed in the month of Zul Hijja, the 12th lunar month of the A.H. Calendar, and the pilgrim must reach Makkah before the 7th day of that month.

As regards the formalities to be observed during the pilgrimage, every Muslim can easily learn them from the instructors, who are usually locally appointed by the authorities to instruct the laity pilgrims as to what to do, although the literate may get all information required on the rites to be observed by consulting the books of laws before leaving for their destination.

The following is a complete summary of the principal rites

in connection with the institution of the pilgrimage as observed by the Sunni or Orthodox Muslims:

Upon the pilgrim's arrival at the last stage near Makkah, he bathes himself, and performs two *rak'ats* and then divests himself of his clothes to assume the pilgrim's robe, which is called *ihram*. This garment consists of two seamless wrappers, one being wrapped round the waist and the other thrown loosely over the shoulder, the head being always left uncovered[12]. Sandals may also be worn, but not boots or shoes. After having assumed the pilgrim's garb, he must not anoint his head, shave any part of his body, pare his nails, nor wear any other than the *ihram*. The pilgrim, having now entered upon the hajj (pilgrimage), faces Makkah and makes a formal declaration of his, intention, (niyya) by saying: "O God, I purpose to perform the hajj; make this devotional service easy to me and accept it from me." He then proceeds on his journey to the sacred city and on his way, as well as at different periods during the pilgrimage, he recites or sings, alone or in the company of his fellow pilgrims, in a loud voice, the pilgrim's supplication called the *talbiya* (a word signifying waiting or standing for orders). In Arabic it runs thus:-

"Labbayka, allahumma labbayk.
Labbayka; la sharika laka, labbayk.
Innal-hamda wan-ni-mata laka.
Wal-mulko.
La sharika lak".

which may be rendered in English as follows:-

"I stand up for Your Service, O God.
I stand up.
"I stand up. There is no partner with You.
I stand up.
Truly, Yours is the praise, the blessing
and the Kingdom.
There is no partner with You."

Immediately on his arrival at Makkah, the *haji* performs the legal ablution in the Masjidul-Haram (the sacred Mosque of Makkah) and then kisses the Black Stone. He then encompasses the Ka'ba seven times; three times at a quick pace or run, and four times at a slow pace. These acts are called *tawaf* or the circuit, and are performed by commencing on the right and leaving the Ka'ba, on the left. Each time the pilgrim passes round the Ka'ba. he touches the Ruknul-Yaman or the Yemen corner, and kisses the Black Stone. He then proceeds to the Maqamu-Ibrahim, or the seat of Abraham, where he recites verse 125 of the second Chapter of the Quran: *"Wat-takhizu min maqam Ibrahima Musallaa,"* i.e. "Take the station or seat of Abraham for a place of prayer," and performs prayers of two *rak'ats.*

He then goes to the gate of the Sacred Mosque leading to Mount Al-Safa, and from it he ascends the hill, reciting in a loud voice verse 158 of the second Chapter of the Quran: "Truly Al-Safa and Al-Marwa are counted as rites of the Divine Service of God." Having arrived at the summit of the hill, turning towards the Ka'ba, he recites the following; *There is no deity save God (Allah). There is no deity but Allah alone. He has no partner. He has executed His promise, and has given victory to his servant (Muhammad), and He has by himself defeated the hosts of infidels. There is no deity save God."*

These words are recited thrice. He then runs from the top of Mount Al-Safa to the summit of Mount Al-Marwa seven times, repeating the aforesaid supplication or prayer.

This is the sixth day, the evening of which is spent at Makkah, where he again encompasses the Ka'ba *once.*

On the seventh day he listens to the *khutba,* or oration, in the Sacred Mosque, on the excellence of the pilgrimage and the necessary duties required of all true Muslims. On the following day, which is called the day of *tarwiya*[13] (satisfying thirst), he proceeds with the fellow-pilgrims to a place called Mina, where he spends the night, performing the usual service of the Muslim rites.

On the next day, it being the ninth of the month, all pilgrims proceed to Mount Arafat where they spend the whole day, performing the midday and afternoon prescribed prayers, and hearing the sermon and spending the time in reciting the Quran or making humble supplication to God, asking His favour of forgiveness of their sins and soliciting His guidance to a virtuous life, etc. Before sunset, the pilgrim leaves Arafat for a stage called Al-Muzdalifa, a place between Mina and Arafat, where he should arrive for the sunset and night prayers.

The next day, it being the tenth of the month and known all throughout the Muslim world as *Yawmul-Nahr*, or the day of sacrifice, and celebrated as the *'Eidal-Adha*, or the great feast known in the West as Kurban Bairam. Early in the morning, having said their prayers at Al-Muzdalifa, the pilgrims proceed in a body to the three monumental pillars at Mina. The pilgrim casts seven small stones or pebbles at each of these pillars, this ceremony being called *ramyal jumar*, or throwing of the pebbles. Holding the pebbles (which he can easily pick up from the sand at the locality), between the thumb and forefinger of the right hand, the pilgrim throws it from a distance of some fifteen feet, and says: "In the name of God, the Almighty, I do this, and in hatred of the devil and his shame." The remaining pebbles are thrown in the same way at each of the other pillars.

The pilgrim then returns to Mina and performs the sacrifice of the Bairam-*'Eidal-Adha*. The sacrificial animal may be a sheep, a goat, a cow, or even a camel, according to the means of the pilgrim.

When slaughtering the animal, the pilgrim says in a loud voice: "God is Great. (*Allahu akbar*) O God, accept this sacrifice from me."

This ceremony concludes the pilgrimage; and the haji, or pilgrim, then gets himself shaved, his nails pared, and the *ihram*, or pilgrim's garment is taken off and replaced by the usual dress. Although the pilgrimage rites are over by this time, he should have rest at Makkah for the following three days, which are known as *ayyamul-tashriq*, or the days of drying up of the blood of the sacrifice—three well-earned days of rest after the peripatetic performance of the last four days.

Before leaving Makkah for good, the pilgrim should once more perform the circuits round the ka'ba and throw stones at the Satanic pillars at Mina seven times. He must also drink water from the famous well near the Ka'ba, known as the Zamzam well.

The throwing of these stones or pebbles at the aforesaid monumental pillars represents a deeply rooted and heartfelt intention on the part of the pilgrim, never again to follow in the foot-steps of wicked, mischievous or bad company or to listen to evil suggestions, usually known as treading the path of the devil or Satan. This practice can by no means be mistaken for a display of idolatry. It is rather a meritorious act of self-suggestion.

Most Muslims then go to Al Madina to visit the shrine of their Holy Prophet, and to distribute alms within their means and according to their ability among the poorer citizens of the revered city.

From the time the pilgrim has assumed the *ihram* until he takes it off, he must abstain from worldly affairs and give himself up entirely to the duties of devotion. He is not allowed to hunt or kill game. He is prohibited from uniting in sexual intercourse, disputing in a vainglorious way, commiting any unlawful act, or using bad language or insulting words.

The appointed pilgrimage known as hajj, as already stated, can be performed only on the appointed days of the months of Zul hijjah. But a visit can be meritoriously made to the Sacred Mosque at Makkah at any time of the year; and in this case it is not called a pilgrimage, but takes the name of 'umra, meaning 'visit to the Holy Mosque.'

If the pilgrim happens to arrive at Makkah as late as the ninth day of the month, he can still perform his dutiful pilgrimage legally, provided he can join the pilgrims when they are at Mount Arafat on that day.

The pilgrimage cannot be performed by proxy according to the sunni or Orthodox School of Law. But if a Muslim on his death-bed bequeaths a sum of money to be paid to a certain person in order to perform the pilgrimage by proxy, this is considered as satisfying the claims of the Muslim Law.

It is regarded as a highly meritorious act to pay the expenses of a poor Muslim who cannot afford to perform the pilgrimage.

If a Muslim has the means to perform the pilgrimage, and omits to do so, he is considered to have committed a great sin.

According to the sayings of the Holy Prophet, the merits of a pilgrimage to the Sacred Mosque (the house of Allah at Makkah) are very great: "He who makes a pilgrimage for God's sake, and does not talk loosely nor act wickedly, shall return from it as pure from sin as the day on which he was born." "Truly, pilgrimage and 'umra (a visit to the Holy Mosque) put away poverty and sin like the fire of a forge which removes dross.' "When you see a pilgrim, salute and embrace him, and request him to ask pardon of God for you, for his sins have been forgiven and his supplications may be accepted."

Summary of the Fundamental Injunctions Relating to Pilgrimage

The principal rites to be observed in connection with the institution of pilgrimage are:

1. *Ihram*, that is entering the sacred land in a state of *ihram* in which the ordinary clothes are put off and all pilgrims wear one kind of apparel, consisting of two seamless sheets, leaving the head uncovered, except in the case of women pilgrims who cover their heads.
2. *Tawaf*, or making circuits round the ka'ba seven times.
3. *Sa'y*, or running seven times between two small hills near the Ka'ba known as Al-Safa and Al-Marwa.
4. Staying in the plain of Mount Arafat on the 9th day of the month of pilgrimage (Zul Hijja), where the noon and afternoon prayers shall be said.

It will be seen that the state of *ihram* makes all men and women stand upon one plane of equality, all wearing the same very simple dress and living in the same simple conditions. All distinctions of rank and colour, of wealth and nationality, disappear; and the prince is now indistinguishable from the peasant. The whole of humanity assumes one aspect, one attitude, before the Master.

Thus the greatest and noblest sight of human equality is witnessed in that wonderful desert plain called "Arafat," which enables man to obtain a better knowledge of his Creator, the word "Arafat" being derived from *arafa*, meaning 'he came to acquire knowledge (of something).' Nowhere in the whole world can we see so noble a picture of real brotherhood and equality.

The condition of pilgrim and the different movements connected with the pilgrimage, the making of circuits and running to and fro, in fact represent the stage in which the worshipper is imbued with the spirit of true love of the Divine Being. That love of God which is so much talked of in other religions becomes here a reality. The fire of divine love being kindled in the heart, the worshipper now, like a true lover, neglects all cares of the body, and finds his highest satisfaction in sacrificing his very heart and soul for the beloved One's sake; and like the true lover he makes circuits round the house of his Beloved and hastens on from place to place. He shows, in fact, that he has given up his own will and sacrificed all his interests for His sake.

The lower connections have all been cut off, and all comforts of this world have lost their attraction for the Lord. The pilgrim, indeed, represents the last stage of spiritual advancement, and by his outward condition and his movements, the pilgrim only announces to the whole world how all the lower connections must be severed in order to reach the great goals of human perfection and nearness to God, which can be attained only by holding true communion with the Unseen Divine Being.

Stanley Lane Pool's Comments

Commenting on the institution of the pilgrimage, Stanley Lane Pool—a prominent Orientalist—makes the following remarkable comment, which may throw still more light on the subject:

"This same pilgrimage is often urged as a sign of Mohammad's tending to superstition and even idolatry. It is asked how the destroyer of idols could have reconciled his conscience to the circuits of the "Kabba" and the veneration of the "Black Stone". But the fact is that Mohammad perceived that the worship in the

"Ka'aba" would prove of real value to the religion. He swept away the more idolatrous and immoral part of the ceremonies, and retained the pilgrimage to Makkah and the old veneration of the temple for reasons the wisdom of which it is impossible to dispute. He well knew the consolidating effect of forming a centre to which his followers should gather; and hence he reasserted the sanctity of the Black Stone. He ordained that everywhere throughout the world the Muslim should pray looking towards the "Ka'aba" and he enjoined him to make the pilgrimage thither.

"Makkah is to the Muslim what Jerusalem is to the Jew. It bears with it all the influence of centuries of associations. It carries the Muslim back to the cradle of his faith, the childhood of his Prophet; it reminds him of the struggle between the old faith of idolatry and the new one (Islam), of the overthrow of the idols, and the establishment of the worship of the one true God. And most of all, it bids the Muslim remember that all the brother-Muslims are worshipping towards the same sacred spot, that he is one of a great company of believers, united by one faith, filled with the same hopes, reverencing the same thing, worshipping the same God"[14].

PART TWO

TRANSACTIONS

5

Marriage

The third section of the Muslim Law concerns transactions, (Arabic: *Mu'amalat*).

Transactions are subdivided into marriage; inheritance; contracts; sale; barter and agency.

Marriage is enjoined by the Prophet upon every Muslim, while celibacy is frequently condemned by him. It is related in the traditions that the Prophet said: *"When the servant of God marries, he perfects half of his religion, let him then strive to perfect the other half by leading a righteous life."*

The following are some of the sayings of the Prophet on the subject of marriage:-

> "The best wedding is that upon which the least trouble and expenses are bestowed."

> 'The worst of feasts are marriage feasts to which the rich are invited and the poor are left out, but he who is invited should nonetheless accept the invitation."

> "Matrimonial alliances (between two families or tribes) increase friendship more than anything else."

"Marry women who will love their husbands and be very prolific, for I wish you to be more numerous than any other people....."

"When anyone demands your daughter in marriage, and you are pleased with his disposition and his faith, then give her to him."

"A woman may be married either for her wealth or her reputation, her beauty or her religion; then look out for a religious woman."

'All young men who have arrived at the age of puberty should marry, for marriage protects them against intemperances."

"When a Muslim marries he perfects half of his religion, and he should practice righteousness to secure the remaining half."

"Beware, do not make large settlements of dowry upon women, because if great settlements were a cause of greatness in the world of righteousness before God, surely it would be most proper for the Prophet of God to make them."

"A woman ripe in years shall have her consent asked in marriage, and if she remains silent (when asked) her silence is her consent, and if she refuses, she shall not be married by force".

"A widow shall not be married until she be consulted, nor shall a virgin be married until her consent be asked." The Companions said: "In what manner is the permission of a virgin?" He replied, "Her consent is by her silence.'"

From the above-mentioned teachings of the Prophet, it is clear that Islam encourages marriage and condemns celibacy.

Men and women must marry, not once in their lives, but so long as they have the strength and can afford to support each other.

In the early days of Islam, women belonging to the most respectable families in Makkah married several times after becoming widows or—contrary to the attitude of Church Christianity—after having been divorced by their husbands.

During the pre-Islamic period of the Arabs, there was no limit to the number of wives a man could take. But Islam limited the number to one, with permission to marry, if necessary, two or three or even four, provided that one can treat them with justice and equality in one's relation with them as husband, which is extremely difficult. Hence the tendency of Islamic law is towards monogamy, though it does not definitely bind a man to take only one wife. In other words, monogamy is the rule, and polygamy is an exception, it being a remedial course to be resorted to in certain cases and under certain conditions. For the circumstances and exigencies ruling polygamy, the reader is referred to the chapter "The Status of Women in Islam," in this book.

At present the concession of marrying more than one wife is enjoyed by very few, as the economic conditions and the practical difficulties involved in bringing up a large family are rather against polygamy. In the early days of Islam, the circumstances were quite different owing largely to the prevailing social and political conditions. Wars of conquests ended in the capture of a large number of women, some of whom were of respectable families, and had to be taken as wives and supported by the conquerors. Polygamy then became a necessity and offered a ready solution to social problems. A certain latitude in those days was necessary. The same solution might be resorted to if similar social conditions would suggest themselves. A number of the faithful followers of the Prophet were being killed in religious warfare. Public policy and morals required that their widows and grown-up daughters should be adequately provided for and given protecting shelter. It was, therefore, in a spirit of self sacrifice on the part of Muslim men that, within the limit of four wives prescribed by the law, the believers took in wedlock the widows and daughters of their friends, who had sacrificed themselves in the cause of their religion. The greatest sacrifice in this respect was made by the Prophet himself, whose additional object in having as many as nine wives—all of whom (except 'A'isha) were elderly women—was to propagate the teachings of Islam through them among the women of Arabia. It was through the Prophet's wives that the Arab women, who embraced Islam, came to know what the institutions of the new religion—as envisaged by the daily life of the Prophet—really were.

Marriage — A Civil Contract

In Islam, marriage is a civil contract made by mutual consent between man and woman. What is necessary among the *sunni* or orthodox Muslims to conclude a match is the presence of two male or one male and two female witnesses and a dower. A woman who has reached the age of puberty is free to choose, to accept, or to refuse an offer, although such conduct may be against the declared wishes of her parents or guardian.

If a girl is married in her infancy, she may renounce and dissolve the contract, if she wills, on reaching her majority. Although the parents are recommended to find a suitable match for their daughter, they cannot legally force her to agree to it. Her consent in any case is necessary. She can make her own terms, before the marriage, as to the amount of dower to be paid to her, the dissolution of marriage in case her husband leaves the locality and goes to some other country, or in regard to any other matter such as the husband taking another wife, etc. All terms conditions and stipulations agreed to mutually must be recorded in the contract of the marriage by the registrar and are binding on the husband.

In the case of impotence, insanity or extreme poverty which renders it impossible for the husband to support his wife, or should he be imprisoned for such a length of time that the wife should suffer a lack of sustenance, she has the right to divorce him by a verdict of the judge.

A man may see the face of his bride, nay, he is encouraged

61

by the law to do, so before the consummation of marriage, though in practice this legal concession is not availed of in certain eastern countries where future husbands receive information about their spouses through their women relations who arrange the marriage.

A man may divorce and re-marry the divorced wife, but if he pronounces divorce on three occasions, she cannot return to him, unless it is after having married another man and lived with him as his wife for a length of time. She may be divorced by the second husband, and then she may be re-married to the first. This, however, happens only in extreme cases. The object of this law is that the husband who has divorced his wife should feel ashamed and disgraced to take her back after she has re-married and lived as the wife of another man. Therefore, in practice, few people take advantage of the right to divorce their wives on the slightest sinful act. Divorce is condemned by the Prophet and is not to be resorted to except in unavoidable circumstances, such as infidelity of the wife, or other similar serious causes.

Kinds Of Divorce

Divorce in Islam is of two kinds: Revocable, and Irrevocable.

A husband has the right to divorce his wife; but this right is not effective until the period of 'iddat, i.e. probation, is over. This period is of three menstrual courses or three months, and during this time the right of the husband to revoke the divorce may be availed of.

Should the wife survive her husband, the period of 'iddat, or probation, is prolonged to four months and ten days; before this period is ended, the widow cannot legally get married to a new husband.

If a woman is pregnant and divorce has to be resorted to, the 'iddat period continues until the delivery takes place. In this case, the wife has the right to reside in her husbands's house and be maintained by him.

A child born six months after the marriage is considered the child of the married husband; but if the child is born earlier than six months after the marriage, it is not considered legitimate.

Different Forms of Divorce

The following are the different forms of divorce current among the *sunnis:*

Besides impotence on the part of the husband, a verdict of divorce may be pronounced by the competent judge on the demand of the wife in the following cases:

1. Inequality of status of the man and woman.
2. Insufficient dower.
3. If the Muslim husband embraces any religion other than Islam.
4. If a husband charges his wife with adultery, even though she swears that she is innocent and the former insists that she is not.
5. If the husband is imprisoned for such a length of time that she suffers from want.
6. If there is continuous disagreement between husband and wife, and the latter is willing to forego some of her own privileges or give a certain ransom to free herself from her husband.(This is known as *khul'* divorce.)

Prohibited Marriages

By one of the fundamental principles of Islam neither can a Muslim marry an idolatress, nor can a Muslim woman marry an idolator.

The direct result of such prohibited marriages is the prevention of any introduction into Islam of idolatry, which it had strenuously striven to eradicate. Otherwise, Islam is quite liberal in this respect, as it permits Muslim men to marry virtuous women from among the Christians or the Jews. However, Islamic Law, for reasons closely connected with policy, does not allow a Muslim woman to marry a Christian or a Jew.

Suggested Reconciliation

In case there is any fear of a breach between a wife and a husband, reconciliation is recommended to be sought through the good offices of two arbitrators: one chosen from the husband's family and the other from the wife's family; if they are desirous of agreement, God may, through His Mercy, effect a reconciliation between them.

Prohibited Marriage Relations in Islam

These prohibitions are detailed in verses 22, 23 and 24, of Chapter 4 of the Quran, which are interpreted as follows:

> "And do not marry women whom your fathers have married: for this is a shame, and hateful and an evil way, though what is passed may be forgiven"[15].

> "Forbidden to you are your mothers, and your daughters and your sisters, and your aunts, both on the father's and mother's sides, and your foster mothers and your foster sisters, and the mothers of your wives, and your step-daughters who are your wards, born of your wives to whom you have gone in (but if you have not gone in to them, it shall be no sin in you to marry them), and the wives of your sons who proceed out of your loins; and you are forbidden to marry two sisters at a time."

> "You are also forbidden to marry any married woman."

Religious Ceremony on the Occasion of Marriage

Islamic Law appoints no specific religious ceremony, nor any religious rites as being necessary for the contraction of a valid marriage.

Legally, a marriage contracted between two persons possessing the capacity to enter into the contract is valid and binding, if entered into by mutual consent, in the presence of witnesses. In all cases, the religious ceremony is left entirely to the discretion of the qualified registrar known as the *ma'zun*, that is, the representative of the court parties.

Below is given, *in extenso*, the nuptial sermon, universally preached on the occasion of marriage, in imitation of the Holy Prophet:

> "O believers, fear God as He deserves to be feared, and do not die without having become true Muslims. O men, fear your Lord Who has created you of one progenitor, and of the same species he created his wife and from these two has spread abroad so many men and women. And fear God, in whose name you ask mutual favour, and reverence the wombs that bore you. Truly, God is watching over you. O believers, fear God and speak with well-guided speech, so that God may bless your doings for you and forgive you your sins. And whosoever obeys God and His Apostle with great bliss he surely shall be blessed."

The sermon is a collection of Quranic verses and their repetition at each and every wedding is meant to remind Muslim men and women of their duties and obligations. It opens with a commandment to fear God, and the same commandment is repeated quite a number of times in the course of the ceremony, showing that the whole of the ceremony is to be carried out in fear of God, so that from beginning to end it may be a pure, moral binding and that no selfish equivocation or hypocritical prevarication may mar the sanctity of the sacred rite.

The registrar, having recited the above verses with certain sayings of the Prophet bearing on the benefits of marriage, and the bridegroom and the bride's attorney (usually the father, uncle or elder brother) and the witnesses having assembled in some convenient place (commonly the bride's domicile) and arrangements having previously been made as to the amount of dower payable to the bride, begins to request the bridegroom to ask God forgiveness for his sins and to declare his belief in the unity of God and the Prophethood of His Apostle the Holy Prophet Muhammad. The registrar then asks the bridegroom whether he accepts to be wedded to (mentioning the name of the bride) against such and such a dower payable to her and on the law principles stated in the Quran and in the sayings of the Holy Prophet. The bridegroom answering in the affirmative, the registrar announces the consummation of the marriage contract and raises his hands and offers the following or similar prayer: "O God, grant, out of Your bounty, that mutual love and agreement may reign between this couple, as it existed between Adam and Eve."

The ceremony being over, the bridegroom shakes hands with his friends and such of his relatives as happen to be present and receives their congratulations.

Marriage Festivals

Marriage is preceded and followed by festive rejoicings which have been variously described by Oriental travellers, but they are not parts of either the civil or religious ceremonies.

The bridegroom is entitled to see his fiancee before the contract of marriage is entered into, though this custom is not usually exercised in many Muslim countries.

Inequality of the Two Sexes Regarding Divorce

Marriage, being regarded as a civil contract and as such not indissoluble, Islamic Law naturally recognizes the right of both parties to dissolve the contract under certain given circumstances. Divorce, then, is a natural corollary to the conception of marriage as a contract, and it is regrettable that it may have furnished European critics with a handle for attack. They seem to entertain the view that the Islamic Law permits a man to repudiate his wife "even on the slightest disgust". Whether the law permits or favours repudiation on the slightest disgust, we shall presently see. But there is another point raised by these critics, namely the inequality of the two sexes in regard to the right of obtaining a divorce, which inequality is in fact more seeming than real. The theory of marriage, no doubt, points to a subordination of the wife to her husband, because of her comparative inferiority in discretionary powers; but in practice the hands of husband are fettered in more ways than one. The theoretical discretion must not be understood as giving tacit sanction to the excesses of a brutal husband; on the contrary, it is intended to guard against the possible dangers of an imperfect judgement. The relations between members of the opposite sex which marriage legalizes are, however, so subtle and delicate and require such constant adjustment, involving the fate and well-being of the future generations, that in their regulation the law considers it expedient to allow the voice of one partner, more or less, predominance over that of the other.

It is perhaps worthy of notice here that in Europe the two sexes are not placed on an equal footing in respect of the right of divorce. Lord Helier, P.C., K.C.B., who was president of the Probate, Divorce and Admiralty Division of the High Court of Justice, 1982-1905, makes this observation: "Much comment has been made on the different grounds on which divorce is allowed to a husband and to a wife—it being necessary to prove infidelity in both cases, but a wife being compelled to show either an aggravation of that offence or addition to it. Opinions probably will always differ whether the two sexes should be placed on an equality in this respect, *abstract justice being invoked, and the idea of marriage as a mere contract, pointing in one direction, and social consideration in the other. But the reason of the legislature for making the distinction is clear. It is that the wife is entitled to an absolute divorce only if her reconciliation with her husband is neither to be expected nor desired. This was no doubt the view taken by the House of Lords*"[16].

Limitation on Divorce

A Muslim is not free to exercise the right of divorce on "the slightest disgust." The law has put many limitations upon the exercise of this power. Then again the example and precepts of the Prophet in this particular instance have rendered divorce most repellent to the Muslim mind. A Muslim is permitted to have recourse to divorce provided that there is ample justification for such an extreme measure. The Quran expressly forbids a man to seek a pretext for divorcing his wife, so long as she remains faithful and obedient to him in matters recommended by the law: "If women obey you (i.e. in lawful matters), then do not seek a way against them." (4:34) That is, do not seek a pretext for separation.

The law gives man, primarily, the faculty of dissolving the marriage, if the wife, by her indocility or her bad character, renders their married life unhappy. But in the absence of serious reasons, no Muslim can justify a divorce either in the eyes of religion or the law. If a man abandons his wife or puts her away from simple caprice, he draws upon himself the divine anger, for *"the curse of God,"* said the Prophet, *"rests on him who repudiates his wife capriciously,"*

In the Quran, there is a most edifying verse (4:19) which is generally overlooked by the critics of Islam: *"Associate with your wives, with goodness; and if you dislike them, it may be that you dislike a thing and God may have put abundant good in it."* (Prolphet Auyyub) Thus the Quran enjoins forbearance, even with a wife the husband does not like. One really wonders at the boldness of the critics who presume that the Islamic Law permits divorce on "even the slightest disgust."

Many and various are the sayings of the Prophet of Islam that teach love, untiring patience, a forgiving disposition and, above all, fear of God in the treatment of women. *"The man who bears the ill-manners of his wife,"* said the Prophet, *"shall receive from God rewards equivalent to what the Lord gave to Job, when he suffered his affliction. And to the woman who bears the ill-manners of her husband, God grants rewards equivalent to what He granted to Assiyah, the righteous wife of Pharaoh."*

It may rightly be observed that divorce in Islam is allowable only when object of divorce is not simply to cause distress to the wife. There are just grounds, such as refractory or unseemly behaviour on the part of the wife, or extreme necessity on the part of the husband.

Islam discourages divorce in principle, and permits it only when it has become altogether impossible for the parties to live together in peace and harmony. It avoids, therefore, a greater evil by choosing a lesser one, and opens a way for the parties to seek agreeable companions and, thus, to accommodate themselves more comfortably in their new homes.

For, under Islam, a divorced woman, like the husband who divorces her, acquires the right of marrying any person she likes, the moment the separation is recognized by the law[17].

Fully recognizing the evils that arise from divorce, the Prophet of Islam took very cautious steps in framing the laws; and the ruling idea seems to be that divorce is justified only when marriage fails in its effects and the parties cease to fulfil the duties that spring from the marriage relations. There is, in fact, no justification for permanently yoking together two hostile souls, who might make themselves quite comfortable in new homes, if they were permitted to effect a separation. To compel them, in pursuance of a most vaxatious law, to live together under the heavy yoke of slavery—for such is marriage without love—would be a hardship more cruel than any divorce whatever. God, therefore, gave laws of divorce, which when properly used, are most equitable and human.

If a woman is chaste and mindful of her duties as a wife, Islamic Law makes it obligatory upon the husband to associate with her on the best terms, and with kindness and courtesy. But if she proves refractory in her behaviour, the law confers on the husband the power of correction, if exercised in moderation[18].

Finally, it is to be remembered that the abuse likely to arise from the laxity of the laws, may conveniently be contracted by other lawful impositions. The wife, or her guardian or attorney, may stipulate, at the time of marriage, against the arbitrary exercise of the power of divorce by the husband. The right to contract out of the marriage, may be stipulated to be with the wife, instead of with the husband, if necessary. The same object may also be achieved indirectly, by fixing the dower at a large sum payable to the wife in case of divorce by the husband, such as may be beyond the means of the husband to liquidate. The wife may also, by stipulation, reserve to herself the power of dissolving the marriage under certain legitimate circumstances, for example, if the husband marries a second wife.

Again, in the event of a divorce, Islamic Law is very particular in providing for the protection of the wife's property against the avarice of the husband: if the cause for divorce is imputable to the husband, he has to make over to her all her property, and pay off the dower that had been settled upon her. If, however, the divorce has been resorted to at the instance of the wife, without any justifiable cause, she has simply to abandon her claim to the dower. The wife thus occupies a decidedly more advantageous position than the husband.

Islamic Law also institutes a procedure known as tafriq, which legally means dissolution of the status of marriage by a judicial verdict. Here are some causes for which the wife can demand a divorce by authority of the court:

a) Habitual ill-treatment of the wife.
b) Non-fulfilment of the terms of marriage contract.
c) Insanity.
d) Incurable Incompetency.
e) Quitting the conjugal domicile without making provision for the wife.
f) Any other causes which in the opinion of the court would justify a divorce.

Islamic Legal Status of a Married Woman

To sum up, the Islamic legal status of a Muslim married woman is decidedly superior to that of a European woman. The former enjoys social immunities which allow the fullest exercise on her part of the powers and privileges given to her by the law. She acts as *sui-juris* in all matters which relate to herself and to her property, in her own individual right, without the intervention of husband or father. She never loses her own identity on becoming wedded, by remaining related to her father's family. She appoints her own attorney, and delegates to him all the powers she herself possesses. She enters into valid contracts with her husband and her male relations on a footing of equality. If she is ill-treated, she has the right to have the marriage tie dissolved, and is entitled to pledge the credit of her husband for the maintenance of herself and her children. She is able, even if holding to a creed different from that of her husband, to claim the free and unfettered exercise of her own religious observance. To enjoy all her rights of action she requires no intermediaries, trustees or next of kin. When she is wronged by her husband, she has the right to sue him in her own capacity.

It is both interesting and instructive to compare the above summary with another, from the writing of J.S. Mill, which gives us an idea of the corresponding position of women under the usages of Church Christianity:

"We are continually told," that civilization and Christianity have restored to woman her just rights. Meanwhile, the wife is the actual bond-servant of her husband; no less so, as far as legal obligation goes, than a slave commonly so-called. She vows a life-long obedience to him at the altar, and is held to it all through her life by law. It may be said that the obligation of obedience stops short of participation in crime, but it certainly extends to everything else. She cannot act, whatever the case, but by his permission, at least tacit. She can acquire no property but for him; the instant it becomes hers even if by inheritance, it becomes *ipso facto* his. In this respect the wife's position, even under the common law of England, is worse than that of slaves in the laws of olden days in other countries. By the Roman Law, for example, a slave might have peculium which, to a certain extent, the law guaranteed him for his exclusive use[19].

6

Law of Inheritance

The law of inheritance is called *'Ilmul-farayid,* or *'Ilmul-mirath,'* i.e. the science of obligations of inheritance. The verses in the Quran upon which the law of inheritance is founded begin at the 11th verse of Chapter 4 of the Quran. They are rendered as follows:

> "With regard to your children, God commands you to give the male the portion of two females, and if there be more than two females, then they shall have two-thirds of that which their father has left: but if there is an only daughter, she shall have the half; and the father and mother of the deceased shall each of them have a sixth part of what he has left, if he has a child; but if he has no child, and his parents be his heirs, then his mother shall have a third; and if he has brothers, his mother shall have a sixth, after payment of any legacies he shall have bequeathed and his debts. As to your fathers or your children, you do not know which of them is the most advantageous to you. This is the law of God. Truly, God is All-Knowing and Wise."

"Half of what your wives leave shall be yours if they have no issue; but if they have issue, then a fourth of what they have shall be yours, after paying bequests and debts.

"And your wives shall have a fourth part of what you leave if you have no issues, but if you have issue, then they shall have an eighth part of what you leave, after payment of bequests and debts, if any."

"If a man or woman makes a distant relation their heir, and he or she has a brother or a sister, each of these two shall have a sixth; but if there are more than this, then shall they be sharers in a third after payment of the bequests and debts."

"Without loss to any one, this is the ordinance of God, and God is All-Knowing and Gracious."

The foregoing general rules of inheritance are detailed in the following[20]:

The property of a deceased Muslim is applicable, in the first place, to the payment of his funeral expenses; secondly to the discharge of his debts; and thirdly, to the payment of legacies not exceeding one-third of the residue. The remaining two-thirds along with that part of the one-third as is not absorbed by legacies, are the patrimony of the heirs. A Muslim is, therefore, disabled from disposing of more than one third of his property by will.

The clear residue of the estate descends to the heirs; and among these the first are persons for whom the law has provided certain specific shares or portions and who are thence denominated 'the sharers' or Za-wul-furud in Arabic.

In most cases, there must be a residue after the sharers have been satisfied; and this passes to another class of persons who, under that circumstance, are termed residuaries or 'asaba in Arabic.

It seldom happens that the deceased has no individuals

connected with him who do not fall into either of these two classes; but to provide for this contingency, the law has recognized another class of persons who, by reason of their remote position with respect to the inheritance, have been denominated "distant kindred" or *za-wul-arham* in Arabic.

Gifts and Donations

During his lifetime a Muslim has absolute power over his property. He may dispose of it in whatever way he likes. But such dispositions, in order to be valid and effective, are required to have been made during the lifetime of the owner. If a gift be made, the subject of the gift must be made over to the done during the lifetime of the donor; he must, in fact, divest himself of all proprietary rights in it and place the donee in possession. To make the handing over of the gift dependent upon the donor's death would invalidate the donation. The same applies to endowments for charitable or religious purposes. A disposition—in favour of a charity,—in order to be valid, should be accompanied by the complete divestment of all proprietary rights. As regards testamentary dispositions, the power is limited to one-third of the property, provided that it is not in favour of one who is entitled to share in the inheritance. For example, the proprietor may devise by will one-third of his property to a stranger; should the bequest, however, relate to more than one-third, or should it be in favour of a legal heir, it would be invalid.

Points of Contract

A Muslim upon his death may leave behind him a numerous body of relations. In the absence of certain determinate rules, it would be extremety difficult to distinguish between the inheriting and the non-inheriting relations. In order to obviate this difficulty and to render it easy to distinguish between the two classes, it is the general rule and one capable of universal application, that when a deceased Muslim leaves behind him two relations, one of whom is connected with him through the other, the former shall not succeed while the intermediate person is alive. For example, if a person on his death leaves behind him a son and son's son, this latter will not succeed to his grandfather's estate while his father is alive. Again if a person dies leaving behind him a brother's son and a brother's grandson and his own daugher's son, the brother's son, being a male agnate and nearer to the deceased than the brother's garndson, takes the inheritance in preference to the others.

The law of inheritance is a science acknowledged even by Muslim doctors to to be an exceedingly difficult object of study.

Although it is not easy to follow it out in all its intricacies, a carefully drawn up table on the *sunni* law of inheritance is given hereunder.

A. Legal Heirs and Sharers

1. *Father*

As a mere sharer, when there is a son or a son's son, how low soever, he takes 1/6.

As a mere residuary, when there is no successor but himself, he takes the whole: or with a sharer, not a child or son's child, how low soever, he takes what is left by such a sharer.

As sharer and residuary, as when there are daughters and son's daughter but no son or son's son, he, as sharer, takes 1/6; a daughter takes 1/2, or two or more daughters 2/3; a son's daughter 1/6; and the father the remainder as residuary.

2. *True Grandfather*

A father's father, his father and so forth, into whose line of relationship to the deceased no mother enters, is excluded by the father and excludes brothers and sisters; he comes into the father's place when there is no father; but does not, like the father, reduce the mother's share to 1/3 of residue, nor entirely exclude the paternal grandmother.

3. Half Brothers by the Same Mother

They take, in the absence of children or son's descendants and father and true grandfather one 1/6, two or more between them 1/3, being those who benefit by the "return".

4. Daughters

When there are no sons, daughters take one 1/2; two or more 2/3 between them; with sons they become residuaries and take each half a son's share, being in this case of those who benefit by the "return".

5. Son's Daughters

They take as daughters when there is no child; take nothing when there is a son or more daughters than one; take 1/6 when only one daughter; they are made residuaries of a male cousin, how low soever.

6. Mother

The mother takes 1/6 when there is a child or son's child, how low soever, or two or more brothers or sisters of whole or half blood; she takes 1/3 when none of these; when husband or wife and both parents, she takes 1/3 of the remaindr after deducting their shares, the residence going to father; if no father but grandfather, she takes 1/3 of the whole.

7. True Grandmother

Father's or mother's mother, how high soever; when there is no mother, she takes 1/6; if more than one, 1/6 between them. The paternal grandmother is excluded by both father and mother; the maternal grandmother by the mother only.

8. Full Sisters

These take as daughters when no children, son's children how low soever, true grandfather or full brother; with a full brother, they take half the share of the male: when there are daughters or son's daughters, how low soever, but neither sons, nor son's sons, nor

76

father, nor true grandfather, nor brothers, the full sisters take as residuaries what remains after the daughter or son's daughter has had her share.

9. Half Sisters by the Same Father

They take as full sisters, when there are no full sisters; with one full sister, they take 1/6; when there are two full sisters, they take nothing, unless they have a brother who makes them residuaries and then they take half of a male's share.

10. Half Sisters by the Mother only

When there are no children or son's children, how low soever, or father or true grandfather, they take one 1/6; two or more 1/3 between them.

11. Husband

If no child or son's child, how low soever, he takes 1/2; otherwise 1/4.

12. Wife

If no child or son's child how low soever, she takes 1/4; if otherwise,1/8. Several widows share equally.

Corollary

All brothers and sisters are excluded by son, son's son, how low soever, father or true grandfather. Half brothers and sisters on the father's side are excluded by these and also by full brothers. Half brothers and sisters on the mother's side are excluded by any child or son's child, by father and true grandfather.

B. Residuaries

1. Residuaries in their own right, being males into whose line of relationship to the deceased no female enters:

(a) Descendants

1. Son.
2. Son's son.
3. Son's son's son.
4. Son of No. 3.
   (4a) Son of No. 4.
   (4b) And so on how low soever.

(b) Ascendants

5. Father.
6. Father's father.
7. Father of No. 6.
8. Father of No. 7.
   (a) Father of No.8.
   (8b) And so on how high soever.

(c) Collaterals

9. Full brother.
10. Half brother by father.
11. Son of No.9.
12. Son of No. 10.
    (11a) Son of No. 11.
    (11b) Son of No. 11a.
    (12a) Son of No. 12.
    (12b) Son of No. 12a.
    And so on how low soever
13. Full paternal uncle by father.
14. Half maternal uncle by father.
15. Son of No. 13.
16. Son of No. 14.
    (15a) Son of No. 15.
    (16a) Son of No. 16.
    And so on how low soever.
17. Father's half paternal uncle by father's side.
18. Father's half paternal uncle by father's side.

19. Son of No. 17.
    (19a) Son of No. 19.
20. Son of No. 20.
    And so on, how low soever.
21. Grandfather's full paternal uncle by father's side.
22. Grandfather's half paternal uncle by father's side.
23. Son of No. 21.
24. Son of No. 22.
    (23a) Son of No. 23.
    (24a) Son of No. 24.
    And so on, how low soever.

Notes

a) A nearer residuary in the above table is preferred to and excludes a more remote residuary.
b) Where several residuaries are in the same degree, they take *per capita* not *per stripes*, i.e. they share equally. The whole blood is preferred to and excludes the half blood at each stage.

2. Residuaries in another's right: being certain females, who are made residuaries by males parallel to them; but who, in the absence of such males, are only entitled to legal shares. These female residuaries take each half as much as the parallel male who makes them residuaries. The following four persons are made residuaries:

a) Daughters made residuary by son.
b) Son's daughters made residuary by full brother.
c) Full sister made residuary by full brother.
d) Half sister by father made residuary by her brother.

3. Residuarries with another: being certain females who become residuaries with other females. These are:

a) Full sisters with daughters or daughter's sons.
b) Half sisters with father.

79

Notes

When there are several residuaries of different kinds of classes, e.g. residuaries in their own right and residuaries with another, propinquity to the deceased gives a preference, so that the residuary with another, when nearer to the deceased than the residuary in himself, is the first.

If there be residuaries and no sharers, the residuaries take all the property.

If there be sharers and no residuaries, the sharers take all the property by the doctrine of the "return". Seven person are entitled to the "return". 1st. mother; 2nd, grandmother; 3rd, daughter; 4th, son's daughter; 5th, full sister; 6th, half sister by father; 7th, half brother or sister by mother.

A posthumous child inherits. There is no presumption as to commorients, who are supposed to die at the same time, unless there be proof otherwise.

If there be neither shares nor residuaries, the property will go to the following class (distant kindred):

C. Distant Kindred

(All Relatives who are neither Sharers nor Residuaries)

Class 1

Descendants: Children of daughters and son's daughters:-

1. Daughter's son.
2. Daughter's daughter.
3. Son of No. 1.
4. Daughter of No. 1.
5. Son of No. 2.
6. Daughter of No. 2 and so on, how low soever, and whether male or female.
7. Son's daughter's son.
8. Son's daughter's daughter.
9. Son of No. 7.
10. Daughter of No. 7.
11. Son of No. 8.

12. Daughter of No. 8, and so on how low soever, and whether male or female.

Notes

a) Distant kindred of Class I take according to proximity of degree; but when equal in this respect, those who claim through an heir, i.e. sharer or residuary, have a preference over those who claim through one who is not an heir.

b) When the sexes of their ancestors differ, distribution is made having regard to such difference of sex, e.g. daughter of daughter's son gets a portion double that of son of daughter's daughter, and when the claimants are equal in degree but different in sex, males take twice as much as females.

Class 2

Ascendants: False grandfathers and false grandmothers.

13. Maternal grandfather.
14. Father of No. 13, father of No.14 and so on as high soever (i.e. all false grandfathers).
15. Maternal grandfather's mother.
16. Mother of No. 15 and so on, how high soever (i.e. all false grandmothers).

Note

Rules (a) and (b), application to class I, apply also to class 2. Furthermore, when the sides of relation differ, the claimant by the paternal sides gets twice as much as the claimant by the maternal side.

Class 3

Parents Descendants:

17. Full brother's daughter and her descendants.
18. Full sister's son.
19. Full sister's daughters and their descendants, how low soever.

20. Daughter of half brother by father, and her descendants.
21. Son of half sister of father.
22. Daughter of half sister by father, and her descendants, how low soever.
23. Son of half brother by mother.
24. Daughter of half brother by mother, and her descendants, how low soever.
25. Son of half sister by mother.
26. Daughter of half sister by mother, and their descendants, how low soever.

Note

Rules (a) and (b) applicable to Class 1, apply also to Class 3, Furthermore, when two claimants are equal in respect of proximity, one who claims through a residuary is preferred to one who cannot so claim.

Class 4

Descendants of the two grandfathers and the two grandmothers.

27. Full paternal aunt and her descendants, male or female, and how low soever.
28. Half paternal aunt and her descendants, male or female, how low soever.
29. Father's half brother by mother and his descendants, male or female, how low soever.
30. Father's half sister by mother and her descendants, male or female, how low soever.

Note

The sides of relations being equal, uncles and aunts of the whole blood are preferred to those of the half, and those connected by the same father only, whether males or females, are preferred to those connected by the same mother only. Where sides of relation differ, the claimant by paternal relation gets twice as much as the

82

claimant by maternal relation. Where the sides strength of relation is equal, the male gets twice as much as the female.

General Rule: Each of these classes as above mentioned excludes the next following class.

Note

In cases where there are no sharers, residuaries, or distant kindred to claim inheritance, the whole property of the deceased shall be given over to the Public Treasury, i.e. The State.

7

Sale and Usury

Sale in the language of the Muslim Law signifies an exchange of property with the mutual consent of the parties. In its ordinary acceptance, sale is a transfer of property in consideration of a price in money. The word has a comprehensive meaning in the law, and is applied to every exchange of property with mutual consent. It, therefore, includes barter as well as sale, and also loan, when the articles lent are intended to be consumed and replaced by a similar quantity of the same kind, to be returned to the lender. This transaction which is truly an exchange of property is termed a *qard* in the law, *i.e.* a loan.

According to the Muslim Laws of contracted transaction of sale and barter, etc., things are divided into (a) Similars; and (b) Dissimilars.

Similar things are those which are sold by weighing and measuring; and dissimilar things which are different in quality but sold in exchange, such as wheat for its price in coin. In the case of similar things such as wheat for rice, when sold after being measured or weighed, delivery should take place at once. When these are sold unconditionally, the buyer has no right to choose the best part of it from the whole, unless the seller consents and desires to please him. Things sold or exchanged cannot remain undelivered or unadjusted on the mere responsibility of the parties. But if a thing is sold against its value in money, time is allowed for payment. Among similar things, there are equivalents in capacity, weight and sale. The seller must express clearly the quantity and quality of the thing exactly as it is, so that any doubt or misunderstanding may not arise in regard to it later on. He must fix the price and say that he is willing to sell to so and so such and such a thing, valued at so much, and on such and such terms and conditions (if there be any); and the buyer must accept the offer in clear language. If the seller himself cannot do this, he must appoint an agent, with sufficient authority to dispose of his goods. If a contract is made through a broker, it must be ratified by the actual buyer. Where a commodity has not been removed from the seller's premises, both buyer and seller have three days in which to opt out of the transaction. If a thing is purchased without inspection or examination and afterwards a difference is found in the quantity or the quality specified by the seller, or asked for by the purchaser, the latter may refuse to take delivery of it. Of the various kinds of recognized kinds of sale, the following are the most important:

1. Sale of a specific thing for a price or by way of barter.
2. Sale of silver for silver or gold for gold or banking in which the exchange of coins, either silver or gold, must be exact in weight or quality, so that there may be no chance of resorting to usury.
3. Sale in advance when the price is deposited before taking delivery of goods.
4. Loan, etc.,

The quality of the thing, when lent, must be specified and the thing to be given back should be of the same quality.

One can mortgage his property, but here also usury is avoided. The theologians have permitted only such bargains in which a lender of money can be benefited without transgressing the law, e.g. by the use of a thing or property which has been mortgaged; or make a condition precedent that if, within a specified time, the money is not repaid, the property mortgaged will be delivered into the possession of the lender, etc. *Riba* or usury is strictly prohibited under Islamic law, It means taking advantage of an individual in distress by giving him momentary relief, with the intention of bringing more misery upon him. One is forced to ask for a loan on the condition that it would be repaid, as agreed, to the lender; often much more has to be paid to the lender than he has actually paid. In some cases it may be deemed harmless, but often it brings ruin to whole families, of which the lender is conscious. Such exaction is against the spirit of Islam. The lender may intentionally lend money to gain possession of the property of one who may, owing to hard circumstances, be forced to seek his help. Islam inculcates moderate socialism and with it prescribes a rational and just mode of dealing as between members of the Muslim community. Each individual has the right to possess what is his own property and enjoy what is his own wealth, but only to the extent that he does not injure others' happiness or interests. He may amass wealth, but the surplus wealth, of which he is not in need for immediate use, must be used for helping those who are badly in need thereof. Usury as practiced in the time of the Prophet, was against such democratic principles and was, therefore, prohibited. It is difficult to say whether the modern method of banking and charging of interest on amounts lent out is based upon the doctrine of mutuality, service and mutuality of benefit between lender and borrower. If the benefits are deemed to be onesided, this cannot be said to be permitted by Islamic Law. If, on the other hand, there is mutuality of service, it would, in the judgement of Muslim theologians, be permissible, as it would be held by them to be a kind of transaction.

Usury

Usury, as an illegal transaction, is judged on the basis of *rate*, *combined with species*, and it includes all gain upon loans, whether from the loan of money, or goods or property of any kind.

The teaching of the Quran on the subject is given in Chapter 2, verse 275 of which the following is a translation:

"Those who live on usury shall arise on the last day as they arise whom Satan has infected by his touch. For they say: 'Trading is no different from usury, and yet God has allowed trading and forbidden usury, and whosoever receives this admonition from his Lord, and abstains from it, shall have pardon for what is past and his lot shall be decided by God. But they who return to usury shall be given over to the Fire—therein to abide forever."

The Prophet is related to have said:

"Cursed be the taker of usury, the giver of usury, the writer of usury, and the witness of usury, for they are all equal."

"Indeed, the wealth that is gained in usury, although it be great, is of small advantage."[21]

Riba, i.e. usury, in the language of the law, signifies 'an excess," according to a legal standard of *measurement or weight* in one of two *homogeneous* articles (of weight or measurement of capacity) opposed to each other in a contract of exchange, and in which such excess is stipulated as an obligatory condition on one of the parties, without any return, i.e. without anything being opposed to it. The sale, therefore, of two loads of barley, for instance, in exchange for one load of wheat does not constitute usury, since these articles are not *homogeneous*; and, on the other hand, the sale of ten yards of cloth in exchange for five yards of another cloth is not usury, since although these articles be homogeneous, they are not estimable *by weight*, or *measurement* of capacity.

Usury, then, as an illegal transaction, is judged to be so on the basis (according to most distinguished doctors) of *rate in conjunction with species* where, however, it must be observed that rate, in the law of Islam, applies only to articles of weight and measurement of capacity, and not to articles of *longitudinal*

87

measurement, such as cloth, etc., or countable items such as eggs, dates, walnuts, etc., when exchanged from hand to hand. Where species correspond and also have the quality of being weighable or measurable by capacity (a possible occasion for), the stipulation of *inequality* as well as the suspension of payment to a future period, are both usurious.

Thus it is usurious to sell either one measure of wheat in exchange for two measures or one measure of wheat for one measure deliverable at a future period. If, on the contrary, *neither* of these circumstances exists (as in the sale of wheat for money), it is lawful either to stipulate a higher rate or the payment at a future period. If, on the other hand, only *one* of these circumstances exists (as in the sale of wheat for barley), then a higher rate may legally be stipulated, but not a suspension in the payment. Thus, against one measure of wheat two measures of barley may lawfully be sold; but it is not lawful to sell one measure of wheat for one measure of barley, payable at a future period.

Items similar in weight and capacity are distinguished from all other categories of property in a very remarkable way. When one article of weight or one of measure is sold or exchanged for another of measure, the delivery of both must be immediate, from hand to hand, and any delay in delivery in one of them is unlawful and prohibited.Where again, the articles exchanged are also of the same kind, as when wheat is sold for wheat, or silver for silver, there must not only be reciprocal and immediate delivery of both before the separation of the parties, but also absolute equality of weight or measure, according to whether the articles are weighable or measurable; any excess on either side is also unlawful and prohibited.

These two prohibitions constitute in brief the doctrine of *riba* (usury), which is a marked characteristic of the Islamic Law of sale. The word *riba*(in Arabic) properly signifies "excess," and there are no terms in Islamic Law which correspond to the words "interest" and "usury" in the sense attached to them in the English language; but the Prophet expressly prohibited his followers from deriving any advantage from loans, and that particular kind of advantage which is called by Westerners "interest" —the receiving back from the borrower a quantity larger than that actually lent to him. This was effectually prevented by the two rules mentioned above.

Lawful Transactions

Items similar in weight and capacity may have features common to other commodities, which mark with further peculiarity their treatment in the Islamic Law, e.g., there may be aggregates of minute parts, which are not exactly alike, but which so closely resemble each other, that the difference between them may be safely disregarded. For this reason they are usually dealt with in bulk, with regard only to the whole of a stipulated quantity, and not to the individual parts of which it is composed. When sold in this manner, they are said to be indeterminate. They may, however, be rendered specific in several ways. Actual delivery, or production with distinct reference at the time of contract, is sufficient for that purpose in all cases. But something short of this would suffice for all similar items, excepting money. Thus flour, or any kind of grain, may be rendered specific by being enclosed in a sack, or oil, or any liquid, by being put into casks or jars; and though the vessels are not actually produced at the time of contract, their contents may be sufficiently particularized by description of the vessels and their equality. Money is not susceptible of being thus particularized. Hence, money is said to be always indeterminate. Other identical items, including those which are countable, are sometimes indeterminate. Dissimilar items, including those which are countable, are always specific.

When similar items are sold indeterminately, the purchaser has no right to any specific portion of them until it be separated from a general mass, and marked and identified as the subject of the contract. From the moment of offer till actual delivery, he has nothing to rely upon but the seller's obligation, which may, therefore, be considered the direct subject of the contract. Similar items taken indeterminately are accordingly termed *dayn* or obligation in Islamic Law. When taken specifically, they are classed with dissimilars under the general term of *'ayn*.

The literal meaning of this term is "substance or thing;" but when opposed to *dayn* it means something determinate or specific. The subject of traffic may thus be divided into two classes: specific and indeterminate; or if we substitute for the latter the word "obligation" and omit the word "specific," as unnecessary, when not opposed to "indeterminate," these classes may, according to the view of Islamic lawyers, be described as things and obligation.

It is a general principle of the Islamic Law of sale that credit cannot be opposed to credit, namely that both the things exchanged cannot be allowed to remain on the responsibility of the parties. Hence it is only with regard to one of them that any stipulation for delay in delivery is lawful. Price admits of being left on responsibility, and accordingly a stipulation for delay in the payment of the price is quite lawful and valid. It follows that a stipulation for delay in the delivery of the things sold cannot be lawful. And this is the case, with the exception of a particular kind of sale, hereafter to be noticed, in which the thing to be sold is always indeterminate, and the price is fixed in advance. It may, therefore, be said of all specific things when subject of a sale, that a stipulation for delay in their delivery is illegal, and would invalidate the sale. The object of this rule may have been to prevent any change of the thing sold before delivery, and the disputes which may in consequence arise between the parties.

There is a kind of sale known as *salam* in Islamic Law. This word literally means an "advance"; and in a *salam* sale the price is immediately advanced for the goods to be delivered at a future fixed time. It is only things of the similar class that can be sold in this way, and as they must necessarily be indeterminate, the proper subject of sale is an obligation, while, on the other hand, the price must be actually paid or delivered, at the time of the contract, before the separation of the parties, and must, therefore, even in the case of its being money, be produced, and in consequence be particularized or specified; a *salam* sale is strictly and properly the sale of an obligation for a thing, as defined before. Until actual payment or delivery of the price is made, however, it retains its character of an obligation, and for this reason the price and the goods are both termed "debts," and are adduced as examples of the principle that the sale of a debt, i.e.

of the money or goods which a person is under engagement to pay or delivery before possession, is invalid.

There is another transaction which comes within the definition of sale; it is that which is called *qard* in Arabic and "loan" in English. The borrower acquires an absolute right of property in the things lent; and comes under an engagement to return an equal quantity of things of the same kind. The transaction is, therefore, necessarily limited to items which are similar in weight, capacity or number, and the things lent and repaid being of the same kind, the two rules mentioned for the prevention of *riba* or usury must be strictly observed. Hence it follows that any stipulation on the part of the borrower for delay or forbearance by the lender, or any stipulation by the latter for interest to be paid by the lender, or any stipulation by the latter for interest to be paid by the former are alike unlawful.

Notwithstanding the stringency of the rules for preventing usury, or the taking of any interest on the loan money, methods were found for evading them, while still keeping within the letter of the law. It had always been considered lawful to take a pledge to secure the repayment of a debt. Pledges were ordinarily of movable property; when given as security for a debt, and the pledge happened to perish in the hands of the pawnee, the debt was held to be discharged to the extent of the value of the pledge. Land, though scarcely liable to this incident, was sometimes made the subject of the pledge, and devices were adopted for enabling the lender to derive some advantage from its possession while pledged to him . If repayments were made at the assigned term, the lender was obliged to return the land; but if not, the property would remain his own, and the difference between its value and the price or sum lent might have been considered an ample compensation for the loss of interest. This form of sale which is call *bay'ulwafa* in Arabic, a term given to a sale of something that may be reconveyed by the seller on repayment, within a fixed period, of the price or sum given. This form of sale seems to be strictly legal according to the most approved authorities, though held to be what the law calls abominable, as a device for obtaining what it prohibits.

In constituting sale, there is no material difference between the Islamic and other systems of law. The offer and acceptance which are expressed or implied in all cases, must be so connected as to obviate any doubt of the one being intended to apply to the other. For this purpose, Islamic Law requires that both shall be interchanged at the same meeting of the parties, and that no other business shall be suffered to intervene between an offer and its acceptance. A very slight interruption is sufficient to break the continuity of a negotiation, and to terminate the meeting in a technical sense, though the parties should still remain in personal communication. An acceptance, after the interruption of an offer made before it, would be insufficient to constitute a sale.

As personal communication may be inconvenient in some cases, and impossible in others, the integrity of the meeting is held to be sufficiently preserved when a party who receives an offer by message or letter declares his acceptance of it on receiving the communication and apprehending its contents.

When a sale is lawfully contracted, the ownership of the things exchanged passes immediately from and to the parties respectively.

In a legal sense, delivery and possession are not necessary for this purpose. Until possession is taken, however, the purchaser is not liable for accidental loss, and the seller has a lien for the price on the thing sold. Delivery by one party is in general tantamount to possession taken by the other. It is, therefore, sometimes, of great importance to ascertain when there is a sufficient delivery; and many cases real or imaginary, on the subject, are inserted in the books of detailed theology[22]. It sometimes happens that a person purchases a thing of which he is already in possession, and it then becomes important to determine in what cases his previous possession is convertible into a purchase. Unless so converted, it would be held that there is no delivery under the sale, and the seller would of course retain his lien and remain liable for accidental loss.

Though possession is not necessary to complete the transfer of property through a legal sale, the case is different where the contract is illegal; for here property does not change hands till possession is taken. The sale, however, though so far effectual, is still invalid and liable to be set aside by a judge, at the instance of either of the parties, without any reference to the fact of the person complaining being able to come before him with what in legal phraseology is termed "clean hands." A Muslim judge is obliged by his law to interfere, for the sake of the law itself, or, as it is more solemnly termed, for the right of God, which is the duty of the judge to vindicate, though by doing so he may afford assistance to a party who personally may have no just claim to his interference.

Quranic Enjoinments Relating to Trade and Usury

"They (the unbelievers) say that trading is just like usury: (tell them that) God allows trade and forbids usury." (2:275)

"God does not bless usury, but He blesses charity and makes it fruitful." (2:276)

"When you contract a debt for a fixed time, record it in writing; let a scribe record it between the two parties in terms of equity. But if a debt or is a minor, weak (in brain) or unable to dictate, call two men to witness; if not, one man and two women...Do not be averse in writing the contract whether small or great and record the term." (2:282)

"If a debtor is in a straightened condition, postpone claim for payment until he finds it easy to pay back the debt, or, better still, if you can, remit the debt as alms giving." (This in case of extreme poverty and inability on the part of a debtor, who instead of persecution and imprisonment,, deserves sympathy and help).

"If you are on a journey and cannot find a scribe, a pledge with possession may serve the purpose, and if one of you deposits a thing on trust with another; let the trustee faithfully discharge his trust." (2:283)

"When measuring, make the measure perfect and weigh with a right balance." (17:35)

"Keep up the balance with equity and never make the measure deficient." (55:9)

"Woe to the defrauders who when they take, they demand, in full measure, but when they give, they measure less." (83:1-3)

Appendix on Usury

The basis of the prohibition on usury is no doubt a sympathetic feeling towards those in distress. The word used in the Quran bearing on the ban on usury is the Arabic word *riba* (literally an excess or addition) which signifies an addition over and above the principle sum lent or borrowed[23]. The term is considered by some broad-minded commentators not to cover certain kinds of interest, where neither the depositor of the money nor the trustee is unfairly treated. Wherever the transaction differs from the common form of usury, it is more likely to obtain the sanction of the law.

It is rightly argued that the prohibition of interest in all forms of transaction would be a serious drawback to trade and business transactions and also to the execution of important national schemes. It is unquestionable that this prohibition, whenever applied in a broad sense in the name of the Mohammadan law, would not fit into the framework of modern world conditions.

The material civilization of the West has given rise to conditions in which usury and interest seem to be unavoidable, and so the Muslims were told more than thirteen centuries ago by the Holy prophet:

"A time will come over people when not a single person will remain who does not swallow down 'riba, and if there be any who refrains from it, still its vapour (or dust) will overtake him."

In the forefront of all these questions is the modern banking system. Some theologians are of the opinion that this system is not in conformity with the Quranic law which prohibits *riba* or usury. Carefully examined and technically studied in the light of the surrounding economic interest of the nation, the banking system should not come within the scope of the prohibitory law of *riba*. The question of trade, which is today no longer a national but an international concern, is entirely dependent on the banking system. Therefore, the Mohammadan Law, which is a mercy from Almighty God to mankind, can never stand as an obstacle in the way of the general national interest.

The banking system, with its legalization of interest, has proved to be a necessary condition of economic life, and in the prevailing conditions this seems to be unavoidable. It is not only the Muslims living in non-Muslim States who cannot avoid it, but even Muslim States seem to be driven to the necessity of employing it.

Therefore, some solution had to be sought to defend the economic question confronting the Muslim nations relating to interest on money lent, borrowed or deposited.

Usury is undoubtedly universally condemned when it becomes oppressive for the debtor, a fact which is borne out by the history of indebtedness in all countries.

In Egypt, the great centre of Islam, the rulers have legalized seven per cent as the maximum interest on money borrowed or lent for *trade transactions and economic ventures*. On such a scale, the Muslims are free to transact business within the banking system. About fifty years ago, when Egypt instituted the Post Office Savings Bank, which ensures 21.2% on individual savings, some objection was raised as to the lawfulness of the institution on the assumption that it legalizes *riba*.

Thereupon, the Muslim Government resorted to *ijtihad*, the third source of Jurisprudence, and referred the matter for legal decision to the Grand Mufti of the State, Imam Sheikh Mohammad Abdou by name. He was a recognized *mujtahid*, entitled to give his verdict on *knotty* questions. He gave his decision to the effect that the interest gained therefrom by the depositors could not be considered *riba*, where the recipient of money contracts a debt, so that the rule about *riba* did not apply to interest gained on savings or on money given to a trustee to employ the same in trade or other economic transactions. This decision was made public throughout the country and no other *mujtahid* at the time gave his opinion to the contrary or opposed the decision. Hence, an *ijma'sukuti* was arrived at, and the Post Office savings Bank has ever since run as a lawful institution.

Bank Deposits

The question of deposits in banks, on which interest is payable, seems to be more like the question on trade, a necessity of modern world conditions, which cannot be avoided. The bank receives the money not as a borrower but as a trustee, where money is safe and can be withdrawn at the time of need. But at the same time it does not allow the money to lie idle, and draws some profit from it, the major portion of which again comes in the shape of interest. Out of this profit, the bank pays a certain amount to the depositors, the rate of which depends generally on the economic conditions prevailing in the country concerned, or in the world at large. It does not make over the entire profit either to the shareholders or to the depositors, but carries a certain amount over to a reserve fund to fall back upon in less profitable years, in cases of loss. So far, therefore, as it is a part of the profit earned by the bank, there is nothing objectionable in it. Some depositors spend the excess amount, which they receive as interest on their deposits on charitable objects. It is really a great pity that hundreds of thousands of guineas of interest are abandoned by Muslim depositors in favour of the banks instead of being made over to some charitable institution, or to help the poorer classes in the Muslim communities, if not to be accepted as lawful earnings in consonance with the *fatwa* (the legal decision), of the "Grand Mufti" referred to before.

Co-operative Banks

The co-operative banks are more in consonance with the spirit of the teaching of Islam, as the idea underlying them is the amelioration of the condition of the poor, who are thus saved from the clutches of the usurer. There is, moreover, this difference between an ordinary bank and a co-operative bank, that the former generally functions for the benefit of the rich and the capitalists, and the latter for that of the poor and the labourers. In the co-operative bank, the shareholders are the depositors as well as the borrowers of money, and the interest paid to the bank is, more or less, in the nature of a contribution by which the borrower of money is also ultimately benefited.

Interest on Business Capital

Interest on the capital with which a business is run, differs from ordinary debt. It is, in fact, a case in which capital and labour are sharers. But it requires that both capital and labour shall be sharers in profits as well as in loss. The payment of interest at a fixed rate means that capital shall always have a profit, even though the business may be running at a loss. It is true that when the business is profitable, the rate of interest may be much less than the profit earned, but in all such uncertainties, the viewpoint of Islam is that neither side should have undue advantage or be made to suffer undue loss. If the business is run at a profit, or if it is being run at a loss, let the capital also share in the loss. The keeping of an account of profit and loss is quite practicable and every business man must keep an account of profit and loss, if only for the purposes of taxation. This method is more advantageous for the general welfare of the community than the method of charging interest on capital.

State Borrowings

Borrowings by a state or a company for the purpose of executing projects, such as the building of railways, canals, etc., stand on a different basis. In such cases the shareholders who supply the capital are generally paid a dividend, which is calculated on the basis of profits. But sometimes the shareholders are paid a fixed rate of interest. The question is whether these cases would come under the Quranic prohibition of *riba!* Considering the above *fatwa* of the Grand Mufti it does not. The rate of interest is no doubt fixed and is generally a part of the profit. Occasionally the profits of the concern may be less than the amount of interest paid, or there may be even a loss, but in such cases there is a reserve fund to fall back upon. It cannot, however, be denied that the payment of a varying dividend is more in accordance with the spirit of the teachings of Islam than the payment of a fixed rate of interest.

8

Ownership

Kinds and Divisions of Property

Ownership, termed *milkiya,*in Arabic, is of two kinds:—

1. Things in common or joint use, such as public roads, gardens, water, pasture, light and fire lighted in a desert to which any man has a right of warming himself.

2. Private concerns, limited to the ownership of an individual. These may be classified under the following headings:

   a) *Milkul-raqaba,* which in Arabic literally means "possession of the neck", or right of the proprietor to a thing.

   b) *Milkul-yadd* or right of being in possession.

   c) *Milkul-tasarruf* or right of disposition.

Property is divided into:

1. *Movable* property, which is subdivided into the following:

   a) That which is *measured,*such as rice, etc.

   b) That which is *weighed,*such as silver, etc.

   c) That which is measured by a linear measure, such as cloth, etc.

   d) That which may be counted, such as animals, etc.

   e) Articles of furniture and miscellaneous things.

2. *Immovable* property, such as buildings, land, etc. A man may not be the owner of a property, but may have a share in its income, through hard labour, or skill, in which case, he is not concerned with the loss. But a full owner or a member of a company is affected both in the loss and the profit. As part-owners in property, each part owner is co-owner and bears the responsibility of sharing in the onus of maintaining it, repairing, it, etc. At the same time, each co-owner enjoys the right of demanding his or her share and resolving to separate his or her own share of it from the joint ownership.

There are partial or temporary rights, such as the right of *murur* or passing through another's land, and the right of *shuf'a* or pre-emption, which means that a co-partner in a certain property must be given preference in the matter of its purchase before the property is sought to be sold to a stranger, and next to him to a neighbour (if the property is immovable, such as a building or land). If there are more partners than one, the preference is to be given according to the proportion of the share or of the need, as between the parties, or on other considerations. But if the sharer or sharers do not assert their claim at the proper time, their claim lapses. Therefore, when the judge announces the sale of such property, he fixes a time for the exercise of the right. Waste land belonging to the State may become private property by cultivation after permission from the authorities concerned. Land belonging to an individual cannot, however, be acquired through cultivation or effecting other improvements on it. The Islamic Law prevents an individual from becoming a nuisance or a source of annoyance to others in exercising one's own right of ownership. For instance, a man may not build his house so close to his neighbour's as to prevent the access of light and air to them; nor can he discharge rain or water on to his neighbour's property etc.

Possession is transferred by *'aqd*, which means, a "tie," by the original possessor proposing its transfer on certain terms, or unconditionally, and the receiver accepting the same. This is called—in the law—*ijab* (proposal), and *qabul* (acceptance). Offers and acceptance of transfers of this kind are classified as follows:

1. *Hiba* or gift—a transfer of property without any exchange. This is effected by a decree of the court (Judge).
2. *Bay'* or sale, which is a transfer of property in exchange for something else. This may be effected by: (a) payment of cash; (b) barter; (c) banding, in which the transaction is cash for cash; (d) sale by payment in advance, so that the goods sought to be bought may be delivered on a future date; and (e) sale in advance, which occurs when goods are made only on receiving an order, its value being paid, in whole or in part, in advance.
3. Mortgage,
4. Rent.
5. Bequest of property, which takes effect after the death of its owner. The testator has the full right of bequest in one-third of his or her property for private and charitable purposes, after paying the debts (if any) and funeral expenses incurred, the remaining two-thirds being distributed according to the law among his heirs. If he or she desires to bequeath more than one-third of the property for charitable purposes, he or she must take the consent of the future heirs. A testator must not be insolvent at the time he or she bequeaths the property in question, or in debt to an extent exceeding the value of the property. He or she must be adult at the time the bequest is made. The bequest can be made in writing or verbally in the presence of two males or one male and two female witnesses. An executor, after accepting the responsibility, cannot decline to discharge it. He must administer the property in case the heirs are minors and distribute the property among them according to the will on their attaining majority. He may sell, pledge, or let the land or house, for absolute advantage or for meeting a necessity. But he cannot trade with it unless specifically permitted by the will. A bequest made must be accepted by the legatee. It may be in favour of one or more persons of his own family or to outsiders, who may be Muslims or non Muslims.

    Duties of an Executor. — Besides generally administering the property, the duties of an executor are:—

a) Paying the funeral expenses.
b) Discharging all debts due, if any.
c) Collecting all dues and debts owing to the testator.
d) Acting according to the intention of the testator.

A bequest may be revoked during the lifetime of the testator, and all changes he desires may be effected by him in regard to it.

6. *Waqf* or endowments. *Waqf*, literally means suspension or standing. It is a word used in the sense of transferring an individual's property and income for some charitable purpose. Endowments among Muslims are made for the erection and maintenance of the following:-

a) Mosques
b) Hospitals
c) Free schools.
d) Sacred shrines.

They are also meant for the benefit of the poor, maintaining reservoirs, water works, etc. carrying out caravans services, hostels, cemeteries and supporting a family (all of it or the poorer members).

The idea of a public charity of this kind began as early as the time of the Prophet; but it developed and took a definite and legal form about the end of the first or the beginning of the second century of the Hijra. Its objects from the very start were the promotion of charity and the encouragement of learning, particularly religious learning. Accordingly, Islamic Law forbids such endowments for purposes opposed to Islamic teachings.

A non-Muslim is permitted to make endowments under the same conditions as a Muslim can. The donor or *waqf* must be in full possession of the property. He must be *'aqil*, a possessor of understanding, i.e. sane; *baligh*, of age; *hurr*, free and of good health at the time he makes the endowment. He must not be in debt for an amount detrimental to the value of his property. The endowment *per se* must be of a permanent nature and, if in the form of objects or property, must yield some profit, i.e. it must be productive or beneficial in some other way, as for instance, the endowment of a library by presenting a number of books which, though they may not yield an income, are lasting and may be studied for a very long time.

Endowments may take the form of immovable property, such as land, buildings, etc., but certain kinds of movable property may also be accepted, such as animals for the milk they may yield.

Divisions of Waqfs

Waqf may be divided into:-

1. *Khayri*, i.e. charitable such as for the benefit of mosques, hospitals, etc..
2. *Ahli*, that is intended to support a family in which the object aimed at is the perpetuation of a family in good circumstances, by affording it the support of an income of an estate.

A *waqf* need not necessarily be executed in writing, but in case it is not in writing, the donor must expressly declare it before witnesses, i.e. state specifically before them:

a) His intention to make the endowment.
b) Description of the nature of the endowment, its income etc.

He must also provide for its coming into force immediately the declaration is made.

A *waqf* can be made of one-third part of the donor's property, the remaining two-thirds being left to his heirs, but the donor may increase the quantity by making a gift during his lifetime. Once a *waqf* is properly made and comes into force, it cannot be revoked even by the donor.

Where a mosque is erected, it becomes public property as soon as any man says his prayers in it. A *waqf* is administered, according to the term of its endowment, by one or more trustees. A single person supervising the administration is called *nazir*, i.e. manager or administrator; he is paid for his services from the income of the estate to the extent of one tenth of the net income. The founder himself can become the *nazir* during his lifetime, if he so provide, and be succeeded by one of his family. But in case another is appointed under the terms of the endowment, the

A HANDBOOK OF MUSLIM BELIEF

founder or his descendants cannot interfere with the management, so long as it is administered according to the terms and conditions laid down in the endowment. If a *nazir* fails to carry out his duties honestly, or if he is proved incompetent, it is left to the magistrate *(qadi)* to dismiss him and to appoint a competent man. If an endowment is not utilized for the intended purpose, it becomes the property of the donor or of his heirs.

The endowed property must be free from the claim of creditors. A man cannot make an endowment of his property in favour of his children if he is in heavy debt, and if his object is to escape payment of his lawful debts.

Th

PART THREE

PENAL LAWS

(UQUBAT OR PUNISHMENT)

9

Criminal Intentional Injury

The third division of the Islamic law is *uqubat* or punishment for intentional injury to the following:

Human body, such as murder or causing wound.
Human property, by usurpation, theft or damage.
Human honour, such as by slander.

It is also applicable to the following:
Breach of public peace, such as rioting, highway robbery, etc.
Offences against religion, such as non-attendance at prayers, or non-payment of *zakat* (legal alms), etc.
Offences against decency, such as adultery, use of intoxicants, and gambling.
Offences against the established government, which means rebellion.

The extent of punishment for the above-mentioned crimes extends from administering a warning, or the infliction of a fine, or bodily chastisement by means of stripes, to imprisonment, transportation, cutting off of hands, feet, and lastly putting to death.

Guilt is proved when a man acts intentionally to cause injury to another man. But if a man is hurt unintentionally, the person causing the injury is not held responsible for it. For example, when a man keeps a dog in his house and a stranger enters, without warning or permission and is bitten by the dog, its owner is not responsible for the consequence. But when a man leaves his horse on the public road and the horse kicks a passer-by and hurts him, the owner is punished for this. In the case of murder, which is called qisas (in Arabic) or retaliation, though the murderer must be put to death, Islamic Law does not insist on such punishment. On the contrary, it recommends that the relatives of the murdered person accept compensation.

Punishment by way of qisas, or the like of a similar injury, is not permitted in doubtful cases. For example, when one causes a fracture in the bone of another, he cannot be punished by inflicting on him the same kind of injury. Thus, the doctrine, of qisas is limited to certain specified cases. Islamic Law, however, punishes, in milder manner, the guilty in cases of such a nature by administering admonition or scorn, by imposing imprisonment, or whipping, and only as a last resort by taking the life of the criminal. It depends upon the character of the offence and the circumstances under which the offence has been committed, the intention of the party and his age. All these are left to the consideration of the qadi (magistrate) whose discretion or judgment is depended upon.

His guide in these matters is the Quran, the hadith (Traditions of the Prophet) and the legal codes as set froth by eminent scholars learned in the law. Moderation may be shown in the type of punishment inflicted but once it is pronounced, there can be no remission in regard to its being carried out. For instance, the magistrate may show leniency in ordering twenty stripes, instead of fifty, but the twenty ordered stripes must be real hard blows, as the Quran orders: "And let not pity detain you in the matter of God's commandments."

Crime Of Murder

Murder

A murderer must either be put to death by order of the magistrate or, if the relations of the murdered man or woman are willing in certain cases to forgive the murderer and forgo their claims, the guilty party may be made to pay compensations as ordered by the court with the mutual consent of the relatives of the murdered man and the murderer. This is prescribed in the Quran, verses 178, and 179, Chapter 2, which may be rendered as follows:

> "Retaliation is prescribed for you in the matter of the slain, the free for the free, and the slave for the slave and the female for the female, but if any remission is made to anyone by his (injured) brother, then prosecution (for the bloodshed) should be made according to usage, and payment should be made to him in a good manner; this (ordinance) is an alleviation from your Lord and a mercy" (2:178).

> *"And there is life for you in (the law of) retaliation, O men of understanding, so that you may guard yourselves against evil." (2-179).*

The meaning is that preservation of life is dependent upon making the law of retaliation work; generally speaking, life cannot be safe unless those who are guilty of homicide are liable to be sentenced to capital punishment.

Qatl (in Arabic), i.e. homicide is classified under the following headings:

1. *Intentional murder:* In this case, the offender is to be punished both in this life and in the next. "Whosoever kills a believer intentionally, his punishment is hell."
2. *Analogous cases of murder, i.e. cases* when the intention to kill may be inferred. For example, when a man strikes another with a stick, he may or may not have intended the strike to

result in death. If it causes the death of the other, the punishment is that if the intention to kill him is not established, then he is fined heavily, but not put to death.

3. *Murder by mistake:* Murder may be committed by a mistake of fact or intention. The former occurs when a man strikes someone other than his intended target and kills him; the latter, when a man has no intention to kill, but accidentally causes the death of a person. The following verse bears on this point. It may be interpreted as follows:

"And it does not behove a believer to kill a believer except by mistake, and whoever kills a believer by mistake, should free a believing captive (or war prisoner) and blood-money should be paid to his people, unless they remit it as alms. But if he cannot find a captive to emancipate, he should fast for two months successively, a penance from God, and God is All-Knowing and Wise" (4:92).

4. *Murder by indirectly causing death:* For example, if a man digs a well outside his compound, on a public road, or where there is the possibility of people having to cross, and a passer-by falls in it and dies, the man is held liable and made to pay a fine. But if this act *per se* is not illegal, the dead man having taken the risk, there is no liability for reparation to be made for his death.

According to Islamic Law, the man who kills is alone held responsible for his guilt. It excludes the relatives from retaliation by the relatives of the murdered man, as was the custom among the pre-Islamic Arabs.

10

Adultery

Adultery/Fornication. Muslim jurists recommend that an eyewitness in a case of this sort should satisfy the court of the truth of the charge by proving what he saw with his own eyes. If he fails to satisfy the court, he is liable to punishment with eighty stripes. The task of becoming a witness is, therefore, onerous under Islamic Law. The object is to discourage such charges which may arise from suspicion, wrong notions, jealousy or other similar causes and which, even if true, have an effect that is not likely to prove healthy on society. Extra marital sex is either committed by an unmarried or a married person. In the former case the punishment is not so severe, but in the latter the punishment is stoning the guilty to death.

A husband may slay his wife, if he finds her with her lover in the act of sexual union. In other cases, an alleged act of adultery or fornication if brought forward by any person must be proved by four witnesses, whose statements should not differ or appear doubtful. If the charge is proved in accordance with the injunctions of the law, the punishment for fornication (for an unmarried person) is one hundred stripes, inflicted on a man while standing, and on a woman while sitting. At present the punishment for adultery and fornication is relaxed in Muslim countries, especially in those occupied or influenced by foreign powers.

The following is an English translation of the text in the Quran relating to fornication:

"As to the fornicatress and the fornicator, scourge each one of them with a hundred stripes and let not pity for them detain you in the matter...and let a party of believers witness their chastisement."[24](24:2)

Punishment for Slander

In the case of slander, one who accuses a woman of adultery must produce the evidence of four witnesses, who must clearly state the crime or else the slanderer himself is to be punished as enjoined by the Quran:

> And those who accuse free women and cannot bring four witnesses, flog them with eighty stripes, and do not admit any evidence from them ever.[25]"(24:4).

> "And as for those who accuse their wives and have no witnesses except themselves, the evidence of one of these should be taken four times, bearing God to witness that he (the husband) most surely tells the truth."

> "And the fifth (time) the curse of God will be upon him if he told lies.[26]" (24:6:7).

> "And it shall avert the chastisement from her (the wife) if she testifies four times, bearing Allah to witness, that he is most surely a liar."

> "And the fifth (time) the wrath of God will be upon her if he told the truth." (24:8:9)

11

Theft and Robbery

Crime of Theft and Highway Robbery. —According to the following text of the Quran, the magistrate may inflict any moderate or severe kind of punishment. It is left to his discretion and depends upon his interpretation of the text and his judgment:

> "The punishment for those who fight against God and his apostle and cause disaster in the land (by highway robbery) is: (1) to be slained; (2) crucified; (3) have their hands and feet cut off crossways; (4) or to be banished from the land—unless he or they repent and reform before falling into the hands of the court." (5:23)

> "And as for the man or woman who steals, cut off his or her hands as a punishment from God." (5:38)

The judge, according to Muslim jurists, may pass the following sentence:

1. If the crime involves making public highways unsafe for travellers and trade caravans, the punishment is deportation from the country.
2. If anything has been stolen, the guilty parties may be

punished by having their right hands cut off, and, for a second offence the left feet.

3.   If, besides interrupting caravans, public highways are made unsafe and those who are guilty are also held to have killed any man or woman, those adjudged guilty may be put to death or crucified, such a sentence being considered a deterrent one. But if those guilty repent before being brought before the officers of the law, they may be forgiven, provided that they restore the stolen property; and if they have killed anyone, they pay the *diyya* (in Arabic), that is the amount of money fixed by the judge and accepted by the murdered person's relatives, as compensation to be given to his heirs.

Islamic Law defines theft in the sense of stealing a thing considered as the property of another man kept in his shop, etc. or in any other safe place such as a house, or left in the care of some guardian. Many things are not considered property, such as:

1.   Things which may decay or be wasted, such as milk, fruits, grain, (not reaped) grass, fish, garden stuff, etc..
2.   Intoxicants, the theft of which a thief may excuse himself by saying he wanted to spilt it.
3.   Trifling things, such as fowls, etc.
4.   Books, including copies of the Quran.
5.   The public treasure, or *baital-mal* (in Arabic) being a property common to all Muslims, the idea being that an individual Muslim cannot be punished by amputation for an offence of this kind, because, as a Muslim, he is entitled when in distress to some share in it.

A creditor may take up to the limit of his claim from a bad debtor without transgression.

In cases where theft is proved and the magistrate passes the judgment of cutting off the hand of the thief, it is cut at the joint of the wrist.

This punishment is exacted nowadays in Saudi Arabia, Yemen and Afghanistan of the Muslim countries. Only a very few hands have been cut off on the charge of robbery or theft during the past twenty years. The punishment is so severe that it has proved an effective deterrent to such transgressions.

In Hijaz, no case of theft or robbery whatever was recorded or judged during the entire decade ending 1957.

Intoxicants, gambling, etc., are forbidden by the Quran and the punishment to be inflicted is whipping, as many stripes as may be ordered by the trying magistrate.

The testimony of a gambler or a drunkard is not to be accepted by the court: the Quran makes this explicit:

"Intoxicants and games of chance (gambling) and sacrificing to idols and divining by arrows are only an abomination, and the devil's work; shun them, therefore, so that you may prosper.

"It is the devil who seeks to cause enmity and hatred to spring up in your midst by means of intoxicants and games of chance, and to keep you from the remembrance of God and from saying your prayers, therefore abstain from them." (90:91)

The punishment for drinking wine or any intoxicating liquor is whipping, which may consist of as many as eighty stripes.

Such, in brief, is the Penal Law of Islam, which has been modified to some extent in modern Muslim States all over the world. No Muslim Government in these days (with the exception of Arabia and Afghanistan) orders the cutting off of the hands of a thief; nor does it allow the ransoming of a murderer. Even as early as the Ummayad rule, Khalifa Hisham modified the punishment for theft by limiting it to ordinary imprisonment extending to two years. With regard to other crimes, the punishment is today left to the discretion of the judge after the nature of the crime has been alleged and proved.

12

Divisions of Punishment

Punishment is divided into three classes:-
1. *Hadd*
2. *Qisas*
3. *Ta'zir*.

1. *Hadd* (pl. *hudud*) (literally that which is defined) is that punishment, the limits of which have been defined in the Quran and *hadith* (the traditions of the Prophet). The following belong to this class:

   a) Adultery, for which the adulterer must be stoned.

   b) Fornication, for which the guilty persons must receive one hundred stripes.

   c) The false accusation of a married person of adultery, for which the offender must receive eighty stripes.

   d) Apostasy, which is punishable with death.

   e) Drinking intoxicating liquor, for which the offender must receive eighty lashes.

   f) Theft, which is punished by cutting off the right hand.

   g) Highway robbery: For robbery only, the loss of hands and feet, and for robbery with murder, death, either by sword or crucifixion. This division of punishment has

already been dealt with at length in the foregoing
chapters.

2.   *Qisas (literally* retaliation) is that punishment which, although
fixed by the law, can be remitted by the person offended
against, or in the case of a murdered person, by his heirs.
It is applicable to cases of murder and wounding.

3.   *Ta'zir*, i.e. punishment which is left to the discretion of the
judge. The following chapter presents a thorough explanation
of the *ta'zir* (punishment).

13

Discretionary Correction or Ta'zir

Ta'zir (Arabic) from 'azr (to censure or repel) is that discretionary correction administered for offences, for which hadd, or fixed punishment, has not been appointed.

According to the Sunni Law, the following are the leading principles of ta'zir:

Ta'zir in the primitive sense means "prohibition" and also "instruction;" in the law, it signifies an infliction undetermined in its degree by the law, on account of the right of Allah (God), or of the individual, and the occasion of it is any offence for which hadd or "stated punishment" has not been appointed, whether that offence consists in word or deed.

1. Chastisement is ordained by the law, the institution of it being established on the authority of the Quran, which enjoins men to chastise their wives, for the purpose of correction or amendment, and the same also occurs in the traditions (examples of the Prophet). It is recorded that the Prophet chastised a person who had called another "perjurer," and all the Companions agreed concerning this. Moreover, both reason and analogy indicate that chastisement had to be inflicted for acts of an offensive nature in such a manner that men might not become habituated to the commission

117

of such acts, for, if they were, they might by degrees be led into the perpetration of others more atrocious. Though in chastisement nothing is fixed or determined, the degree of it is left to the discretion of the *qadi, (judge)*, because its purpose is correction, some being sufficiently corrected by reprimands, whilst others, more obstinate, require confinement or even blows.

2. There are four degrees of chastisement: First, the chastisement proper to the most noble of the noble, (or, in other words, the most eminent and men of learning), which consists merely in admonition, as if the *qadi* were to say to one of them: "I understand that you have done this or that," so as to make him ashamed. Secondly, the chastisement proper to the noble (namely commanders of armies and chiefs of districts) which may be performed in two ways, either by admonition (as stated above) or by *jarr* (Arabic), that is by dragging the offender to the door and exposing him to scorn. Thirdly, the chastisement proper to the middle order (consisting of merchants and shopkeepers, etc.), which may be performed by *jarr* (as above) and also by imprisonment; and fourthly, the chastisement proper to the lowest order in the community, which may be performed by *jarr* or by imprisonment and also by blows.

3. It is recorded that the ruler of a country may inflict chastisement by means of property, that is by the exaction of a sum of money in the manner of a fine, proportioned to the offence.

4. Chastisement, which is incurred purely as the right of God, may be inflicted by any person whatever. For instance, a man, finding another in the act of adultery with his wife, may slay him; but if the husband knows that expostulation or beating will be sufficient to deter the adulterer from a future repetition of his offence, he must not slay him; if, on the other hand, he sees reasons to suppose that nothing but death will prevent a repetition of the offence, in such a case the husband is allowed to slay that man, and if the woman is consenting to his act, her husband is also allowed to slay

her, from which it appears that any man is empowered to chastise another by blows for such offences against the right of God, even though there be no magistrate present; the reason for this is that the chastisement in question is of the class of the removal of evil with the hand. The Prophet has authorized every Muslim to remove evil with the hand, if possible, as he has said; *"Whoever among you sees evil, let him remedy it with his own hands; but if he be unable so to do, let him forbid it by his tongue."* Chastisement, therefore, is evidently different from punishment, since authority to inflict the latter does not appertain to any but a magistrate or a judge. This species of chastisement is also different from the chastisement which is incurred on account of the right of the individual (such as in cases of slander and so forth), since that depends upon the complaint of the injured party, in which case no one can inflict it but the magistrate, even under a private arbitration where the plaintiff and defendant may have referred the decision of the matter to a third person.

5. Chastisement in any instance in which it is authorized by the law, is to be inflicted, where the *imam*, the legal ruler, sees it as advisable.

6. If a person accuses of whoredom a male or female slave or an infidel, he is to be chastised, because this accusation is offensive, and punishment for slander is not incurred by it, as the condition of *ihsan* (*i.e.* marriage for a free Muslim or woman in the sense which induces punishment for slander) is not attached to the accused; chastisement, therefore, is to be inflicted. And in the same manner, if any person accuses a Muslim of anything other than whoredom (i.e. abuses him by calling him a reprobate, a villain, an infidel, or a thief), chastisement is incurred, because he injures a Muslim and defames him; and punishment cannot be considered as due from analogy, since analogy has no concern with the necessity for punishment; chastisement, therefore, is to be inflicted. In the case of abusing a Muslim, the measure of the chastisement is left to the discretion of the magistrate, be it more or less; and whatever he sees proper, let him inflict it.

7.   If a person abuses his Muslim brother by calling him an ass or a dog, in this case chastisement is not incurred, because these expressions are in no respect defamatory of the person towards whom they are used, it being evident that he is neither an ass nor a dog. Some jurists assert that even on such occasions, in our time chastisement may be inflicted, since in the modern acceptation, calling a man an ass or a gog is held to be abuse. Others, again, allege that it is esteemed as such, only where the person towards whom such expressions are used happens to be of dignified rank (such as a noble man or a man of letters), in which case chastisement *must* be inflicted upon the abuser, as by so speaking he exposes that person of rank to contempt; but if he be only a common person, chastisement is not necessarily incurred, but the case is, however, left to the discretion of the *qadi* and this is the most approved doctrine.

8.   The largest number of stripes in chastisement is thirty-nine, and the smallest number is three. This restriction is founded on a saying of the Prophet: *"The man who shall inflict scourging to the amount of punishment, in a case where punishment is not established, shall be counted an aggravator"* (meaning a wanton aggravator of punishment), from which saying it is to be inferred that the infliction of a number of stripes in chastisement equal to the same number as in punishment is unlawful. This being admitted, the Muslim jurists, in order to determine the utmost extent of chastisement, consider what is the smallest punishment—and this is the punishment for slander with respect to a slave, which is forty stripes—and establish thirty-nine as the largest number to be inflicted in chastisement. Abu Yusif, the eminent jurist and authority, on the other hand, considering the smallest punishment with respect to free men (as freedom is the original state of man), which is eighty stripes, deducts five and establishes seventy-five as the largest number to be inflicted in chastisement as aforesaid. This is because the same is recorded of Imam 'Ali, the fourth Khalifa, whose example Abu Yusuf follows in this instance. The more modern doctors of divinity assert that the

smallest degree of chastisement must be left to the judgement of the *imam* or *qadi*, who is to inflict whatever he may deem sufficient for chastisement, which is different with respect to different men. It is agreed that the degree thereof is in proportion to the degree of the offence; and it is also established that the chastisement for petty offences should be inflicted to a degree approaching to the punishment allotted for offences of a similar nature; thus the chastisement for libidinous acts (such as kissing and touching) is to be inflicted to a degree approaching to the punishment for whoredom, and the chastisement for abusive language to a degree approaching to the punishment for slander.

9.   If the *qadi* (judge) deems it fit in chastisement to combine imprisonment with scourging, as in cases of most vicious offences (such as committing sodomy), it is lawful for him to do both, since imprisonment may of itself constitute chastisement, and had been so employed, for the Prophet once imprisoned a person by way of chastising him. However, imprisonment is not lawful before the offence be proved, merely upon suspicion: unlike the case of offences which incur punishment, for there the accused may be lawfully imprisoned upon suspicion. It is also agreed that the *qadi*, according to his discretion, may combine imprisonment with blows in offences deserving the same.

10.   The severest blows or stripes may be given in chastisement, with no leniency as regards the amount of force used for otherwise the design would be defeated; and so leniency is not shown in chastisement by inflicting the blows or stripes upon different parts of the body. And next to chastisement, the severest blows or stripes are to be inflicted in pushishment for whoredom, as that is instituted in The Quran. Whoredom, moreover, is a deadly sin, so much so that lapidation for it has been ordained by the law. And next to punishment for whoredom, the severest blows or stripes are to be inflicted for wine-drinking, as the occasion of punishment is there fully certified, and next to that comes slander, where the severity of the blows or stripes must be given some

121

consideration, because there may be some doubt in respect to the occasion for the punishment (namely the accusation), as an accusation may be either false or true. And also because severity, if observed, may discourage the slanderer from appearing to give evidence; severity is not, therefore to be observed also in the nature of the blows or the stripes.

11. If the magistrate inflicts either punishment or chastisement upon a person, and the sufferer dies in consequence of such punishment or chastisement, his blood is *hadar*, that is to say, no reparation is required, because the magistrate is authorized therein, and what he does is done by decree of the law; and an act which is decreed is not restricted by the condition of safety. This is analogous to a case of phlebotomy; that is to say if any person desires to be bled, and consequently dies, the operator is in no respect responsible for his death; and so here also. It is different, however, in the case of a husband inflicting chastisement upon his wife, for his act is restricted by consideration of safety, as a husband only is allowed to chastise his wife. In the case of the fine of blood, according to the Shaf'i School of Jurisprudence, this is due from the public treasury (*bait-el-mal*). Because although (where chastisement or punishment proves destructive) it is homicide by misadventure (as the intention is not destruction, but the amendment of the sufferer), a fine is due from the public treasury, since the advantage of the act of the magistrate extends to the public at large; reparation is due, therefore from their property, namely from the public treasury. On the other hand, according to the Hanafi School of Theology, whenever the magistrate inflicts a punishment ordained by God upon any person, and that person dies, it is the same as if he had died by the visitation of God, without any visible cause, in which case no responsibility for this devolves upon the magistrate. In any case, the matter is left to the ruler to decide according to his discretion.[27]

14

Sinful Acts Classification

Sins are classified into:

    1. *Kabira* or great. 2. *Saghira* or small.

    This division is based upon the following interpreted text in the Holy Quran:

> "To those who avoid the great sins and scandals
> but commit only the lighter faults, the Lord will
> indeed be profuse in His mercy."

    According to Islam, a human being does not possess evil in his true nature or self but has the weakness of being tempted into evil. Therefore, evil, is not a human disposition but an acquired habit. It is a mental disease and may be cured through right preaching and training. Satan, who is evil by nature, was the first to sin. *i.e.* to disobey the command of God. His sin was self-conceit and pride, enumerated among the gravest sins. The evil tendency is the bidding of an animal soul.

    Joseph, the Prophet, is quoted in the Holy Quran to have said to himself: "I do not declare myself free from (human) weakness: most surely it is the animal soul that commands evil (and hence man does evil) but God is so Merciful to forgive as He is the most Merciful." (12:53)

Therefore, if the carnal (animal) soul is brought under the control of true self, one may become free from evil. Among the great sins are:—

1.   Associating any being with God.
2.   Wilful murder.
3.   Adultery.
4.   Theft or robbery
5.   Unnatural crime.
6.   Drunkenness.
7.   Telling lies.
8.   Usury.
9.   Disobedience to one's parents.
10. Groundlessly charging a Muslim woman with fornication.
11. Bearing false witness.
12. Defrauding orphans.
13. Despairing of God's mercy in the face of the hard trials of destiny.
14. Cowardice in defensive religious warfare.
15. Neglect of prayers or of fasting without any justification.
16. Gambling.

Sincere repentance for any sin may bring God's mercy and salvation. If a non-Muslim embraces Islam, his past shortcomings are all forgiven. A Muslim, by committing a great sin, becomes a sinner, but not an infidel. According to *sunnis*, the Prophets, all of them, including those of the Old and the New Testaments, did not commit any great sin, but were prone only to slight imperfections in action. For example, in the case of Adam, his action in eating the forbidden fruit was not disobedience but weakness of the understanding, or rather forgetfulness of the divine commandment and not intentional disobedience thereof. Therefore, he is not to be treated as one who was disallowed from seeking pardon from God. Nor does seeking pardon of God necessarily mean committing any sin. It is only a sign of humility towards Almighty God. It is admitted that human beings in any stage of human perfection are not perfect and their imperfection is in itself sufficient reason to seek God's pardon.   There is a tradition that the Holy Prophet said: *"I ask pardon of God and repent towards Him so many times every day."* Thus "sin" is human imperfection, a weakness in being tempted, though the real self remains pure in its essence.

Suicide. Suicide is a great sin, because it is considered a wilful act to kill oneself. According to the tradition of the Prophet, *"Whoever kills himself will suffer in hell."* In Islam, life is respected and its destruction, though it may be in one's own care, is forbidden. Accordingly, cases of death by suicide are very rare in Muslim countries. A true Muslim must submit to the decrees of God and accept cheerfully all unavoidable events. According to the teachings of the Holy Quran, some of these happenings should be taken to be trials ordered by Almighty God. The following is an English translation of the Quranic text bearing on the subject:

> "And He will most certainly try you with some fear, hunger, loss of property, lives and fruits (i.e. results of your strivings), and the Prophet is ordered to give good news to the patient in all such trials; they, who, when a misfortune or a loss of property or lives befalls them, should say nothing but that surely they belong to God and to Him they shall return. Upon those who remain patient Almighty God will shower His blessings and mercy, whence they prove to be submissive and dutiful to their Lord.' (2:155-156)

From this point of view, a Muslim, in attempting to commit suicide, is really revolting against the trials sent down to him by God in the form of misfortunes.

Permissible and Prohibited Food

Food is also divided in Islamic religion into permissible and prohibited.

Among the forbidden food are the following:

Quadrupeds that seize prey with their paws and teeth or talons, such as cats, tigers, etc.; and among birds: crows, kites, eagles, etc. Besides these, the flesh of elephants; the flesh of any animal dying a natural death; the blood and flesh of swine; and the flesh of those animals over which names other than God's name have been invoked when slaughtered.

The following is an interpretation of the text in the Holy Quran bearing on the subject:

> "Forbidden to you is that which dies of itself; and blood and flesh of swine, and that on which any name other than that of Allah (God) has been invoked (while the animal is being slaughtered) and the strangled (animal), and that beaten to death and that killed by a fall and that killed by being smitten with the horn, and that which beasts have eaten, except what you slaughter in the proper manner.[28]"(5-3)

An animal to be fit for food must be slaughtered with a sharp knife; in using it, care must be taken to avoid suffering to the animal as far as possible. *Before* killing, the name of God must be recited before using the knife (the formula *Allahu akbar*—God is Greater —is usually said), signifying that it was God who allowed animals to be slaughtered for the nourishment of human beings.

PART FOUR

MORALITY

15

Muslim Ethical Basis of Social Life

The ethical Muslim social life is rather a difficult subject to write about in anything like adequate fashion. Islam is international, and Muslims, who inhabit different parts of the world and live in different stages of social development, are attached to their inherited age-old customs, some of them of pre-Muslim origin. The ethical basis on which Muslim society is built up may be traced back to the last address delivered by the Prophet soon after his farewell pilgrimage, in which he said:

> "O men, listen to me, for I may not be with you after this year in this place. Let it be well understood that your lives and property are sacred and inviolable to each other. Everyone will have his share of inheritance. The child belongs to his parents. You have rights over your wives and they have rights over you. They should not be faithless to you and you must treat them with loving kindness. Do not transgress, and be faithful to any trust placed in you. Usury is prohibited and also vengeance for blood. Treat your slaves (servants) with kindness, feed them with what you eat, and clothe them as you do yourselves. Forgive them if

they make mistakes. The slaves in your possession,
who perform prayers, are your brothers and all
Muslims are brothers to one another. I ask you all
to guard yourselves against all sorts of injustice."

Such was the fraternal spirit in which Muslim society came to be first established and later developed, first and foremost in Arabia and then Central and South Asia, North Africa, and Southern Europe. The same spirit made itself felt to a greater or lesser degree, wherever Islam permeated, even if in a mild or attenuated form.

Among the more important factors which influence the development of any society is the status assigned to men and women as members of the family.

In Islam man is the maintainer of the family and as such has greater power and responsibility, though women take a prominent part in it. In fact, one of the most striking features in Muslim culture is the position assigned to women in social life.

Position of Women in Islam

Among the pre-Muslim Arabs, the custom of polyandry was prevalent. A woman could break off her relations with her husband, simply by turning the side of her tent. She was free, too, to choose her husband either directly or through her parents, and dismiss him at her pleasure. A woman could possess several husbands, and children were born to an unknown father, and not knowing the father they had to live with the mother. Thus kinship was recognized from the mother's side and the affection of children was built up more among the relatives of the mother than of the father. The eldest member of the family was recognized as the head, and several brothers had one wife in common between them, and the man who was with her at any time, used to fix his stick on the door of the tent, which was a sign for others not to enter it.

Women among the pre-Islamic Arabs were included in the property inherited, and on the father's death, a son could marry his stepmother. Mothers-in-law were also taken as wives. Islam, however, definitely abolished all these relations, and made the father's side stronger to safeguard the chastity of women, to prevent polyandry and to make a man responsible for the support of his wife and children. Thus, while Arab women lost certain indecent privileges and freedom, they gained security in livelihood, and a higher social position.

Islam also abolished the evil custom of female infanticide, which was common among the pre-Islamic Arabs, where a father used to consider it his sacred duty to take his daughter of tender age and bury her alive.

Islam contributed towards the improvement of the position of women in various ways:

1. Retaining certain of the more ancient healthy customs, such as respect and good treatment of a foster mother.
2. Making a woman the mistress of her own property, in which the husband had no right to interfere, except with her permission.
3. Giving her the right of claiming divorce on the following grounds: impotence of the husband; leprosy or insanity on his part; inferior social status; non-payment of the dowry; and conversion to any religion other than Islam. Divorce is allowed to a woman in certain other cases. Thus, if the wife is suspected and accused by her husband of adultery, but cannot prove her guilt and swear that she is guilty, and she swears she is not guilty, she becomes free from her husband. If she accepts marriage on certain conditions, which cannot be fulfilled by her husband, she secures freedom of action[29]. If, again, she is not paid her *nafaqa*, (maintenance), or if she is badly maltreated, or if she can establish sufficient reason why she should be allowed to have recourse to divorce proceedings, she becomes free.
4. She need not take part in fighting lines in case of war, though she may help the fighting men and nurse or encourage them against the enemy.

5.   She is free to re-marry after divorce.
6.   She is encouraged to study and acquire learning.
7.   Then, again, if the husband remains absent from home in an unknown place for a very long time and does not pay for her maintenance, the wife may procure a decree of divorce from the judge, etc.

Divorce was very common among the pre-Islamic Arabs and, though a lawful act, it was condemned by the Prophet who said: *"The thing most disliked by God (of lawful acts) is divorce."* He has also praised a good wife by saying: *"The world and its pleasure are valuable, but more valuable than all pleasure is a virtuous wife."* The Holy Prophet also said: *"The best of you in the consideration of Almighty God is the man who treats his wife best."*

16

Muslim Ethics and Morality

Muslim ethics and morality, as stated in the Quran, embrace the consideration of all those forms of moral excellence known to any advanced civilization, such as sincerity, honesty, humility, justice, patience, straightforwardness, keeping a promise, chastity, meekness, politeness, forgiveness, goodness, courage, veracity, sympathy, and other ethical instructions and rules of conduct, which are recommended, praised and enjoined upon Muslims in the Holy Quran and in the teachings of the Holy Prophet.

But the Quran does not simply enumerate such moral qualities and distinctions as God is pleased to enjoin upon his servants; nay, it further gives us ethical teachings as to how man may acquire these forms of moral excellence and shows the straight way leading to their achievement. It teaches that there are three springs, out of which the physical, moral and spiritual conditions flow. Now, what is the effect of the teachings of the Holy Quran upon the physical state of man, how does it guide us with respect to it and what practical limits does it set to natural inclination? It may be remarked at the outset that, according to the Muslim Scripture, the physical conditions of man are closely connected with his moral and spiritual states, so much so that, even his modes of eating and drinking play a part in the moulding of his moral and spiritual qualities. If, therefore, his natural desires are subjected to the directions of the law, they become invested with moral qualities and this deeply affects the spiritual state of the soul. It is for this reason that in all forms of devotion and prayer and in all the injunctions relating to internal purity and moral rectitude, the greatest stress has been laid upon external purity and cleanliness and the proper attitude of the body. The relation between the physical and spiritual nature of man would become evident on a careful consideration of the actions of the outward organs and the effect they produce upon the internal nature of man. Weeping, even when artificial, at once saddens the heart, while an artificial laugh makes it cheerful. Likewise, a prostration of the body, as is done in prayer, causes the soul to humble itself and adore the Creator; whereas strutting produces vanity and vainglory. Experience also shows the strong effect of food upon the heart and brain powers. For instance, vegetarians ultimately may lose courage. There is not the least doubt that food plays an important part in the formation of the character. Furthermore, just as it is wrong to exclude meat from the diet altogether, an excess of meat is also injurious to character and badly affects the admirable qualities of humility and meekness. But those who adopt the middle path are heirs to both the noble qualities of courage and meekness. It is with this great law in view that the Holy Quran gives the instructions: *"Eat (meat as well as other food) and drink but do not give way to excess (in any particular form of diet so that your character and health may not suffer from it)"* (7:31). In fact, there is a mysterious relation between the body and the soul of man, and the solution of the mystery is all but beyond human comprehension.

Directions Relating to Reformation of Man's External Life

The directions relating to the reformation of the external life of man and his gradual advancement from savageness to civilization until he reaches the highest pinnacles of spiritual life are based on the following method: Almighty God has been pleased to lead man out of darkness and raise him up from a savage state by teaching him the rules relating to his ordinary daily actions and modes of social life. Thus they begin at the lowest point of man's development, first of all, drawing a line of distinction between man and the lower animals, teaching him as well the first rules of morality which may go by the name of sociability. Next they undertake to improve upon the low degree of morality already acquired by bringing his habits to the level of moderation, thus turning them into an expression of sublime morality.

Therefore, in the first stage we are concerned with the more ignorant savages, whom it is our duty to raise to the status of civilized men by teaching them the social laws embracing their daily mutual relations.

The first step towards civilization, therefore, consists in teaching the savage not to walk about naked, or devour carcasses, or indulge in barbarous habits. This is the lowest grade in the reformation of man. In humanizing people upon whom no rays of the light of civilization have yet fallen, it is necessary, first of all to take them through this stage and make them accustomed to morals of the most basic type. When the savage has learned the elementary manners of society, he is then prepared for the second stage of reformation. He is then taught the high and excellent moral qualities pertaining to humanity, as well as the proper use of his own faculties and of whatever lies hidden beneath them. Those who have acquired excellent morals are now prepared for the third stage. After attaining the outward perfection, they are made to taste the real knowledge and love of God. These are the three stages which the Holy Quran has described as necessary for anyone who has embraced Islam.

Our Holy Prophet was raised at a time when the whole world had sunk to the lowest depth of ignorance. Utter darkness and barbarism at that time prevailed over the whole of Arabia. No social laws were observed, and the most despicable deeds were openly committed. An unlimited number of wives was taken, and all prohibited things were made lawful. Raping and incest reigned supreme and mothers were not infrequently taken for wives. It was to prohibit this horrible custom that the words of the Quran were revealed: i.e. *"Your mothers are prohibited to be taken as your wives.'* Like beasts, most Bedouin Arabs did not even hesitate to eat carcasses and to practise cannibalism. There was no vice which was not freely practiced by them. The great majority of them did not believe in a future life, and not a few were atheists. Infanticide prevailed throughout the whole peninsula, and they mercilessly butchered orphans to rob them of their properties. Their thirst for wine was excessive and fornication was committed unscrupulously. Such was the dark picture of the time and the land in which the Holy Prophet of Arabia appeared, and it was to reclaim this wild and ignorant people that the word of God came upon him. It is for this reason that the Holy Quran is claimed as the perfect book of guidance to mankind: for it alone the path was cleared to bring about reformation complete on all sides, the other Scriptures never having been given such an opportunity. The Quran had a grand aim before it. It had first to reclaim human beings from savagery and to make good men of them, then to teach them excellent morals and make them good, and last of all to take them to the highest pinnacles of advancement and make them godly. The Holy Quran gives excellent and distinct teachings on these three points.

It is to be observed that the first stage of a moral being, *i.e.* one whose actions can be classed as good or bad morally, is that in which he is capable of distinguishing between good and bad actions or between two good or two bad actions of different degrees. This takes place when the reasoning faculty is sufficiently well developed to form general ideas and perceive the omission of a good deed and feels repentance or remorse after doing a bad one. This is the second stage of man's life which the Holy Quran terms "*nafsil-lawwama,*" i.e. that of the self-blaming soul (or conscience). But it should be borne in mind that for the primitive-minded man or the savage to attain this stage of the self-blaming soul, mere admonition is hardly sufficient. He must have so great a knowledge of God that he does not look upon his own creation by God as an insignificant or meaningless thing. This soul-ennobling sense of God can greatly help to lead to actions truly moral. And it is for this reason that the Holy Quran inculcates a true knowledge of God along with the admonitions and warnings, and assures man that every good or bad action is watched and seen by God and that accordingly it bears fruit which causes spiritual bliss or torture in this life, while a clear and more palpable reward or punishment awaits him in the next. In short, when man reaches this stage of advancement, which we have called the self-blaming soul, his reason, knowledge, and conscience reach the stage of development, in which a feeling of remorse overtakes him in doing unrighteous deeds and he is very anxious to do good. This is the stage in which the actions of man can be said to be moral.

Thus in the earliest stage in man's civilization, the Quran teaches this particular portion of morals which we term "manners." Quranic Laws are laid down to guide the actions of daily life; and all that is necessary to make the primitive-minded person a social being is inculcated. Examples of the injunctions of the Holy Book on this point are as follows:

> "Your mothers are forbidden to you (as wives) and so are your daughters and sisters and your aunts, both on the father's side and the mother's side; and your nieces on the brother's and sister's side, your foster-mothers, and your foster-sisters, and the mothers of your step-daughters who are your wards, born of your wives to whom you have gone in (but if you have not gone into them,, it shall be no sin); and the wives of your sons who proceed out of your loins; and it is also forbidden that you should have two sisters together (as two wives at one and the same time); this that you did before (in the time of ignorance) is now forbidden to you and forgiven by the All-Forgiving and All-Merciful God." (4:23)

> "And do not marry women whom your fathers have married, but what is passed shall be forgiven (for you did it in ignorance)." (4:22)

"This day (all) the good things are allowed to you, and the food of those who have been given the Scriptures (Jews and Christians) is lawful for you and your food is lawful for them; and the chaste from among the believing women and the chaste from among those who have been given the Scriptures before you (are lawful for you), when you have given them their dowries, taking them in marriage, not fornicating nor taking them for paramours in secret...[30]." (5:5)

"Do not commit suicide." (17:33)

"Do not kill your children." (17:31)

"Do not enter houses other than your own (like savages) without permission, but wait until you have asked leave; and when you enter, salute the inmates; and if the house is empty, do not enter till the owner of the house gives you leave; and if the owner asks you to go back, return forthwith; that is more decent for you." (24:27-28)

"Enter houses by their doors (not by clambering over their walls)."

"When you are met with a salutation, just greet the person with a better salutation or at least return the same."

"Wines (including all intoxicants) and games of chance and idols and divining arrows are but an abomination of Satan's mischief, avoid them, therefore, so that you may prosper." (5:90)

"You are forbidden to eat that which dies of itself, and blood, and flesh of swine." (5:3)

"And when they (the new converts) ask what is lawful for them to eat, say: "Everything good and clean is allowed to you (only the dead and the unclean things which resemble the dead are forbidden)." (5:4)

"When you are told to make room in your assemblies for others, then make room (so that others may sit)."

"Eat and drink, but be moderate in your diet and do not exceed the proper limits." (7:31)

"Do not indulge in idle talk, but speak rightly when the occasion requires it."

"And let your clothes be clean and let not anything that belongs to you (your body, your dwellings, etc) be dirty."

"Bear witness with justice and let not hatred of some people induce you to act inequitably...."

"Act equitably and be just, God is aware of all that you do."

"When speaking, do not shout, and when walking, walk gently." (31:19)

17

The Moral Conditions

Having briefly indicated the directions given by the Holy Quran in the first stage of reformation, we now come to the second. After it has given to the savage and the primitive such rules as are necessary for his guidance, it undertakes to teach him high morals. We shall, therefore, mention, as a specimen, only a few of the moral qualities upon which the Holy Quran laid stress. All moral qualities fall under two heads: (1) those which enable man to abstain from inflicting injury upon his fellow-men, and (2) those which enable him to do good to others:

1. To the first class belong the rules of conduct which direct the intentions and actions of man so that he may not injure the life, property, or honour of his fellow-beings by means of his tongue or hand or eye, or any other part of his body.

2. The second class comprises all rules calculated to guide the intentions and actions of man in doing good to others by means of the faculties which God has granted him, or in declaring the glory or honour of others, or in forbearing from punishing an offender, or in punishing him in such a manner that the punishment turns out to be a blessing for him.

Chastity

The moral qualities which fall under the heading of abstaining from doing wrong or harm are chiefly four in number. Each of these is denoted by a single word in Arabic, the language of the Holy Quran, which is so rich in vocabulary that it supplies a different word for all different human conceptions, manners and morals. First of all, we shall consider the quality of *ihsan* (in Arabic). This word signifies the virtue which relates to the act of procreation in men and women. A man or a woman is said to be *"muhsan"* or *"muhsana"* when he or she abstains from illegal intercourse and its preliminaries which bring disgrace and ruin upon the heads of the sinners in this world and severe torture in the next. None is more wicked than the infamous villain who causes the loss of a wife to a husband and that of a mother to her children, and thus violently disturbs the peace of the whole household, bringing ruin upon the heads of both the guilty wife and the innocent husband and children.

The first thing to remember about this moral quality which we call chastity is that no one oculd deserve the credit for refraining from satisfying his carnal desires illegally if nature had not given him these desires. The expression "moral quality", therefore, cannot be applied to the mere act of refraining from such a course unless nature has also granted the capacity of committing the bad deed. It is refraining under such circumstances, *i.e.* against the power of such passions as nature has vested in man, that deserves to be credited with being of a high moral quality. Immaturity, impotence, emasculation or old age nullifies the existence of the moral quality we termed chastity, although refraining from the illegal act takes place in these cases. But the fact is that in such cases it is a natural condition, and there is no resistance of passion, and, therefore, no propriety in the act. This is a distinction of importance between acting under natural conditions and acting where a moral choice is necessary. In the former there is no tendency to go in the opposite direction, while in the latter there is a struggle between the good and evil passion, which necessitates the application of the reasoning faculty as well as obedience to the restrictions of the law together with a true feeling that Almighty God is aware of all human deeds. There is no doubt that the action of children below the age of puberty and men who have lost the power upon which restrictions are to be imposed, cannot be said to possess a moral quality of so great a value, though they might resemble those of chaste men and women. But their chastity, if it might at all be called chastity, is only a natural condition over which they have no need to exercise control.

For this reason the Holy Prophet announced that *"He is not the true courageous one who overcomes his enemies, but the most true is he who overcomes and controls his lower passions."* Again the implication of Muslim precepts is that no man should deserve God's reward for acting in accordance with the ordinances of religion unless he be naturally capable of disobeying them.

The directions contained in the Holy Quran for attainment of the noble quality of chastity are given in the following ordinances:

"Ask (O Prophet) the believing men to lower their gaze (to strange women) and be modest. That is purer for them. (Let them know) that God is aware of all that they do." (24:30)

"And tell the believing women to lower their gaze and be modest, and to display of their adornment only that which is apparent, and to draw their veils over their bosoms, and not to reveal adornment save to their own husbands and husbands' fathers, or their sons or their husbands' sons, or their brothers or their brothers' sons or sisters' sons, or their women or their slaves or male attendants who lack vigour, or children who know naught of woman's nakedness. And let them not stamp their feet so as to reveal what they hide of their adornment. Tell the believing men and women to observe these ordinances, so that they might lead a successful life." (24:31)

The Holy Quran also instructs Muslims "Not to draw near to fornication, but that they should keep aloof from occasions which give rise to such injurious ideas, and keep away from paths which might lead to commission of sin, for he who commits fornication does an extremely wicked deed, and it is an evil way (for it holds one back from attaining the desired perfection)." (17:32)

In another verse, the Holy Quran directs those who cannot find a match to employ other means to preserve their continence such as fasting or taking light food, or to try to apply themselves to the remembrance of the fear of God's punishment to the evil-doers. Furthermore, the Quran states that some of the Christians have devised methods of their own for restraining themselves from sexual relations as by adopting celibacy or monasticism (and thus depreciating marriage,) or by submitting themselves to castration, but all these methods have been invented by the people themselves and not decreed by God, and the result was that they could not observe these innovations as they ought to.

Here, Almighty God declared that He did not prescribe the method of castration, etc., for had this been among the commandments of the Almighty, the people would have had to observe these rules and then the human race would long since have disappeared from the face of the earth. In addition to the immorality attaching to such an evil practice, it is an objection against the Creater for having given man such a power. Moreover, it can be easily seen that there is no merit in having been unable to act, and credit is due to him only who has to resist the evil tendency and to overcome the evil passions from fear of God. The person who has the energy in him to do so deserves twofold credit, *viz.* for the application of the energy in the proper place and for refraining from applying it where there is no proper occasion for it. But the man who has lost it is not entitled to any of these. He is like a child and deserves no credit for refraining from what he has lost the power to do. There is no resistance, no overcoming and consequently no merit or glory.

The foregoing Quranic verses not only contain excellent teachings for the attainment of charity, but point out certain remedies for observing continence: Refraining from casting unrestrained looks upon strangers and refraining from listening to the love stories of strange men and women exciting lust; avoiding every occasion where there may be fear of being involved in the wicked deed and, last of all, resorting to fasting or light food and constant remembrance of the fear of God's punishment upon evil-doers and wicked transgressors.

Here we can confidently assert that the teachings about chastity, together with the remedies for continence, as contained in the Holy Quran, are peculiar to Islam. One point deserves special attention. The natural propensity of man, in which carnal appetite takes its root and over which man cannot have full control except by undergoing a thorough transformation, is — whenever there is occasion for it— to lead the object of his desire into serious and lamentable consequences. The divine injunction in this respect is, therefore, that it is unlawful for a Muslim to cast unnecessary free glances, whether with pure or impure looks, upon strange women. We must avoid every circumstance which may make us stumble at any time. Unrestrained looks are almost sure to lead to danger.

The word of God, therefore, constrains the lascivious desires of man and woman to avoid the very occasion where there is danger of the excitement of the passions.

This is the secret underlying the institution of the seclusion of women in Islam. It is sheer ignorance of the noble principles of that religion to take seclusion in the sense of shutting up women like prisoners in a goal. The object of seclusion is that both men and women should be restrained from intermingling freely, and that members of the fair sex should not display their adornments and beauty freely to strangers.

It should further be borne in mind that *"to restrain the looks,"* in the Quranic verse, means, in the Arabic language of the Holy Book, the averting of one's eyes when the object in sight is not one which it is proper for one to look at freely, and not total restraint on one's glances on the proper occasions. The casting down of the eyes on proper occasions is the first requirement of pure social life. This habit, without causing any serious disadvantages to man in his social relations, has the invaluable advantage of making him perfect in one of the highest morals, which we call chastity.

Honesty

We come next to the second moral quality of refraining from injuring others by cheating them or taking unlawful possession of their properties. An infant, free as it is from every bad habit, is averse to sucking the milk of a woman other than his mother, if he has not been entrusted to her while still young enough to be quite unconscious of the relationship. This propensity in the infant is the root from which grows the natural inclination to be honest, and which is later developed into the moral quality known to advanced civilization as "honesty." The true principle of honesty is that there should be the same aversion to the dishonest taking of another's property. In the child, however, this is not a moral quality but only a natural condition, in as much as it is not regulated by any principle or opted for on the proper occasion. The child has no choice in the matter. Unless there is a choice, the action of a moral being cannot be included in the category of moral conditions. One who inclines towards honesty in obedience to the requirements of his own nature, without having to consider any questions of propriety, does not earn the title of "honest man." His actions may, to outward appearances, resemble Those of a moral being, and may appear to have a moral quality, but without his having had to consider their advisability, they do not necessarly entitle him to be thought of a "moral being." It is only by virtue of his making correct moral choice that he can merit that application. We cite in Illustration some versess from the holy Quran:

> "And if there are among you any owners of property who are weak of understanding, being minors or orphans, and have not sufficient prudence for the management of their affairs, you (i.e. the Muslims) should assume full control over their property as a Court of Wards, and do not make over to them that which God has placed with you

as a means of support and as a stock of trade, but assign them a portion of it such as is necessary for their maintenance and clothing; and speak to them words of kindness such as may sharpen their intellects and mature their understanding and train them for the business which is most suited to their capacities, giving them full instruction in these respects. And test the orphans in whatever you instruct them, so that you may be able to see if they have made any progress. And when they attain the age of majority (for which the proper limit is eighteen)[31] and you perceive that they are able to manage their affairs well, release their property to them. And do not waste it profusely, nor consume it hastily for fear that they will shortly be of age to receive what belongs to them. If the guardian is well off, he should abstain entirely from taking remuneration from the orphans' estate, but if he is poor, he may take a reasonable remuneration. When you make over their property to them, do it in the presence of witnesses; and know well that God takes sufficient account of all your actions.

"Let those who are guardians over orphans' property have the same fear in their minds as if, after their demise, they have left a weakly offspring behind them. Let them then fear God and speak words of appropriate comfort." (4:5, 6,9)

What Almighty God has preached is true honesty and faithfulness, and its various requisites are clearly set forth in the verses quoted above.

Elsewhere the Holy Quran teaches us: Not to consume each other's wealth unjustly, nor offer it to judges as a bribe, so that with their aid you might seize other men's property dishonestly." (2:188)

And again we are instructed thus: "God enjoins upon you to give back faithfully any trust to its owner. God hates the unfaithful." (4)

In another instance the Holy Quran gives the following instructions:

> "Give just measure and do not be of those who give less. And weigh (things) with an exact and right balance. And do not defraud any people, of their substance and do not act corruptly in the earth, making mischief. And guard yourselves against the punishment of God for all sorts of corruption." (26:180-183).

> "And give to the orphans their property, and do not substitute worthless things for (their) good ones and do not devour their property (as an addition) to your property; this is surely a great crime." (4:2)

These are comprehensive injunctions against all sorts of dishonest dealings, and every breach of trust comes within them. Separate offences are not enumerated in this chapter, for a comprehensive list of them would have required much space; and even then it would have been very hard to set a limit to them. But it was the mission of the Holy Prophet of Islam to explain in full detail any and all ordinances referred to in the Quran; and Muslims are instructed by the Quran to obey the rules and abide by the explanations and instructions laid down by God's Prophet, whose sayings are to be treated by all believers as if they were from God Himself. The Holy Quran says "He who has obeyed the Prophet has in fact obeyed God." and again the Quran teaches that the Prophet is charged with explaining and pointing out any precepts revealed to him.

We hope to publish later a separate volume containing the various rules of conduct, touching on all aspects of life and social affairs and democratic dealings, which the Holy Prophet has laid down for the instruction of his followers.

Peacefulness

Let us now turn to the third class of morals falling within the first division, namely refraining from causing injury to others. This moral quality is known as peacefulness. It consists in refraining from causing harm or injury of any sort to another person and thus living a peaceful life upon earth. Peacefulness is, no doubt, a blessing for humanity and must be valued for the great good which proceeds from it. The natural inclination, out of which this moral quality develops, is witnessed in the youth of a human being in the form of attachment. A natural inclination towards submission and attachment so early witnessed in the young human is only the germ, out of which flows the high moral quality of peacefulness. But it is plain that, divested of reason, man cannot realize peacefulness or hostility. That which is not consciously resorted to upon the recommendation of reason cannot be regarded as having a moral quality.

Some examples of directions enshrined in the Holy Quran are given briefly below:

"Live peacefully with one another."

"If they (the other party) incline to peace, you should also incline to it."

"There is much good in coming to agreeable reconciliation, i.e. to live peacefully."

"And the servants of the Compassionate (God) are those who walk peacefully upon the earth."

"And when they hear frivolous discourse which they fear might lead to some quarrel, they do not listen to it, but pass on with dignity, and do not pick quarrels on trifling matters," i.e. they do not take a hostile attitude so long as no material injury is caused to them. The guiding principle of peacefulness is that one should not be offended at the slightest opposition to one's feelings. The word frivolous in the above teaching requires some explanation. A word or deed is said to be 'frivolous' when it causes no substantial loss or material injury to its object, although it be said or done with a mischievous or bad intention. But if the injury is not trivial and causes material loss of life, property or honour, the Islamic moral quality required to meet this emergency is not peacefulness or meekness but forgiveness, which shall be treated later.

The Quran also teaches us to: *"Repel the evil deed which is vain or frivolous with so much better an answer, that the person between whom and ourselves there was enmity or discord will turn into bosom friend."* (41:34)

The overlooking of trivial injuries is inherent in the moral quality of peacefulness.

Politeness

The fourth and last class of moral qualities is politeness, or gentlemanliness. The preliminary stage of this quality as witnessed in the child, is cheerfulness. Before the child learns to speak, the cheerfulness of its face serves the same purpose as kind words in a grown-up man, but the propriety of the occasion is an essential condition in classing politeness as "a high moral quality". The teaching, of the Quran on this point are as follows:

"Speak gently and politely with one another."

"Let no man deride another man, who may be better than himself, neither let women deride other women who may be better than they; neither defame one another, nor insult one another not even by calling him or her by a nickname." (49:11)

"Avoid immoderate suspicion, for some suspicions are surely sinful, neither backbite one another. Would any one of you love to eat the flesh of his brother, certainly not, you abhor that: so abhor the other." (49:12)

"They are most honoured by God who are the best

in conduct," (i.e. Those who are most dutiful to
God and are......fraternally polite with one another."
(49-13).

In these fine verses, Almighty God enjoins believers to lead
a polite life, not to defame one another, to avoid entertaining
frequent suspicions, not to traduce any person in his absence and
to embrace the best conduct in our social life. He urgues believers
"not to accuse any person of committing sinful deeds or crimes
without having sure proof of his or her guilt" and "not to walk
on the earth exultantly or arrogantly (17:37).

Forgiveness

We now turn to the second heading of morals which relate to
doing good to others as taught by the Holy Quran. The first of
these morals is forgiveness. The person to whom a real injury has
been caused has the right to redress by bringing the offender to
law for punishment or himself dealing out some punishment to
him, and, therefore, when he foregoes his right of redressal and
forgives the offender, he truely does him good. The Holy Quran
gives the following injunction on this point:

"Praised are they who restrain their anger and
pardon the faults of others; and God loves those
who do good to others." (3:134)

"God loves those who shun transgressions and
indecencies, and whenever they get angry they
forgive (him who caused their anger)." (42:37)

The Holy Quran also teaches that: "The recompense
for an evil deed is punishment proportionate to it,
but whoever forgives (the injury caused to him
thereby) and seeks reconcilement shall have his
reward from Allah (God): Surely God does not
love the wrongdoer." (42:40)

149

Here is a golden Islamic rule for forgiveness of evil. The rule laid down is that evil must be requited by punishment proportionate to the amount of wrong committed. This is a very just and necessary deterrent. But the verse also furnishes a guiding rule as to the occasions of forgiveness. There is in Islam neither the one extreme of "a tooth for a tooth" nor the opposite one of "turning the left check when the right is smitten" or "giving away the cloak to one who has already taken the coat of his brother." Forgiveness in Islam is highly commended, but it is preached in such a manner as to make it not impracticable; it means that forgiveness may be exercised if it will mend matters and do good to the wrongdoer himself. The object is to make "amends" whether this may be attained by giving proportional punishment or by exercising forgiveness. The course which is calculated to mend matters should be adopted. The offender would under certain circumstances benefit by forgiveness and mend his ways for the future. But, on other occasions, forgiveness may produce the contrary effect and may embolden the culprit to do worse deeds. The word of God does not, therefore, enjoin that we should go on forgiving faults quite blindly. It requires us to consider and weigh the matter first and see what course is likely to lead to real good. Jus as there are persons of a vindictive nature who carry the spirit of revenge to excess, there are also others who are ready to yield and are too prone to forgive on every occasion. Excess in mildness, like excess in vengeance, leads to harmful consequences. The mere giving up of a claim to requital from an offender, whatever the circumstances and however serious the nature of the offence done by an attack upon the honour or chastity, is far from being a great moral quality to which men should aspire. The mere presence of this quality in a person, therefore, does not entitle him to real credit unless he shows by its use on the right occasion that he possesses it as a moral quality. The distinction between natural and moral qualities should be clearly borne in mind. The inborn or natural qualities of man are transformed into moral qualities when a person does, or refrains from doing, an act upon the right occasion and after due consideration of the good or evil that is likely to result from it. Many of the lower animals are quite harmless and do not resist when evil is done to them. A cow may be said to be innocent and a lamb meek, but to neither do we attribute the high moral qualities which man aspires after, for they are not gifted with reason and do not know right from wrong. It is only the occasion upon which anything is done that justifies or condemns a deed; and the wise and perfect Word of the Omniscient God has therefore, imposed this condition upon every moral quality.

Goodness

The second moral quality is that known as goodness, *i.e.* to do good to others, or, in other words, to do good for good, which represents justice in its simplest sense. Then comes in the wake of moral development—the higher quality of kindness, followed by the highest quality named tenderness. Thus in the Holy Quran, Almighty God commands men to repay good for good and (if we can avail ourselves of an opportunity of doing more than mere justice), to do good for the sake of goodness, *i.e. without having received any benefit and* (if it befits the occasion) to bestow gifts with the natural tenderness of kindred. He forbids rudeness and abomination and wrongdoing (16:90).

These commandments call attention to three stages in the doing of good. The lowest stage is that in which man does good to his benefactors only. Even an ordinary man who has the sense to appreciate the goodness of others can acquire this quality and do good in return for good. From this there is an advancement to the second stage in which man takes the initiative to do good to others. It consists in bestowing favours upon persons who cannot claim them as a right. This quality, excellent as it is, occupies a middle position. To it often attaches the infirmity that the doer expects thanks or prayers in return for the good he does, and the slightest opposition from the object of compassion is termed ungratefulness. He would have an acknowledgement of the benefit conferred and is led sometimes to take advantage of his position by laying upon him some burden, which the other could not have otherwise willingly borne. To remedy this effect, the Holy Quran has warned the doer of goodness saying, *"Do not make your alms or benefits void by reminding those whom you relieve of your obligation, and by injuring them."* (2:264). If there is no sincerity in the deed, alms are of no avail, being mere show. In brief, this is an infirmity attaching to the noble deed of doing good to another that the doer is led sometimes to remind the person relieved of the obligation, or to boast of it. A third stage has, therefore, been taught by the Holy Word of God which is free from every imperfection. To attain this perfection man should not think of the goodness he had done, nor expect even an expression of thankfulness from the person upon whom the benefit is conferred.

The idea of doing good should proceed from sincere sympathy like that which is shown by the nearest relatives: by a mother, for instance, towards her children. This is the highest and the last stage of showing kindness to the creatures of God. Such sympathetic and sincere benefactors are highly praised by the Lord in the Quran where it states that: The servants of God (whom He loves) are those who on account of their love for God bestow their food on the needy *wretch* and the *orphan* and the *bondsman*, though longing for it themselves, and who say "we do not confer any obligation upon you, but our desire is that God may be pleased with us and we do it only for the sake of God, and this is a service for which we   seek from you neither recompense nor thanks" (76:8,9); "God loves those who, when they spend, are neither prodigal nor niggardly and keep the golden mean" (25:67); "and those of whose property there is a due portion for those who beg and for those who are needy and outcast" (25:19); "and those who spend in ease and in adversity" (3:134); "you shall by no means attain goodness till you expend in the cause of your fellow-being out of that which you love" (3:92); "and give your kindred what they require in time of need and also to the poor and the wayfarer and do not squander wastefully." (17:26) This verse forbids prodigality and the squandering of wealth in luxury or otherwise withouth occasion. Therefore, any excess in the doing of that which would otherwise have been most beneficial is condemned by the law. Nor, it should be borne in mind, is the mere doing of good in any of the above mentioned forms a high moral quality of goodness unless attested to as such by the propriety of the occasion as by exercise of judgment.

In another verse the word of God enjoins the believers to "be good to parents and kindred and to the orphans and to the poor and to the neighbours who are your relatives and to the neighbours who are strangers and the companions on a journey and to the wayfarer; and whatever you rightly possess (be they your servants or horses or other domestic animals)"; "this is what God loves you to do, and He does not love the vain boasters and the selfish and does not like those who are niggardly themselves and bid others to be niggards, and hide away what God of His bounty has given them, saying to the poor and the needy, "We have nothing to give you."" (4:36,37)

Courage

Courage is a virtue resembling the instinct of audacity. The very young human being, when it lacks sufficient reason, is apt to display audacity and is ready to thrust its hand into the fire, because having no knowledge of the consequences, the instinctive quality is predominant in it, and its action is by no means a noble quality. The virtue which we call courage cannot be displayed only after a good deal of reasoning and reflection and a full consideration of the propriety of the act. The Holy Quran contains the following elaborations upon this point:

> "The truly brave are those who are true to their
> promises and steadfast in trial and adversity and
> in times of war. Such are the true believers; such
> are the God-fearing." (2:177)

> "They who do good to others and guard against
> evil shall have a great reward from their Lord;
> those who, when threatened with the mustering
> of people against them and are told to fear the
> forces gathering around to crush them, are not
> dispirited thereby." *This circumstance, on the other
> hand, increases the faith of true believers and they say;*

*"God is sufficient protector and excellent guardian,"
since they were to fight in the cause of truth and in
obedience to their Lord." (3:172-174)*

Therefore, the moral quality of courage, according to the
teachings of Islam is not a mechanical movement depending upon
passion and flowing in one direction only: it is rather a signal
virtue which enables the faithful resist and overcome the passions
of the flesh, and, moreover, to resist the attacks of transgressors
when it is advisable to do so in the cause of the truth.

The truly courageous do not display their bravery in an
insolent manner and with a view to appearing superior to other
men; their only consideration is the pleasure of God who wishes
them to resist evil by their courage and to be patient in hardship.
All this leads to the conclusion that true courage takes its root in
patience and steadfastness. The courageous man resists his passions
and does not fly from danger like a coward, and before he takes
any step, he looks to the ultimate consequences of his action.

Between the daring dash of a savage and the indomitable
courage of a civilized man, there is this vast difference that the
latter is prepared to meet real dangers but he reasons and reflects
even in the fury and tumult of battle, before he proceeds to take
the course best suited to avert the evil, while the former, in
obedience to an irresistible passion, makes a violent assault in one
direction only.

Veracity

The next virtue, which is developed out of natural conditions, is
veracity. So long as there is no motive to tell a lie, man is naturally
inclined to speak the truth. He is, by his very nature, averse to
lying, and hates the person who is proved to have told a plain lie.
But this natural condition cannot claim our respect as one of the
noble moral qualities. Unless a man is purged of the low motives
which bar him from truth, his veracity is questionable. For he
speaks the truth only in matters where his interest or property or
honour are at stake or in which the utterance of truth does him

no harm, and rather than tell a lie, simply holds his tongue, he can claim no superiority over the untruthful. In fact, no one speaks an untruth without a motive, and there is no virtue in refraining from this while there is no apprehension of harm. The only circumstance which can serve as a test of truthfulness is that in which one's life or honour or property is in danger. The Holy Quran sets forth the following injunctions on this subject:

> "Shun you the pollution of idols and shun you the
> word of falsehood." (22:30)

The shunning of idols and falsehood is enjoined in the same breath: it indicates that falsehood is an idol and the person who trusts in it— as the idolators and the heathen used to do—does not trust in God for he bows in submission to an idol and does not worship God.

> "The witnesses among the true believers shall not
> refuse to present themselves whenever they are
> summoned to give witness; and do not conceal
> true testimony, for he who conceals it has surely
> a wicked heart." (2:282)

> "When you speak a word or pronounce a judgment,
> be true and just, though the person concerned be
> your relative. Stand fast to truth and justice and
> let your testimony be only for the sake of God and
> do not speak falsely, although the declarations of
> truth might be against your own interest or against
> your parents or your near relatives, such as your
> children." (4:135)

> "Let not hatred towards any person induce you to
> act unjustly against him." (5:8)

> "The truthful men and the truthful women shall
> find a rich reward." (33:35)

> "They are beloved and blessed who enjoin truth

and patience upon each other;" "and they who do
not give false evidence and who maintain their
dignity when histening to profance abuse." (25:72)

Patience

Another virtue which develops out of the natural condition of man
is patience. Everyone has more or less to suffer misfortunes,
diseases and other afflictions which are the common lot of
humanity. Everyone, too, has, after much sorrowing and suffering,
to make his peace with the misfortune which befalls him. But such
contentment is by no means a noble moral quality. It is a natural
consequence of the continuance of affliction that weariness at last
brings about conciliation. The first shock brings about depression
of spirit, inquietude and wails of woe, but when the excitement
of the moment is over, there is necessarily a reaction, for the
extreme has been reached. But such disappointment and consequent
contentment are both the result of natural inclination. It is only
when the loss is received with total resignation to the *will* of God
and in complete *resignation to His predestination* that human resolve
deserves to be seen as having virtuous moral qualities. The word
of God thus deals with that noble quality of patience. "We shall
test you by afflicting you in some measure with fear, hunger, and
decrease of wealth and loss of lives, and fruits. Those who prove
patient under such misfortunes are to be given good tidings of
God's reward—to those who, when a misfortune befalls them, say:
'Surely we are God's creatures and his charges, and, therefore,
must return to our owner.'" (2:155:156).

This is the true expression of a true Muslim: "We are God's
creatures and his charges and to Him must the charges return; we
come from God and He is our goal, therefore no trial or misfortune
can disturb the course of our life, which has a much higher aim
than mere comfort."

Sympathy

Another quality falling into the same category is sympathetic zeal.
People of every nationality and religion are naturally endowed

with the feeling of national sympathy, and in their zeal for the interest of their countrymen or co-religionists, they do not hesitate to wrong others. Such sympathetic zeal, however, does not proceed out of moral feelings, but is an instinctive passion and is witnessed even in the lower animals, especially the ravens, of which the call of one, brings together numerous others, or in sheep in which case the rush of one though it be towards a precipice, brings the whole flock to follow its example. To be classed as a moral quality, it must be displayed in accordance with the principles of justice and equity and on the proper occasion. Only under certain conditions is sympathy to be shown. The injunction of the Holy Quran on this point are: "Sympathy and co-operation are enjoined upon you towards deeds of goodness and piety, but you must not co-operate in sinful or transgressive deeds." (5:2). Again the Holy Word of God teaches every Muslim not "to be a pleader for the treacherous" (4:105). "And do not plead on behalf of any people who deceive themselves; God does not love anyone who is treacherous and sinful." (4:107)

18

True Believers

Their Manners and Characters as Described in the Quran

The Holy Quran describes the Muslims, *i.e.* the true believers as follows:

> "Believers are they who fear God and fear nothing else." (3:102)

> "They hold together and unite together." (3:103)

> "They are protected from harm since they abide by the instructions of their Lord and Benefactor, the True God, Allah."

> "Their lives, honour and property are sacred."

> "Believers should not disregard those who salute them and wish them peace, even if the saluters are unbelievers." (4:95)

> "They should not sit and listen when God's attributes are ridiculed." (4:140)

They prefer their co-religionists for true friends: "O you who believe, do not take the unbelievers for guardians (true friends) rather than the believers." (4:144).

Their behaviour when giving witness is "to be upright and bear witness with justice and let no hatred of people incite them to act inequitably." (5:8)

Believers are not to ask inquisitive questions: "O you who believe! Do not put questions about things which, if declared to you, may give you trouble; but wait until things are revealed to you by the Quran." (5:101).[32]

Their duties to God are given in the following verses:

"O you who believe! Be careful of your duty to God, and seek means of being near to Him and strive hard in His way, so that you may prosper." (5-35)

"O you who believe! Turn sincerely to God (from your own passions) so that He will pardon your past evil-doings and will cause you to enter paradise in the hereafter." (66:8)

Believers' exalted grades are describes as follows:

"They are true believers whose hearts become full of loyalty when Allah (God) is mentioned; and when His communications are recited to them, this increases their faith, and in their Lord they put wholly their trust; those who pray steadfastly and spend benevolently out of what Almighty God has granted them. These are the true believers surely; they shall have from their Lord exalted grades and forgiveness and honourable sustenance." (8:2:4)

The righteous are described as those: "who walk on the earth in humbleness, and when the ignorant (i.e. the foolish) address them, they say (nothing but) peace! and they who pass the night (before going to bed) prostrating themselves before their Lord (through love and good hope)..." (25:53:64)

"And those who when they spend, are neither extravagant nor parsimonious, but always in the moderate and middle way. And they who do not worship or bow down to any but Allah... and they who do not kill any soul, except in the requirement of justice. "And those who do not commit fornication. And those who do not give false witness, or bear witness to what is false." (25:67-68)

"And when they pass by vain scenes they pass by nobly and in a gentlemanly way, i.e. they take no part in such vain matters. And those who, when reminded of the enjoinments of their Lord, do not fall down deaf and blind. And those who say, "O Our Lord! grant us joy in our wives and our offspring and make us guides to those who seek to be righteous.'" (72-73)

The above Quranic description of the righteous shows how great was the transformation wrought by the advent of the Holy Prophet: a people once sunk in degradation were converted into the righteous servants of the only true God:

True believers are also those:

"Who should be firm against the enemies and not lose heart but rely upon God for victory."

"O you who believe! When you meet a party (of the enemies), be firm and keep praying fervently to God to help you and make you victorious. And obey God and His Apostle and do not quarrel

among yourselves, for if you do, you will be weak
in heart and your power will depart; so be patient,
as God supports those who are patient." (8:45:46)

And also those who are neither cowards, nor weary nor faint-
hearted against their enemies:-

"Do not falter or cry for peace when fighting
against the enemies, while you have the upper
hand. God is with you, and He will not bring your
struggle to naught" (47:35).

True believers should help each other and give asylum to
those who go into exile for the cause of God:

"Surely those who believed and fled their homes
and struggled hard in Allah's way with their
property and their souls, and those who gave
shelter and help, should be the guardians of each
other" (8:72).

Also those who do not ask for exemption from joining the
army of the Muslims when at war:

Those who believe in God and the Last Day will
not beg you to exempt they from fighting hard
against the offending enemies—with their property
and their persons.[33]" (9:44)

And those who unite with those who are true in
works and deeds:

"O you who believe! Be careful of your duty to
God and be united only with those who are
truthful." (9:119).

Believers are they who study and teach others:

"Believers are to practise prayer and charity." and
say what is best:

"Say, O! Prophet, to my servants that they should speak the truth and what is best to be said." (17:53).

They should never despair or exult:

No misfortune befalls the earth nor your own souls but it is predestined and recorded before God brings it into existence...so that you may not despair (of God's mercy) or grieve for what has escaped you, nor should you be exultant at what God has granted you: Allah does not love any arrogant boaster." (57:22:23).

They are to make peace and act equitably:

"If two parties of believers should quarrel, make peace between them; but if one of them acts wrongfully towards the other, fight that one who acts wrongfully until he returns to submit to God's command; then if he returns, make peace between them with justice and act equitably. Surely Allah loves those who act equitably. The believers are but brethren; therefore, make peace between your brethren and be of righteous conduct, so that Almighty God may shower His blessings and mercy upon you." (49:9,10).

They must avoid suspicion and spying:-

"O you believers! avoid immoderate suspicion, for surely suspicion is a sin, and do not spy, on one another, or backbite others... (49:12);

"and ...... remember God in humility" (57:16).

They are sincere lovers of truth:

"Those who believe in Allah and the message of His Apostles are the lovers of truth and are themselves truthful and faithful... (57:19).

They do what they say:

> "O you who believe! it is most hateful in the sight
> of God that you say what you will not put into
> action; believers are they who fulfil their promise
> and do not simply talk without confirming by
> deeds what they say with their lips." (2-3).

They are helpers in enforcing God's ordinances:

> "O believers! Be helpers of God's ordinances."[34]
> (61:14).

They put their trust wholly in God:

> "There is no deity but Allah; therefore, let the
> believers put their trust in God alone" (64:13).

> "and ... do righteous deeds." (85:11)

They do what they say.

"O you who believe! It is most hateful in the sight of God that you say what you will not put into action. ...believers are they who fulfil their promise and do not simply talk without confirming by deeds what they say with their lips." (3:3)

They are ... in entering God's ordinances.

"O believers! Be helper of God's ordinances." (61:?)

They put their trust wholly in God.

"There is no deity but Allah, therefore, let the believers put their trust in God alone." (64:13)

"...and ... do righteous deeds." (65:11)

PART FIVE

MUSLIM JURISPRUDENCE AND THEOLOGY

19

The Quran and Jurisprudence

Islamic theology begins with the Prophet's acceptance to settle down at Madinah, which synchronized with an increas in the numbers of Muslims there and elsewhere. The Prophet was the spirtual as well as the temporal head of the community. His orders, revealed from God, were obeyed. Within the short space of ten years from that time, almost all the passages, with which future theology has been concerned, had been revealed. As the Muslims led simple lives and their needs were few, the Islamic Laws were extremely simple. In certain cases the prohibition was introduced gradually. Beginning with a recommendation, it ended in an injunction, as in the case of the use of intoxicants and gambling. The following passages indicate the manner in which the recommendation eventually merges into prohibition:

> First Stage. Recommendation: "They ask you (the Prophet) about wine and games of chance. Say! In both are great evil, although they have certain advantages to men, but their evil is far greater than their advantages." (2:219)

Second Stage. *A first step towards prohibition:*

"O you believers! Do not pray when you are intoxicated, so that you may know well what you say." (4:43)

Third Stage-Total prohibition:

"O believers, intoxicants and games of chance and (sacrificing to) idols and divining arrows are abominations and the work of the devil; therefore; shun them." (5:90)

As the Quranic passages relating to rituals, ceremonies and laws were brief, they needed further explanation, which was given by the Prophet. In this manner, the Prophet himself was the first commentator of the Quran. His explanations may be divided into two parts:

1. Reflection on passages occurring in the Quran.
2. Answers to questions, or relation to some particular occasion.

The rise of the Muslim Arabs after the death of the Prophet was rapid. Within a period of less than sixty years, they became masters of North Africa, including Spain, Syria and the whole of Iran; in fact, of all central Asia as far as China in the East. A large number of non-Arabs also embraced Islam. They were quite ignorant of the Arabic language and hence were unable to understand the Quran, and even when they learnt it, many words, sentences and passages in it were not clear to them. The inhabitants of Makkah and Madinah, particularly those who had served under the Prophet and had occasion to learn the Islamic doctrine directly from the Prophet, came to be held as authorities on the subject of the religion. The regular development of theology might thus be said to begin with the subjugation of the countries mentioned above. As in the case of Sufism, the development of theology was gradual. The period of that development may be divided as indicated below:

1. The life of the Prophet after the announcement, of prophethood, which lasted from A.D. 608 to A.D. 632, *i.e.* about 25 years.

2. The reign of the first four Khalifas, from A.D. 632 to A.D. 661, *i.e.* about 30 years.
3. Umayyad Khalifas, from A.D. 661 to A.D. 750
4. 'Abbaside Khalifas, from A.D. 750 to A.D. 1258.
5. Non-Arab period, from A.D. 1258 to the present time.

The first period is conterminous with the revelation of the Quran itself and the instructions given by the Prophet in person. The second period is rendered noteworthy by the following:-

1. The earliest collection of the Traditions or sayings of the Prophet.
2. The building-up of the system of Muslim Jurisprudence under the guidance of the first four Khalifas.
3. The arrangement of the Quran into chapters as we have it now. Of these achievements, the last is perhaps the most important.

20

Quran—
The First Source of Jurisprudence

The word "Quran" is derived from the Arabic *Qara'a*, i.e. to read, to recite. It is designated *"al-Furqan"* (the distinguisher), *Kalamul-Lah* (the word of God), the *Kitab* (the Book), *Nur* (the light) and *al-Huda* (the guidance). It has a large number of other names, some mentioned in the Quran itself and others given by Muslims. The Quran is held in the greatest respect by all sects of Islam. It is never touched without ablution being performed beforehand. It is considered the eternal miracle of Islam, as the expounder of the most sublime truth; as superior to what was laid down by all past religions; as the best guide for seeking God and for obtaining emancipation; the perfection of all moral codes; as the word of God, uncreated in its origin, and existing before being conveyed to the Prophet; as noble and complete in itself. It has been revealed in parts at different times during a period of twenty three years, as necessity demanded. Some chapters were revealed in complete form; others in portions. It was divided into thirty parts, containing 114 chapters, known in Arabic as *suras*. Some were very long and others very brief. The chapters were arranged under the personal direction of the Prophet, who used to ask the scribe present to insert the revealed passage in a particular chapter and before or after a particular verse of the chapter. It was neither arranged in chronological order nor at random, but as commanded by the Prophet himself.

The work of compilation was first undertaken by order of Abu Bakr, a copy of the Sacred Book having been left in the custody of Hafsa, the widow of the Prophet and daughter of 'Omar, the second Khalifa. The third Khalifa, Osman, ordered the revision and comparison of the various fragments in the possession of different people with the original copy, and the arrangement of the whole Sacred Book into its chatpers under the supervision of the following experts:

1. Zaid Ibn Thabit, who also was the first compiler.

2. 'Abdullah ibn Zubair.

3. Sa'id ibn Al-'As.

4. 'Abdul-Rahman ibn Haris.

With the exception of the first, the other three belonged to the Quraishite tribe. The work was completed after careful scrutiny and comparison with other fragments and presented to the Khalifa who caused a number of copies of it to be made and sent to the different centres of Islam, and these became texts for all subsequent copies of the Holy Book. The fragments in the possession of different people were recovered and burnt. As a number of Companions such as 'Abdullah ibn Mas'ud, Salim, 'Ali (the fourth Khalifa), Mu'az ibn Jabal, Ubayy ibn Kab, 'Abdullah ibn 'Omar, had committed the whole Quran to memory and a large number had each learned by heart a sizeable portion of it, hardly any difficulty was experienced in the matter of producing a correct text or in arranging it as required. The Prophet used to encourage his Companions to write and learn the text of the *suras* by heart. The attachment of the Muslim to the Sacred Book is so great that it has retained its purity, without the least change, for the last over fourteen hundred years. Its contents were revealed in the dialect of the Quraish of Makkah, and the object of 'Osman was to make people read it in this self-same dialect.

A Muslim believes in the Quran as the word of God revealed

in a manner which is unsurpassable in the beauty of its language and in the declaration of the truth of the doctrines inculcated by it. Non-Muslim writers and critics in Europe are unanimous in admitting its high literary merit. George Sale, whose translation of the Quran is well known, writes that it was "so strongly captivating to the minds of his audience that several of his opponents thought it to be the effect of witchcraft and enchantment."

'Omar, the second Khalifa, before embracing Islam, was an opponent of the Prophet; and once he left his place with the intention of killing him. On his way he met his own sister, who had embraced Islam, and found her reading some passage from the Quran. He took these passages and read them, and was so much affected by them that he immediately became a Muslim.

In describing the great world Flood (Deluge), the passages in the Quran became extremely figurative and sublime. According to Arab writers on rhetoric, the following few lines taken from these passages contain twenty-three figures of speech in them. These lines cannot, for obvious reasons, retain their original beauty in the translation offered here:

> "And the ark moved in with them amid waves like mountains, and Noah called out to his son (when) he was apart: `O my child! Embark with us, and do not be with unbelievers.' He said. `I will betake myself to a mountain, that shall save me from water.' He (Noah) said: 'None shall be saved this day from God's decree, save him on whom He shall have mercy,' and a wave passed between them and he (the son) was drowned and God said: `O Earth! Swallow down your water and O Heaven! Withhold your rains; and the water abated, and God's decree was fulfilled and the ark rested on al-Judi (a mountain)." (11:42-44)·

Such is the style of the Quran, most beautiful, fluent, concise, persuasive, possessing great force of expression; in some instances

171

composed for hearing rather than for reading; magnificent when describing the majesty and sublimity of God, encouraging to warriors, seekers of the truth and undetermined hearts. It is composed neither in poetry nor in simple prose. The sentences generally end in rhyme; words being well selected and beautifully placed. Each chapter has its own rhymed words, coming at the end of each sentence.

Apart from the beauty of its composition, it contains original ideas, especially in connection with the unity, existence or the singleness of God.

Divisions Of The Quran

The Chapters of the Quran are divided into Makkan and Madinite. The Makkan chapters are usually in brief sentences, full of enthusiasm, poetical, lofty and brilliant; denouncing idol worship, promising paradise and threatening with the dire punishment of hell; describing the unity and majesty of God, the day of judgment, with allusions to some of the earlier Prophets and the events of their time; rich in eloquence, with appreciation of objects in nature; and with most of them beginning with one or a number of oaths, very attractive to Arabs, as in the following:

> By the sun and its noonday brightness;
> By the moon when she follows it;
> By the day when it reveals it;
> By the night when it enshrouds it;
> By the heaven and Him who built it;
> By the earth and Him who spread it;
> By a soul and Him who perfected it, and
> inspired in it what is wrong and what is right
> for it." (91:1-8) [1]

The Madinite Chapters narrate the same subjects but generally in greater details, the verses being more prosaic and the chapters much longer. They are chiefly noted for the addition of (1) civil and criminal laws; (2) directions and rituals, such as prayer, fasting, giving alms, making the pilgrimage, etc.; (3) social reform; (4) moral regulations; (5) brief description of some of the important battles fought with the Quraishites and the Jews; (6) criticism and condemnation of hypocrites who professed Islam but worked against it; (7) exhortation to defend the cause of Islam; and (8) a brief description of past Prophets, and events illustrating the fundamental principles of Islam.

Orientalists Reviewing The Quran

Speaking of the Quran in his *West-Ostlicher Divan,* Goethe states:

"However often we return to it (the Quran), at first disgusting us each time afresh, it soon attracts, astounds and, in the end, compels our reverence. Its style, in accordance with its contents and aim, is stern, grand, terrible —ever and anon truly sublime. Thus, this book will go on exercising, through all ages, a most potent influence."[36]

Dr. Steingass, the learned compiler of the English-Arabic and Arabic-English Dictionary (W.H. Allen and Co.), has recorded his opinion on the Quran in Dr. Hughes' 'Dictionary of Islam.' After alluding to the words of Goethe, Dr. Steingass writes: 'These words seem to me so much the more weighty and worthy of attention as they are uttered by one who, whatever his merits or demerits in other respects, may be deemed to be, indisputably belong to the greatest masters of language of all times and stands foremost as a leader of modern thought and the intellectual culture of modern times. A work, then, which calls forth so powerful and seemingly incompatible emotions, even in the distant reader—distant as to time, and still more so, as to mental development—a work (*i.e.* the Quran) which not only conquers any repugnance with which the reader may begin its perusal, but changes this adverse feeling into astonishment and admiration, must be a wonderful production of the human mind indeed and a problem of the highest interest to every thoughtful observer of the destinies of mankind. We may well say, *it is one of the grandest books ever written, because it reflects the character and life of the greatest man that ever breathed."* "Sincerity," writes Carlyle, "in all senses, seems to me the merit of the Quran." This same sincerity, this ardour and earnestness in the search for truth, this never flagging perseverance in trying to impress it, when patently found, again and again upon his unwilling hearers, appears to me the real and undeniable, 'seal of prophecy' in Muhammad.'[37]

21

The Tradition

Second Source of Jurisprudence

The Traditions of the Holy Prophet, better known as *sunna* or *hadith*, are the second and undoubtedly secondary source, from which the teachings of Islam are drawn. *Sunna* literally means 'a way' or 'rule' or 'manner' or 'example of acting,' or 'mode of life;' and *hadith*, a saying conveyed to man either through hearing or through revelation[38]. In its original sense, therefore, *sunna* indicates the doings, and *hadith* the sayings of the Holy Prophet, but, in effect, both cover the same ground and are applicable to his actions, practices, and sayings; *hadith* being the narration record of the *sunna* but containing in addition, various prophetical and historical elements.

There are three kinds of *sunna*: (1) a saying of the Holy Prophet, which has a bearing on a religious object; (2) an action or practice of his; or (3) his silent approval of the action or practice of some person. We shall now consider to what extent the teachings of Islam, its principles, and its laws, may be drawn from this source. The Quran generally deals with the broad principles or essentials of religion, going into details only in rare cases.

The details were generally supplied by the Holy Prophet himself, either by showing in his practice how an injunction should be carried out, or by giving a verbal explanation.

The *Sunna* or *hadith* of the Holy Prophet was something for which the need had been felt after his death and which was much needed in his lifetime. The two most important institutions of Islam, for instance, are prayer and *zakat* (*alms-giving*); yet when injunctions relating to prayer and *zakat* were delivered and they were repeatedly met with both in the Makkah and Madinah revelations, no details were supplied. "Keep up prayer" is the Quranic injunction, and it was the Prophet himself who by his own actions gave the details of the service. "Pay the alms" is again an injunction frequently repeated in the Holy Quran, yet it was the Holy Prophet who gave the rules and regulations for its payment and collection. These are just two examples; but since Islam covered the whole sphere of human activities, hundreds of points had to be explained by the Holy Prophet by his example in action and word, while on the moral side, his was the pattern which every Muslim was required to follow.

"Indeed in the Messenger of God, you have a good example to follow." (33:21)

The man, therefore, who embraced Islam stood in need of both the Holy Quran and the *sunna*.

22

Transmission of the Hadith in the Prophet's Lifetime

The transmission of the practices and sayings of the Holy Prophet from one person to another became necessary during the Prophet's lifetime. In fact, when a deputation of a certain tribe came to wait upon him in the early days of Madinah, the Prophet concluded his instructions to them with the words: "*Remember this and report it to those whom you have left behind.*[1]" His instructions were similar in other cases: "*Go back to your people and teach them these things.*[39]" There is another report according to which, on the occasion of a pilgrimage, the Holy Prophet, after enjoining on the Muslims the duty of holding sacred each other's life, property, and honour, added: "*He who is present here should carry this message to him who is absent.*[40]" Again there is ample historical evidence that whenever people embraced Islam, the Holy Prophet used to send to them one or more of his missionaries, who not only taught them the Quran, but also explained to them how the injunctions of the Holy Book were to be carried out in practice. It is also on record that people came to the Holy Prophet and demanded teachers who could teach them the Quran and the *sunna,* saying. "Send us men to teach us the Quran and *Sunna.*" The companions of the Holy Prophet knew full well that the injunctions and practices were to be followed, should no express direction be met with in the Quran. It is related that when Mu'az ibn Jabal, on being appointed governor of Yemen by the Holy Prophet, was asked how he would judge cases, his reply was, "By the Book of God."Again he was asked, "what he would do if he did not find a direction in the Book of God. He replied "By the *Sunna* of the Prophet of God." The *Sunna* was, therefore, recognised in the lifetime of the Prophet as affording guidance in religious matters.

The popular idea in the West that the need for the *sunna* was felt and the force of law given to the *hadith* after the death of the Holy Prophet is opposed by the facts[41].

Why the Hadith was not Generally Written

It is, however, a fact that the sayings of the Prophet were not generally written, and memory was the chief means of their preservation.

The Holy Prophet sometimes objected to the writing down of *hadith*. But this disapproval clearly showed nothing other than fear lest the *hadith* be mixed up with the Holy Quran. There was nothing essentially wrong in writing down the *hadith*, nor did the Holy Prophet ever forbid its being done.

Nor was memory an unreliable means for the preservation of *hadith*, for the Holy Quran itself was safely preserved in the memory of the disciples of the Prophet in addition to committing it to writing. In fact, had the Quran been simply preserved in writing, it could not have been handed down intact to future generations. The aid of memory was invoked to make the purity of the text of the Quran doubly sure[42].

The Arab had a wonderfully retentive memory and he had to store up his knowledge of countless things in his memory. Indeed, before Islam, writing was but rarely resorted to, and memory was chiefly relied upon in all important matters. Hundreds and even thousands of verses could be recited from memory by one man, and the reciters would also remember the names of the poets through whom these verses had been transmitted to them. It is recorded of a later renowned transmitter, Asma'i by name, that he learned twelve thousand verses by heart before he reached majority. Another transmitter was reported to have recited verses from a hundred poets in a single sitting. Sha'bi, a famous transmitter proved that he could continue reciting verses which he knew by heart for a month; and these verses were the basis of the Arabic vocabulary and even of Arabic grammar.

23

The Earliest Preservation of Traditions

Collection of Hadith

First Stage

The first step in the preservation of *hadith* was thus taken during the lifetime of the Holy Prophet, but all his followers were not equally interested in the matter, nor had they an equal chance of being so. Everyone had to work for his living, while most of them faced overwhelming odds when the additional burden of the defence of the Muslim community was placed on them. There was, however, a party of disciples called *As-habus-Suffah* who lived in the Madinah Mosque itself, and who were specially equipped for the teaching of religion to the tribes outside Madinah. Some of these would go to the market and do a little work to earn their living; others would not care even to do that. Of this little band, the most famous was Abu-Huraira, the Prophet's faithful attendant, who would remain in the Prophet's company at all costs and store up in his memory everything which the Holy Prophet said or did.

'A'isha, the Prophet's wife, was also one of those who sought to preserve the *Sunna* of the Prophet. She, too, had a marvellous memory, and was, in addition, gifted with a clear understanding. She had narrated over 160 traditions. 'Abdullah ibn 'Abbas and Abdullah ibn 'Omar were two other companions who were specially engaged in the work of preserving and transmitting the *hadith*, as also was 'Abdullah ibn 'Amr, who used to write down the sayings of the Prophet. And in addition to these, every disciple of the Holy Prophet did his utmost to preserve such of his words and deeds as came to his knowledge. 'Omar, the second Khalifa, was reported to have made arrangements with a neighbour of his that they should be in the company of the Holy Prophet on alternate days, so that each might report to the other what happened in his absence. And most important of all, the Holy Prophet had repeatedly laid an obligation on every one of his followers to transmit his words to others: *"Let him who is present deliver to him who is absent"*, was the concluding sentence of all his utterances, all of which afford a clear proof that the work of preservation and transmission of the *"sunna"* had begun during the lifetime of the Holy Prophet.

Second Stage

With the Holy Prophet's death, the work of the collection of *hadith* entered on a second stage. Every case that came up for decision had now to be referred either to the Holy Quran or to some judgment or saying of the Holy Prophet which had gained an extensive reputation. There were numerous cases on record, in which a right was claimed on the basis of a judgment or saying of the Prophet, and evidence was demanded as to the authenticity of the saying[43]. Thus, there was a double process at work; not only was the trustworthiness of the particular *hadith* established beyond all doubt, but the *hadith* also obtained a wide circulation and, from being the knowledge of one only, it passed to many. The particular judgment might not be on an exact parallel with the circumstances of the case to which it was to be applied, and an analogy might then be sought from one or more sayings. Thus, the multiple needs of a rapidly growing and widely spreading community, whose necessities had increased tenfold on account of its onward march to civilization, brought into prominence a large number of *hadith*, knowledge of which had been limited to one or a few only, with the seal of confirmation of their truth, because at that time direct evidence of that truth was available.

Yet this was not the only factor that gave an impetus to a dissemination of the knowledge of *hadith*.

There was also the influx into Islam of large numbers of people who had never seen the Holy Prophet himself, but who could behold for themselves the astounding transformation brought about by him, and who, therefore, held his memory sacred in the highest degree; this in itself formed an important factor in the general eagerness to discover everything which the great reformer had said or done. It was natural that each new convert should be anxious to know all that was to be known about the Great Prophet who had given quite a new life to a dead world. Everyone who had seen him would thus be a centre to whom hundreds of enquirers would resort, and since the incidents were fresh in their memories, they would be conveyed with fair accuracy to their whole generation.

Moreover, it was to the companions of the Holy Prophet that the religion he brought and his teachings were things which they valued above anything else in the world. For the sake of their new religion, they had given up their business, their kinsfolk, nay, their very homes; to defend it, they had laid down their lives. To carry this divine blessing, the greatest gift of God, to other people, had become the supreme object of their lives; hence a dissemination of its knowledge was their first concern. In addition to this, the Holy Prophet had laid on those of his companions or attendants who were present and on those who saw him or listened to his sayings and teachings, the duty of carrying what they saw or heard to those who were absent. *"Let him who is present carry this to him who is absent"* was the phrase which, on account of the frequency of its repetition, rang continually in their ears. And they were faithful to the great charge laid on them, in whichever direction they went and in whichever country they settled. They went eastward and westward and northward, carrying with them the Quran and the *sunna*.

Every one of them who had the knowledge of even a single

incident relating to the Prophet's life deemed it his duty to deliver it to another. And individuals like Abu-Huraira, 'A'isha, 'Abdullah ibn 'Abbas, 'Abdullah ibn 'Omar, 'Abdullah ibn 'Amr ibn el-'As ibn Malik and many others who had made the preservation of the *sunna* the first object of their lives, had become as it were centres, to whom people resorted from different quarters of the kingdom of Islam to obtain knowledge of the *hadith*. Abu-Huraira alone had eight hundred disciples. 'A'isha's house, too, was resorted to by hundreds of ardent students. The reputation of 'Abdullah ibn 'Abbas (cousin of the Prophet), was equally great, and, notwithstanding his youth, he had a prominent place among the counsellors of the Khalifa 'Omar, on account of his knowledge of the Quran and the *sunna*.

The zeal of the new generation for the acquisition of religious knowledge was so great that students were ready to travel from one place to another to complete their knowledge of the *sunna*, and some would journey long distances to obtain first-hand information about even a single *hadith*[44].

Thus an arrangement existed both for the collection of the knowledge of *hadith* in different centres of learning, and for the spread of it far and wide, through the disciples who gained their knowledge at such centres.

Third Stage

With the passing of the generation that had seen and heard the Holy Prophet directly, the work of collection of *hadith* entered upon a third stage. There were no more reports to be investigated from different teachers who taught at different centres. There was no single centre at which the whole store of the knowledge of *hadith* could be obtained, for companions of the Prophet had spread far and wide. But in the second stage, *hadith* had undoubtedly passed from the individual into public possession, and, therefore, in the third stage the whole of the *hadith* could be learned by repairing to the different centres instead of enquiring about it from individuals. Moreover, at this stage the writing down of *hadith* became more common. The large number of the students of the *hadith* at the different centres, having an abundance of material to digest, to which was also added the further different charge of remembering the names of the transmitters, sought aid from the pen, so that the work might be easier. By this time, writing had become general and writing materials plentiful. Moreover, there was no fear of the *hadith* being confused with the Quran. It must, however, be remembered that at this stage, the *hadith* were written merely as an aid to memory; the mere fact that a written *hadith* was found among the manuscripts of a person was no evidence of its authenticity, which could only be established by tracing it to a reliable transmitter. 'Omar ibn 'Abdul-'Aziz, commonly known as 'Omar II, the Omayyad Khalifa, who ruled towards the close of the first century of Hijra, was the first man who issued definite orders to the effect that written collections of *hadith* should be made. He is reported to have written to Abu-Bakr ibn Hazm, the Khalifa's governor at Madinah: "See whatever sayings of the Holy Prophet can be found, and write it down, for I fear the loss of knowledge and the disappearance of the learned men; and do not accept anything but the true *hadith* of the Holy Prophet, and people should make knowledge public and should sit in companies, so that he who does not know should come to know, for knowledge does not disappear until it is concealed from the public.[45]" The importance of this incident lies in the fact that the Khalifa himself took an interest in the collection of *hadith*.[46] But 'Omar II died after a short reign of two and a half years. After his death, the work of collection of *hadith* in written volumes was taken up independently of government patronage in the next century, and this brings us to the fourth stage in the history of the collection of the traditions of the Holy Prophet.

Fourth Stage

Before the middle of the second century, *hadith* began to assume a more permanent shape, and written collections began to see the light of day, as such collections had become indispensable. The first known work on the subject is that of *Imam* Ibn Juraij. He lived at Makkah, while other authors who wrote books on *hadith* in the second century are *Imam* Malik ibn Anas and Sufyan ibn 'Uwayna at Madinah, 'Abdullah ibn Wahb in Egypt, Ma'mar ibn

'Abdul-Razzak in Yemen, Sufyan Thawri and Muhammad ibn Fudail in Kufa, Hammad ibn Salma and Rauh ibn 'Ubada at Bisra, Hushaim ibn Wasit and 'Abdullah ibn Mubarak in Khurasan (now Afghanistan).

The Book of *Imam* Malik, known as the *Muwatta* Book, is considered the most important of the collections of these authors. However, all these books were yet unexhaustive writings on *hadith*, the object of their compilation was simply the collection of such reports as touched on the daily life of the Muslims. Reports relating to a large number of topics, such as faith, or knowledge, or the life of the Prophet, or wars or comments on the Quran, were outside their scope. Also, every author had collected only such reports and traditions as were taught at the centre at which he worked. Even the *Muwatta* Book, which stood in the first rank, contained only the *hadith* which came through the citizens of Hijaz. All these works on *hadith* which came through the citizens of Hijaz were, therefore, incomplete, but they were a great advance on the oral transmission of the *sunna*.

Fifth Stage

The great work was brought to completion in the third century of the Hijra. It was then that two kinds of collection of *hadith* were made, the *Musnad* and the *Jami*. The *Musnad* was the earlier and the *Jami'* the later. *Musnad* meant the tracing of any one *hadith* back through various transmitters to the companion of the Prophet on whose authority it rested. The most important of this class is the *Musnad of Imam* Ahmad ibn Hanbal (164-241 A.H.) which contains thirty—thousand reports. This great *Imam* divine is one of the four recognized *Imams* of the *Sunni*-Muslim School. The collections, the *Musnad hadith*, however, contains reports of tradition of all sorts. As to the *Jami'*, also known as *Musannaf*, it literally means a work that gathers together; it arranges reports according to their subject-matter and, moreover, it is of a moral critical tone. It is to the *Jami'*, or the *Musnad* that the honour is due of bringing the knowledge of *hadith* to perfection.

Six books are recognized by the *sunni Muslims* as authoritative works on the traditions of the Prophet. These are the collections of: (1) Muhammad ibn Ismail, commonly known as Al-Bukhari (died 256 A.H.), (2) Abu'l Husain Muslim, son of al-Hajjaj al-Qushairi (died 261 A.H.) (3) Abu-Dawud (died 275 A.H.), (4) Tirmizi (died 279 A.H.), (5) Ibn Maja (died 283 A.H.), and (6) An-Nasa'i (died 303 A.H.) The works of the third and the last two are generally referred to by the name of *Sunan*, i.e. practices. These books classified reports under various heads of subjects and thus made *hadith* easy for reference, not only for the judge and the lawyer, but also for the ordinary and the research students.

It may be noted that among the six collections of *hadith* mentioned above, which are known as the six reliable *Hadith Books*, Bukhari holds the first place in several respects, while Muslim's collection comes second and the two together are known as *Sahihain* or the two most reliable *Hadith Books*. Bukhari's collection has the distinction of being the first. Its author is the most critical of all. He did not accept any *hadith* unless all the transmitters were reliable and until there was proof that the later transmitter had actually met the first; the mere fact that the two were contemporaries (which is Muslim's test) did not satisfy him. Moreover, Bukhari heads the more important of his chapters with a text from the Holy Quran and thus shows that a *hadith*, or tradition of the Prophet, is but an explanation of the Quran, and as such secondary of the teachings of Islam.

European criticism of *hadith* has often mixed up *hadith* with the reports met with in the biographies of the Holy Prophet and certain commentaries on the Quran. The fact is that no Muslim scholar has ever attached the same value to the biographical as *hadith* narrated in the above-mentioned collections.

There is no doubt that the collectors of *hadith* attached the utmost importance to the trustworthiness of the narrators. Inquiries were made as to the character of the guarantors, whether they were morally and religiously satisfactory, whether any of them was tainted with heretical doctrines, whether they had a reputation for truthfulness, and had the ability to transmit what they had themselves heard. Finally, it was necessary that they should be competent witnesses whose testimony would be accepted in a court of civil law.[47] But more than this, they tried their best to find out that the report was traceable to the Prophet through the various necessary stages. Even the companions of the Holy Prophet did not accept any *hadith* which was brought to their notice until they were fully satisfied that it came from the Holy Prophet. The collectors went beyond the narrators, and they had rules of criticism which were applied to the subject matter of the *hadith*.

In judging whether a certain *hadith* was spurious or genuine, the collectors not only made a thorough investigation regarding the trustworthiness of the transmitters, but also applied other rules of criticism which were in no way inferior to modern methods. According to these rules, a report of a tradition was not accepted under any of the following circustances:

1. If the report was opposed to recognized historical fact.
2. If the reporter was a *Shi'a*, and the *hadith* was in the nature of an accusation against the companions of the Prophet, or if the reporter was a *Khariji*[48] and the *hadith* was in the nature of an accusation against the Prophet's family. If, however, the *hadith* was corroborated by independent testimony, it was accepted.
3. If the hadith was reported by a single man despite its being of such a nature that to know it and act upon it was incumbent upon all Muslims.
4. If the time and the circumstance of the narration of the *hadith* showed evidence of its forgery.
5. If it was *against reason* or against the plain teachings of Islam.
6. If the subject matter or words of a certain Tradition were unsound or not in consonance with the Arabic idiom, or the subject matter was unbecoming to the Prophet's dignity.
7. If the report mentioned an accident, which, had it happened, would have been known to and reported by large numbers, while as a matter of fact that incident was not reported by any one except the particular reporter[49].
8. If it mentioned threats of heavy punishment for ordinary sins or promised a mighty reward for slight deeds.
9. If the narrator confessed that he was in doubt of what he reported.
10. If the report dealt with the reward of prophets and messengers to the doer of good[50].

24

The Quran is the Greatest Test for Judging Hadith

In addition to the above rules of criticism, which left little to be desired, there is another very important test whereby trustworthiness of *hadith* may be judged, and it is a test the application of which was commanded by the Holy Prophet himself. *"There will be narrators,"* the Prophet is reported to have said, *"reporting hadith from me, so judge by the Quran; if a report agrees with the Quran, accept it, if otherwise, reject it."* There is another saying of the Prophet:

> "My sayings do not abrogate the word of God (the Quran) but the word of God can abrogate my sayings."

As already stated, *hadith* is but an explanation of the Quran; and hence also the Quran must take precedence over the *hadith*.

It is unquestioanble that the Quran had been handed down intact, every word and every letter of it, while *hadith* could not claim that purity, and it was chiefly the substance of sayings that was reported.

Again the Quran deals with the principles of Islamic Law

while *hadith* deals with details, so that only such details should be accepted as are in accordance with the principles.

The *sunni* Muslim community are agreed on the principle that a *hadith* may be unacceptable either on account of there being some defect in its transmitters or because its subject matter is unacceptable. Thus, all trustworthy collectors of traditions of the Holy Prophet are at one that among the most important reasons for which a *hadith* may be rejected is its subject matter. For instance, if a reported tradition contradicts the Holy Quran or the recognized *sunna* or the unanimous verdict of the Muslim community or ordinary commonsense, it is not accepted.

The following sayings of the Holy Prophet will explain the position, which he intended to assign to the oral law of *hadith* or *sunna*:

> "That which the Prophet of God has made unlawful is like that which God Himself has made unlawful."

> "I am no more than a man, but when I enjoin anything respecting religion, receive it, and when I order anything about the affairs of the world, then I am nothing more than a man."

> "Truly, the best word is the word of God, and the best rule of life is that delivered by His Prophet Muhammad."

> "I have left you two things, and you will not go stray as long as you hold them fast. The one is the Book of God and the other the law (sunna) of His Prophet[51]."

25

The Style of Composition
Employed in the Imparting
of Traditions

For the purpose of expressing how a tradition had been communicated from one person to another, certain introductory verbal forms were selected by duly qualified persons. And it was incumbent upon everyone about to narrate a tradition, to commence by the particular form appropriate to the said tradition; this was done with a view to securing for each tradition the credit to which it might be justly entitled.

These introductory verbal forms are as follows: (1) "He told us"; (2) "I heard him saying"; (3) "He said to us"; (4) "He related to us"; (5) "He informed us"; (6) "From".

The first four introductory forms were to be used only in the case of an original narrator communicating the very words of the Tradition to the next below him. The fifth introductory verbal form was used when a narrator inquired of the narrator immediately above him whether such and such a fact, or circumstance, was or was not correct. The last form was not sufficiently explicit, and the consequence was that it could not be decided to which of the two persons the tradition related belonged, so that unless other facts were brought to bear upon it, it could not be satisfactorily proved whether there were any other persons, one or more than one intermediary between the two narrators. As to any eternal facts that might prove what was required to be known, the learned scholars gave the following opinions:

First: If it be known with certainty that the narrator was not notorious for fraudulently omitting the names of other parties forming links in the chain of narration and who also lived at such a time and in such a locality that it was possible, although not proved, that they visited each other, it might be taken for granted that there were no other intermediary narrators between these two.

Secondly: Other learned authorities add that it must be proved that they visited each other at least once in their lifetime.

Thirdly: Others assert that it must be proved that they remained together for such a time as would be sufficient to enable them to learn the tradition, one from the other. The aforesaid restrictions simply tend to show how far the collectors of *hadith* have gone to admit as reliable any tradition of the Holy Prophet.

26

Degrees of Authenticity of the Narrators

The associates of the Prophet, and those persons who lived immediately after them used to relate, with the exception of the Quran, the sense of the Prophets words in their own language, unless they had to use some phrase containing prayers, or when they had to point out to others the very words of the Prophet. It is natural to suppose that deeply learned persons would themselves understand and deliver to others the sense of the sayings better than persons of inferior grade, and they, therefore, have been divided into seven grades:

1. Persons highly conspicuous for their learning and legal acquirements, as well as for their retentive memory. Such persons are distinguished by the title of *Imams of hadith*, i.e. leaders or great scholars of tradition.
2. Persons who, as to their knowledge, rank below the first, but who very rarely committed a mistake.
3. Persons who as to their knowledge still rank after the first and the second, but respecting whose integrity and honesty there is no doubt.

4.   Persons respecting whom nothing is known.
5.   Persons who have made alterations in the pure religion of the Prophet and, actuated by prejudice, have carried them to extremes.
6.   Persons who are pertinaciously sceptical, and have not a retentive memory.
7.   Persons who are notorious for inventing spurious Traditions.

Learned divines are of the opinion that the Traditions related by persons of the first three classes should be accepted as genuine and reliable, according to their respective merits, and, also that Traditions related by persons falling into the three last classes should be at once rejected; and the Traditions related by persons of the fourth[52] class (*i.e.* "from") should be passed over unnoticed so long as the narrator remained unknown.

27

Rules for Distinguishing False Traditions

The following procedures were adopted by the learned scholars of *hadith*:

The actual words employed in Transmitting suspect traditions as well as their style of composition were examined. The contents of each Tradition were compared with the commands and injunctions contained in the Quran and with those religious doctrines and dogmas that had been deduced from the Quran, and with those Traditions which had been proved to be genuine. The learned scholars investigated the nature of the import of each related *hadith* as to whether it was unreasonable, improbable, or impossible.

It will, therefore, be evident that the *hadith*, considered as genuine by the *sunni* Muslims, must meet the following standards: "The narrator must have plainly and distinctly mentioned that such and such a thing (a saying or an action) was either said or done by the Prophet; the chain of narrators from the link up to the Prophet must be unbroken; the subject related must have come within the actual knowledge of its narrators; all the narrators, from the last up to the Prophet, must have been persons conspicuous for their piety, virtue and honesty; every narrator must have received more than one tradition from the narrator immediately preceding him; every one of them must be conspicuous for his learning so that he might be safely presumed to be competent both to understand correctly, and faithfully deliver to others, the sense of the tradition; the import of the tradition must not be contrary to the injunctions contained in the Quran, or to the religious doctrines deduced from that Holy Book, or the traditions proved to be correct; and the nature of the import of the tradition must not be such as persons of good opinion might hesitate in accepting.

Any tradition thus proved genuine can be made the basis of any religious doctrine; but notwithstanding this, another objection may be raised against it, which is that the tradition is the statement of one person only, and therefore, cannot, properly, be believed in implicitly. In order to obviate this, three grades have been again formed of the *hadith* proved as genuine. These three grades are: *mutawatir; mash-hur; and khabarul-ahad.*

Mutawatir is an appellation given to those traditions only that have always been, from the time of the Prophet, and ever afterwards, recognized and accepted by every associate of the Prophet, and every learned individual, as authentic and genuine, and to which no one has raised any objection. All Muslim learned divines of every period have declared that traditions of the grade of *mutawatir* are implicitly believed and ought to be religiously observed.

Mash-hur is a title given to those traditions which, in every age, have been believed to be genuine by a number of learned scholars. These are the traditions which are found recorded in the best collections and having been generally accepted as genuine, form the nucleus of certain Muslim doctrines.

Khabarul-ahad (*or hadith* related by one person) is an appellation given to traditions which do not posses most of the qualities belonging to the traditions of the first two grades; in which case they were considered as not authentic.

There is some difference of opinion as to who first attempted to collect the traditions, and to compile them in a book. Some scholars say 'Abdul-Malik ibn Juraij of Makkah, who died in 150 A.H., whilst others assert that the collection, which is still extant made by the *Imam* (Divine doctor) Malik ibn Anas, who died in 179 A.H., was the first collection. The work of the latter is still held in very great esteem, although it is not generally included in the standard six *Sahih* books, *i.e.* the "six correct" books accepted unanimously by *sunni* Muslims. Previously mentioned in this work they are as follows:

1. *Al-Imam* Muhammad ibn Isma'il Al-Bukhari, 256 A.H.
2. *Al-Imam* Muslim ibn Al-Hajjaj, 261 A.H.
3. *Al-Imam* Abu-Dawud Soliman, 275 A.H.
4. *Al-Imam* Muhammad ibn Isa Al-Tirmizi, 279 A.H.
5. *Al-Imam* Ibn Maja, Abu-'Abdullah Muhammad, 283 A.H.
6. *Al-Imam* An-Nasa`i, Abu-'Abdul-Rahman, 303 A.H.

Besides these, the collections of *Imam* (Divine Dr.) *Al-Shaf'i* (204 A.H.), Ibn Idris, Imam Ahmad ibn Hanbal (241 A.H.). *Imam Malik* ibn Anas (179 A.H.) are also considered authentic by *sunni* Muslims.[53]

28

Ijma'—The Third Foundation of Islamic Laws

Ijma' literally means 'unanimity' of opinion on a certain conclusion. The *sunni* Muslims style themselves *ahlus-sunna wal-jama'*, i.e. the people of tradition and congregation. In Muslim theology, the term *ijma'* expresses the unanimous consent of the learned doctors of theology, who are termed *mujtahids* or those who exert themselves to the utmost. A *mujtahid* is a Muslim divine of the highest degree of learning. The necessary qualifications for a *mujtahid* of the first degree are essentially three: a comprehensive knowledge of the Quran in its different aspects; a knowledge of the *sunna* with its lines of transmission, text and varieties of significance; and a knowledge of the different aspects of *qiyas*[54] or analogy: In addition to these fundamentals, a *mujtahid* must be qualified in the science of *soul*, i.e. the essential principles of the Muslim law, based on the Quran, tradition, consensus of opinion and analogy.

Hence a *mujtahid* is a Muslim divine of the highest degree of learning. This title is usually given by the Muslim rulers to those distinguished doctors of divinity among the community, such as the grand rector of Al-Azhar University in Egypt and to the Members of the Body of Grand Jurists forming the Legislative Council of the said University and to grand *qadis*

197

(judges); also to grand *muftis* or Muslim counsellors in the different Muslim states.

Ijma,' being the exercise of judgment and reason in theological as well as legal matters, plays a very important part in the establishment of the religion of Islam. The value of reason is expressly recognized in the Holy Quran. Although the Quran recognizes revelation as a source of knowledge higher than reason, it admits at the same time that the truth of the principles established by revelation may be judged by reason, and hence it repeatedly appeals to reason and common sense and denounces those who do not use their reasoning faculties: it is full of exhortations like the following: *"Do you not reflect[55]?" "Do you not understand[56]?" "Have you no sense[57]?" There are signs in this for people who reflect." "There are signs in this for people who understand.[58]"* Those who do not use their reasoning faculty are condemned in various verses of the Quran. On the other hand, it praises those who do so[59]. The Quran also recognizes the necessity for the exercise of judgment in order to arrive at a decision: *"And when there comes to them news of security or fear, they spread it abroad; and if they had referred it to the Apostle and to those in authority (the jurists) among them, those among them who can search out the knowledge of it would have known its true purport.[60]"* The original Arabic word in the verse for "search out" reads *"yastanbituna"* from *"istinbat"*, which signifies the searching out of the hidden meaning by the use of judgment and reason. The verse thus recognizes the principle of the exercise of the judgment, which is the same as *ijtihad* and is also the same as *istikhraj* or deduction by analogy[61]; and though the occasion on which it was revealed was a particular one, the principle recognized is considered by all jurists and learned scholars as a general principle.

The Holy Prophet allowed the exercise of judgment in religious matters, where there is no express direction in the Holy Quran or the *sunna*[62].

Establishment of Ijtihad

The exercise of judgment to meet the new circumstances had begun, as already shown, in the Prophet's lifetime, since it was impossible to refer every case to him. After the Prophet's death, the principle of *ijtihad* obtained a wider prevalence, and as new areas of population were added to the material and spiritual realm of Islam, the need of resorting to *ijtihad* became greater. During the reign of Abu-Bakr, when a case came before him, he used to consult the Book of Allah (the Quran); if he found anything in it by which he could decide, he did so; if he did not find it in the Book, and he knew of a *sunna* of the Messenger of Allah, he decided according to it; and if he was unable to find anything there, he used to question the Muslims around him if they knew of any decision of the Holy Prophet in a matter of this kind, and every one of them stated what he knew from the Prophet, and Abu-Bakr would say 'Praise be to Allah who had kept among us those who remembered what the Prophet had said;' But if he was unable to find anything in the *sunna* of the Prophet, he gathered together the leading companions and consulted them, and if they agreed upon one opinion (by a majority) he decided accordingly[63].

The above illustration represents the principle of *ijma* or consensus of opinion, as a source of Islamic Law.

The same rule was followed by 'Omar, the second Khalifa, who resorted to *ijtihad* very freely, but took care always to gather the most learned companions and consult with them. When there was a difference of opinion, that of the majority was made the basis of decision.

Besides the Khalifas among whom the foremost was 'Ali, cousin of the Prophet, there were great individual teachers, such as lady 'A'isha—the Prophet's widow, Ibn 'Abbas, Ibn 'Omar, and other great *mujtahids* of the day, whose opinion was highly revered. Decisions were given according to their own judgment and laws promulgated subject only to the one condition that they were neither contrary to the Holy Quran nor to the *sunna* of the Prophet. And decisions of those earlier jurists were followed by the later jurists.

The Four Great Divine Doctors

In the second century of Hijra arose the great four doctors of jurisprudence who codified the Islamic Law according to the needs of their time.

Imam Abu-Hanifa

The first of these was Imam Abu-Hanifa Al-Nu'man ibn Thabit, born at Basra (80 A.H.) (A.D. 699) and died in A.D. 767. His centre of activity was at Kufa. The basis of his analogical reasoning, known as *qiyas* (analogy), was the Holy Quran, and he accepted a *hadith* only when he was fully satisfied as to its authenticity. The great collectors of *hadith* had not yet commenced their work of collection, and Kufa itself was not a great centre of learning. It was Imam Abu-Hanifa who first directed attention to the great value of *qiyas*, or analogical reasoning, in legislation, which was held by Muslims to be the fourth foundation of Islamic jurisprudence after the source of *ijma'*. (The principle of *qiyas* will be dealt with later.) *Imam* Abu-Hanifa had two renowned disciples, Imam Muhammad and *Imam* Abu Yusuf, and it is mostly their views of the great master's teaching that now form the basis of the Hanafi School system.

Imam Malik

Next comes Imam Malik ibn Anas, the second great Divine. He was born at Madinah in the year 93 A.H. (A.D. 713); he worked there and died at the age of 82. He limited himself almost entirely to the *hadith*, which he found and collected at Madinah, relating more especially to the practice which prevailed there, and his system of jurisprudence is based entirely on the customs and practices of the people of Madinah. His book, known as *Muwatta*, is the first collection of *hadith* and one of the most authoritative books of tradition and *sunna*.

Imam Shaf'i

The third Divine, Imam Muhammad ibn Idris Al-Shaf'i, was born in Palestine in the year 150 A.H. (A.D. 767). He passed his youth at Makkah but he worked for the most part in Egypt, where he died in 204 A.H. In his day, he was unrivalled for his knowledge of the Holy Quran, and took immense pains in studying the *sunna*, travelling from one place to another in search of information. His school was based chiefly on *sunna*. Over the *Maliki* system, which is also based on *sunna*, the *Shafi* system has the advantage that the *hadith* made use of by Imam Shaf'i was more extensive, and was collected from different centres, while Imam Malik contented himself only with what he found at Madinah.

Imam Ahmad Ibn Hanbal

The last of the four great *imams* was Ahmad ibn Hanbal, who was born at Baghdad in the year 164 A.H. and died there in 241 A.H. He too made a very extensive study of *hadith*. His famous work on the subject is known as the *Musnad* of Ahmad ibn Hanbal, and contains thousands of *hadiths*. This monumental compilation is based on the material collected by the *Imam* himself. His collection of *hadiths* is not arranged according to subject matter, but under the name of the companion to whom a *hadith* is ultimately traced.

While the system of Abu-Hanifa applied reasoning very freely and sought to deduce the solutions to all questions from the Holy Quran by the help of reason, the system of Ibn Hanbal is distinguished by the fact that it makes reserved use of reason and judgment.

Different Methods Forming New Laws

The four *above*-mentioned *Imams* who are accepted by the entire *sunni* world of Islam, are thus agreed in giving to *ijtihad* a very important place in legislation. *Ijma'* and *ijtihad* are thus looked upon as two more sources of the Islamic Law along with the Holy Quran and the *sunna* of the Prophet, though the latter two are regarded as *al-adillal-qat'iya*, or absolute arguments or authorities the former two sources being called ˌal-addillal-ijtihadiya, or agruments arrived at by exertion.

The sphere of *ijtihad* is a very wide one, since it seeks to fulfil all the requirements of the Muslim community which are not met with expressly in the Holy Quran and the *hadith*. The great *mujtahids* of Islam have endeavoured to meet these demands by various methods, technically known as *qiyas*, or analogical reasoning, *istihsan*, i.e. equity, *istislah*, i.e. public good, and *istidlal*, i.e. inference. A brief description of these methods may be given to show how new laws are evolved by adopting them.

29

Degrees of Ijtihad

There are three degrees of *ijtihad*. They are: *ijtihad fish-Shar,'* *ijtihad fil-Mazhab*, and *ijtihad fil-masa-il*, or exercise of judgment in legislation, in a juristic system and in particular cases.

The first kind of *ijtihad*, or exercise of judgment, in the making of new, infallible laws is recognized by the *sunni* Muslims to have been limited to the first three centuries and, practically, it centres in the four great revered Imams. They have confined all laws and included in their systems whatever was reported from the Companions and the *tabi'in*, i.e. the next generation of the Companions. It is the general opinion that the conditions[64] necessary for a *mujtahid* of the first degree have not been met with in any person after the first four grand Imams. It is further supposed, for obvious reasons, that they will not be met with in any person in the later generation[65].

The second degree of *ijtihad* belongs to such earlier *mujtahids* as Imam Abu-Yusuf and Imam Muhammad, the two famous disciples of the head Imam Abu-Hanifa whose unanimous opinion on any point of jurisprudence must be accepted by the scholars and followers of the Hanafi system, even if it goes against that of their master.

The third degree of *ijtihad* was and is still attainable by later acknowledged *mujtahids* and local jurists who could solve questions or special cases that came before them, which had not been decided by the *mujtahids* of the first two degrees. But such solutions of new cases must be in absolute accordance with the opinions of the greater *mujtahids*. In fact, *ijtihad* is a great blessing of which the Muslim religion can ever boast; it is the only way by which the needs of the succeeding generations and the requirements of the different races merging into each other could be met.

To fulfil these needs and requirements, the *mujtahids* have laid down the foregoing methods, technically known as *qiyas* (analogical reasoning); *istihsan* (equity); *istislah* (public good); and *istidlal* (inference).

A brief description of these methods is now given to show how new secondary laws are evolved by adopting them:-

'Qiyas or Analogy

The most important of these methods and the one which has almost universal sanction, is *qiyas*, which literally means measuring by or *comparing with* or judging by *comparing with, a thing*, while the jurists apply it to "a process of deduction by which the law of a text is applied to cases which, though not covered with the language, are governed by the reason of the text[66]. Briefly it may be described as reasoning based on analogy. A case might come up for decision, which is not expressly provided for either in the Holy Quran or in the *hadith*. The jurist looks for it in the Quran or in the hadith and by reasoning on the basis of analogy, arrives at a decision. Thus, it is an extension of the law as met with in the Holy Quran and *hadith*, but it is not of equal authority with them, for no jurist has ever claimed infallibility for decisions based on analogical deductions. It is a recognized principle of *ijtihad* that the *mujtahid* may err in his judgment. Many differences of juristic deductions exist, therefore, even among the highest authorities. From its very nature the *qiyas*, of one generation may be rejected by a following generation. However, *ijma'* is in all cases binding on the community.

Istihsan or Equity

Istihsan, which literally means considering a thing to be equitable, is in the technology of the jurists the exercise of private judgment, not on the basis of analogy, but on that of public good or in the interests of justice. According to the Hanafi system, when a deduction based on analogy is not acceptable, either because it is against the broad rules of justice, or because it is not in the interest of the public good, and is likely to cause undue inconvenience to those to whom it is applied, the jurist is at liberty to adopt, instead, a rule which is considered to be in consonance with the broader rules of justice.

This method of *istihsan* is rather peculiar to the Hanafi system.

Istislah or Public Good

This method, a similar rule to that of *istihsan*, and adopted by Imam Malik and the Maliki School at large, entails *a deduction of the law based on consideration of public good.*

Istidal or Inference

Istidlal has two chief sources which are recognized for the purpose of inference. These are the customs and usages which prevailed in Arabia prior to the advent of Islam, and which were not abrogated by Islam; they have the force of law. On the same principle, customs and usages prevailing anywhere, when not opposed to the spirit of the Quranic teachings or not expressly forbidden by the *sunna*, would be admissible, because according to a well-known maxim of the jurists, "permissibility is the original principle", and, therefore, what has not been declared unlawful is permissible. In fact, wherever a custom is recognized by a vast majority of the people, it is looked upon as having the force of *ijma'* and hence has precedence over a rule of a law derived from analogy. The only condition required is that it must not be opposed to a clear text of the Quran or a reliable *hadith*.

The Hanafi School lays special stress on the value of customs, so much so that it is taken as a principle of law[67].

As regards laws revealed to the people of the Book (Jews and Christians) previous to Islam, they also have the force of law even now, so long as they have not been expressly abrogated by the Quran or the *sunna*.

It is to be noted that differences of opinion between acknowledged jurists were never ignored by the Islamic Law, nay, this was encouraged and praised since such differences are naught but the ripe fruit of the use of the reasoning faculty, so long as the oppos it opinions expressed on certain secondary points are not contradicted by the Quran, the Book of God or the practice and teaching of the Holy Prophet.

On this principle, the Messenger of God is quoted to have said that when a *qadi* (qualified judge or jurist) gives a judgment and he exercises his reasoning faculty and is right, he has a double reward, and when he gives a judgment and exercises his reasoning faculty and makes an innocent mistake, there is still a reward for him[68].

Again the Holy Prophet is reported to have said: *"The differences of my people are a mercy.[69]"* Difference of opinion is called a mercy, i.e. a blessing, because it is only through encouraging difference of opinion that the reasoning faculty is developed, and the truth ultimately discovered. There were certain differences of opinion among the Companions of the Holy Prophet, and there were also matters on which a single Companion used boldly to express his dissent from all the rest. For example, Abu-Zarr was alone in holding that to have accumulated wealth in one's possession was a sin. His opinion was that no one should amass wealth unless he had distributed tha most of it to the needy. All the other companions were opposed to the view; and though the authority of *ijma'* was quoted against him, no one did dare say that Abu Zarr had committed a sin for expressing an opinion different from that of the whole body of Companions[70].

Thus the Holy Quran is the fountainhead of Islamic Law, supported and explained by Traditions of the Prophet, agreement, analogy and preference, on which all Muslim schools are unanimous.

The difference only arises in regard to the selection of a

particular tradition or to the preference given to a certain tradition over any other, or to the interpretation of certain of the Quranic passages[71].

Ways Of Inferring "Ijma"

Before concluding this Chapter on the subject of *ijma*, it is necessary to point out the ways by which *ijma'* and its subsequent enjoinment upon the *sunni* Muslims are inferred.

As already stated, the *sunni* Muslim theologians and jurists are unanimous in considering the agreement of the *mujtahids* a source of jurisprudence and one of the foundations of Islamic Law.

The expression and terminology of the general agreement of *mujtahids* is supposed to imply the collection of the opinion of all living *mujtahids* at any certain age. But this is not the case. In fact, the said agreement is inferred in three ways: first by *qawl* (word), *i.e.* when the *mujtahids* express an opinion on the point in question; secondly by *fi'l* (deed), *i.e.* when there is unanimity in practice; thirdly by *sokut* (silence), *i.e.* when the *mujtahids* of a certain age do not oppose an opinion expressed by *one* or more of them; as for example, when the rector of Al-Azhar or any other acknowledged *mujtahid* expresses an opinion on a point of law, and his (or their) opinion was not expressly opposed by some *mujtahids*, but was received by unanimous silence on their part.

30

Payment of the Tribute Called "Jizia"

Foreign writers on Islam have generally assumed that while the Quran offered one of the alternatives, Islam or death, to other non-Muslims, the Jews and Christians were given a somewhat better position since they could save their lives by the payment of a tax known as *jizia*. This conception of *jizia*, as a kind of religious tax of which the payment entitled certain non-Muslims to security of life under the Muslim rule, is as entirely opposed to the fundamental teachings of Islam as is the myth that the Muslims were required to carry on aggressive wars against all non-Muslims till they had accepted Islam. Tributes and taxes were levied before Islam, and have been levied to this day by Muslim and non Muslim states, yet they had nothing to do with the religion of the people affected. The Muslim State was as much in need of finance to maintain itself as any other State in the world, and it resorted to exactly the same methods as those employed by other States. All that happened was that certain small non-Muslim states were, when subjugated, given the right to administer their own affairs, but only if they would pay a small sum by way of tribute towards the maintenance of the central government at Madinah. It was an act of great magnamity of the Holy Prophet to confer complete autonomy on a people who having waged war against the Musims but were

207

ultimately conquered by them, and a paltry sum of tribute (*jizia*) in such conditions was not a hardship but a boon. There was no interference at all with their administration, their own laws, their customs and usages, or their religion; and, for the tribute paid, the Muslim state undertook the responsibility of protecting these small states against all enemies.

There are cases on record in which the Muslim state returned the *jizia*, when it was unable to afford protection to the people under its care. Thus when the Muslim forces under the Muslim commander Abu-'Ubaida were engaged in a struggle with the Roman Empire at Syria, they were compelled to beat a retreat at Homs, which they had previously conquered. When the decision was taken to evacuate Homs, Abu-'Ubaida sent for the chiefs of the place and returned to them the amount which he had realized as *jizia*, saying that as the Muslims could no longer protect them, they were not entitled to the payment of *jizia*[72].

It further appears that exemption from military service was granted only to such non-Muslims as wanted it, for where a non-Muslim people offered to fight the battle of the country, they were exempted from *jizia*. The Bani-Taghlib and the people of Najran, both Christian, did not pay the *jizia*[73]. Indeed, the Bani-Taghlib fought alongside the Muslim forces in the battle of Buwaib in 13 A.H. Later on, in the year 16 A.H., they wrote to the Khalifa 'Omar offering to pay the *zakat* (the legal alms) which was a heavier burden, instead of the *jizia*. "The liberality of Omar", writes Sir Muir in his *'Caliphate'*, "allowed the concession, and the Bani Taghlib enjoyed the singular privilege of being assessed as Christians at a double tithe, instead of paying the obnoxious badge of subjugation[74]."

From the foregoing, it is quite clear the *jizia* was levied not as a penalty for refusal to accept the faith of Islam, but was paid in return for protection given to non-Muslims by the Muslim army, to which they were not compulsorily conscripted like the Muslims. This tribute was levied only on able-bodied men and not on women or children; the aged and the indigent, the blind and the maimed were specially exempted, as were the priests and the monks.

Islam, Jizia or the Sword

It is generally thought that the Muslims were out to impose their religion at the point of the sword, and that the Muslim hosts were overrunning all lands with the message of Islam, *jizia* or the sword. This is, indeed, a distorted picture of what really happened.

The fact that there were people who never became Muslims at all, nor ever paid *jizia*, and yet were living in the midst of the Muslims, even fighting their battles, explodes the whole theory of the Muslims offering Islam or the *jizia* or the sword. The truth of the matter is that the Muslims, finding the Roman Empire and Persia bent upon the subjugation of Arabia and the extirpation of Islam, refused to accept terms of peace without a safeguard against a repetition of the aggression; and this safeguard was demanded in the form of *jizia* or a tribute, which would be an admission of defeat on their part. No war was ever started by them otherwise. History contradicts such an assertion. But when a war was undertaken on account of the enemy's aggression—his advance on Muslim territory or help rendered to the enemies of the Muslim State—it was only natural for the Muslims not to terminate the war before bringing it to a successful conclusion. They were ever willing, but only if he admitted defeat and agreed to pay a tribute, which was to avoid further bloodshed after inflicting a defeat on the enemy. This was really a token tribute as compared with the crushing war indemnities of the present day. The offer to terminate hostilities on payment of *jizia* was thus an act of mercy towards a vanquished foe. But if payment of the token tribute was not agreed to by the vanquished power, the Muslims could do nothing but have recourse to the sword until the enemy was completely subdued.

The only question that remains is whether the Muslim soldiers invited their enemies to accept Islam; and whether it was an offence if they did so. Islam was a missionary religion from its very inception, and every Muslim deemed it his sacred duty to invite other people to embrace Islam. The envoys of Islam, wherever they went, looked upon it as their first duty to spread the message of Islam, because they felt that Islam imparted a new life and vigour to humanity, and offered a real solution to the problems of every nation. Islam was offered, no doubt, even to the fighting enemy, but it is a distortion of facts to assume that it was offered at the point of the sword, when there is not a single instance on record of Islam being enforced upon a prisoner of war, nor of Muslims sending a message to a peaceful neighbouring people to the effect that they would be invaded if they did not embrace Islam. All that is recorded is that in the midst of war, and after defeat had been inflicted on the enemy in several battles, when there were negotiations for peace, the Muslims in their zeal for the faith related their own experience before the chiefs of the enemy. They stated how they themselves had been deadly foes to Islam, and how ultimately they found Islam to be a blessing and a power that had raised the Arab race from the depths of degradation to great moral and spiritual heights, and had wielded their warring elements into a solid nation. In such words did the Muslim envoys invite the Persians and the Romans to Islam, not before the declaration of war but at the time of negotiation for peace. If the enemy had then accepted Islam, there would be no conditions for peace, and the two parties would live as equals and brethren. It was not offering Islam at the point of the sword, but offering it as a harbinger for peace, equality and brotherhood. The early Khalifas had to wage wars, but these wars were never aggressive, nor were they engaged in with the aim of propagating the faith of Islam by force. They could not do anything which their Holy Master never did, and which the Holy Quran forbade them to do.

Directions Relating to War

The following instructions were given by the Holy Prophet to the troops despatched against the Byzantine forces who threatened to invade the Muslims:

"In avenging the injuries inflicted upon us, do not molest the harmless inmates of domestic seclusion; spare the weakness of female sex; do not injure the infant at the breast, or those who are ill in bed. Refrain from demolishing the dwellings of the unresisting inhabitants; do not destroy the means of their subsistence, nor their fruit trees and do not touch the palm[75]."

Khalifa Abu-Bakr also gave the following instructions to the commander of an army in the Syrian battle:

"When you meet your enemies, acquit yourselves like men, and do not turn your backs; and if you gain the victory, kill neither the little children, nor the old people, nor the women. Destroy no palm-trees, nor burn any fields of corn or wheat. Cut down no fruit trees, nor do any mischief to cattle, only such as you kill for the necessity of subsistence. When you make any covenant or treaty, stand by it, and be as good as your word. As you go on, you will find some religious persons who live retired in monasteries and who propose to themselves to serve God that way. Let them alone, and neither kill them nor destroy their monasteries[76]."

Similar instructions were given by the succeeding Khalifas to their respective commanders of the troops, all tending to the treatment of the hostile enemies with justice and mercy.

Treatment of the Prisoners of War

If the wars, during the time of the Holy Prophet or early Khalifas had been prompted by the desire to propagate Islam by force, this object could easily have been attained by forcing Islam upon prisoners of war who fell helpless in the hands of the Muslims. Yet this the Holy Quran does not allow; on the contrary, it expressly lays down that prisoners of war better be set free. To this effect we read in the Holy Quran the following instruction:

"When the Muslims meet in battle those hostile disbelievers, they have to kill them in battle. But when the Muslims have overcome the enemies, they have to make them prisoners of war; and afterwards either set them free as a favour, or let them ransom themselves until the war terminates."
(47:4)

Here we are told that prisoners of war can only be taken after meeting an enemy in regular battle, and even in that case they may

211

either be set free, as a favour, or after taking ransom. The Holy Prophet carried out this injunction during his lifetime. In the battle of Hunain, six thousand prisoners of the Hawazin tribe were taken, and they were all set free simply as an act of favour[77]. A hundred families of Bani Mustaliq were taken as prisoners in the battle of Mura'isi, and they were also set at liberty without any ransom being paid[78]. Seventy prisoners were taken at the battle of Badr, and it was only in this case that ransom was exacted; but the prisoners were granted their freedom, while war with the Quraishites was yet in progress[79].

The form of ransom adopted in the case of these prisoners was that they should teach some of the illiterate Arab Muslims how to read and write[80]. When war ceased and peace was established, all war prisoners would have to be set free, according to the verse quoted above.

Prisoners of War not Slaves

The treatment accorded to prisoners of war in Islam in unparalleled. No other nation or society can show a similar treatment. The golden rule of treating the prisoner of war like a brother was laid down by the Holy Prophet:

> "They are your brethren. Allah has put them under
> your......hands; so whosoever has his brother under
> his hand, let him give him to eat whereof he
> himself eats and let him give to wear what he
> himself wears, and do not impose on them a task
> they are not able to do, and if you give them such
> work, then help them in the execution of it[81]."

The prisoners were distributed among the various Muslim families, as no arrangements for their maintenance by the state existed at the time, but they were treated mercifully. A prisoner of war states that he was kept in a family whose people gave him bread while they themselves had to live on dates[82].

Prisoners of war were, therefore, not only set free but, so long as they were kept prisoners, they were treated generously.

War as a Struggle to be Carried on Honestly

It will be seen from the foregoing statements concerning the injunctions relating to war and peace, that war is recognized by Islam as a struggle between nations which is sometimes necessitated by the conditions of human life. But Islam does not allow its followers to provoke war, nor does it allow them to be aggressors, yet it commands them to put their entire strength into the struggle when war is forced on them. If the enemy wants peace after the struggle has begun, the Muslims should not refuse, even though there is doubt about the enemy's honesty of purpose. But the struggle, so long as it exists, must be carried on to the end. In this struggle, honest dealing is enjoined even with the enemy throughout the Holy Quran; verse 2, Chapter 5, runs thus:

"And let not hatred of a people --------- incite you to exceed the proper limits; and help one another in goodness and piety, but do not help one another in sin and aggression."

Again verse 8 of the same Chapter reads thus:

Let not hatred of a people incite you not to act equitably; see that you act equitably, that is nearer to piety."

The tradition of the Holy Prophet too enjoins honest dealing in war:

"Fight and do not exceed the limits and do not be unfaithful and do not mutilate bodies and do not kill children.[82]"

Such are some of the directions given which purify war of the elements of the barbarity and dishonesty in which western warring nations generally indulge. Neither inhuman nor immoral practices are allowed by Islam in war or peace.

PART SIX

SPIRITUAL ASPECT
OF ISLAM

31

The Treasures of Happiness

Man was marvellously created, not in jest or at random, but for some great end. Although he is not everlasting, he lives for ever, and though his body is mean and earthly, his spirit is lofty and divine. When, in the crucible of abstinence he is purified of carnal passions, he attains the highest plane, and in place of being a slave to lust and anger, he becomes gifted with angelic qualities. Attaining that state, he no longer finds his real happiness in sexual delights, but in the contemplation of Eternal Beauty. The spiritual medicine which heals earthly passions is not to be bought with gold or money. It is to be sought in the hearts of Prophets; its methods of operation are explained to people by the instructions given and practical life led by the Messengers of God. The loving Creator has sent various messengers to teach men the prescription of this cure and how to purify their hearts of baser qualities in the crucible of abstinence. In fact, men will find free treasures of happiness open before them once they turn away from the world to God, and it is to do so that Islam has formed itself also into a moral science.

Islamic medicine is many-sided, but its main constituents are as follows:

1. The knowledge of self.
2. The knowledge of God.

3. The knowledge of this world.
4. The knowledge of the next world.
5. The three stages of man's development.
6. Self-examination, the recollection and love of God.

We shall now proceed to explain these constituents hereinafter as briefly as possible.

1. The Knowledge of Self

Nothing is nearer to man than himself, and if he does not know himself, he cannot know anything else. Knowledge of self is the key to the knowledge of God: The Holy Prophet says: *"He who knows himself well, knows God."* In the Quran we read:

"God will show men His signs in the world and
in themselves, so that the truth may be manifest
to them." (41:53)

Now, if one says "I know myself," meaning his outward shape, body, face, limbs and so forth, such knowledge can never be a key to the knowledge of God or the truth. And if man's knowledge of what is within only extends to recognizing that when he is hungry he eats, and when he is angry he attacks, he will progress no further towards enlightenment along this path, for in this regard, he is on no higher a plane than the animals.

Real self-knowledge consists in solving the following problems:

What is man in himself and from whence did he come? Whither is he going, and for what purpose has he come to tarry here a while, and in what does his real happiness and misery consist?

Some of man's attributes are those of animals, some of devils, and some of angels, and he has to find out which of these attributes are accidental and which are essential. Till he knows this, he cannot come to a real knowledge of himself.

The occupation of animals is eating, sleeping and fighting. Therefore, if man is an animal, let him busy himself in these things. Devils are busy in stirring up mischiefs, and in guile and deceit;

217

if he belongs to their species let him do their work. Angels contemplate the beauty of God, and are entirely free from animal qualities; if man is of angelic nature, then let him strive towards his own origin, so that he may know and contemplate God, and be delivered from the animal thraldom of *passion* and *anger*. He should also discover why he has been created with these two animal instincts; whether they should subdue him and lead him captive, or whether he should subdue them, and, in his upward progress, make of one his steed and of the other his weapon.

The first step in man's knowledge is to know that he is composed of an outward shape, called the body, and an inward entity called the heart, or soul. By "heart" we do not mean the piece of flesh resting in the left of our bodies, but that which uses all other faculties as its instruments and servants. In truth, it does not belong to the visible world, but to the invisible, and has come into this world as a traveller who visits a foreign country for the sake of trade and will presently return to its native land. The knowledge of this entity and its attributes is the key to the knowledge of God. Of this the Holy Quran says:

"We (God) have created Jinn and Men only so that
they may serve Us." (and obey His Messengers)
(51:56)

The Reality of the Heart

Some idea of the reality of the heart or spirit may be obtained by a man closing his eyes and forgetting everything around except his individuality. He will thus obtain a glimpse of the unending nature of that individuality. An exact philosophical knowledge of the heart or spirit is not a necessary preliminary to striving in the path of God, but comes rather as the result of self-discipline, and perseverance in that path, as it is taught in the Quran:

"Those who struggled themselves for God's sake,
We will surely guide them to Us, they having been
righteous and Allah loves the righteous." (29:69)

This much is known of the heart that it is an indivisible essence belonging to the world of decree, and that it is not everlasting, but a created spiritual entity.

For the carrying on of this spiritual struggle by which the knowledge of oneself is to be obtained, the body may be figured as a kingdom, the soul as its king, and the different senses and faculties as the king's army. *Reason* may be called the minister, *passion* the revenue-collector, and *anger* the police-officer. On the pretext of collecting revenue, passion is continually prone to plunder on its own account, while anger, the police-officer, is always inclined to harshness and extreme severity. Both of these two, the revenue-collector and the police-officer, have to be kept in due subordination to the king, but not killed or expelled, as they have their own proper functions to perform. But if passion predominates over reason, the ruin of the soul indubitably ensues.

Man's Highest Faculty

A soul which allows its lower faculties to master the highest is like one who commits his wealth to the custody of thieves, or his only son to the care of base, wicked servants. The aim of Islamic discipline is but to purify the heart of the lust of passion and resentment, till as clear as a mirror, it reflects the light of God.

It is questionable that man has been created with animal and demoniac as well as angelic qualities, but it is this latter which constitutes *his real essence*, while the former are merely accidental and transitory. The essence of each creature is to be sought in that which is highest in it and peculiar to it.

For instance, the horse and the ass are both beasts of burden, but the superiority of the horse to the ass consists in its being adapted for use in battle. If it fails in this, it is degraded to the rank of a pack animal. Similarly with man: the highest faculty in him is reason, which fits him to the contemplation of God. If this faculty predominates in him when he dies, he leaves behind him all tendencies to passion and resentment, and becomes capable of association with angels. As regards his mere animal qualities, man is inferior to many animals, but reason makes him superior to them. However, if man's lower tendencies have been triumphant, after death he will ever be looking towards the earth and longing for worldly delights.

The Power of the Soul

Now the rational soul in man abounds in marvels, both of knowledge and power. By means of it he masters arts and sciences and can pass in flesh from earth to heaven and back again; he can map out the skies and measure the distances between the stars. By it also, he can draw the biggest fish from the sea and the remotest birds from the air, and can subdue beasts to his service like the elephant, the camel, the horse and the like. His five senses are like five doors opening on the external world; but, more wonderful than this, his heart has a window which opens on the unseen world of spirits. In the state of sleep, when the avenues of the senses are closed, this window is opened and man receives impressions from the unseen world and sometimes foreshadowings of the future. His heart is then like a mirror which reflects what is pictured in the Table of Fate. But even in sleep, thoughts of worldly things dull the mirror so that the impressions it receives are not clear. After death, however, such thoughts vanish and things are seen in their naked reality, and the word of God is fulfilled:

> "You were heedless of this (end); We have now
> removed the veil from your eyes and so your sight
> today is piercing." (50:22)

This opening of a window in the heart towards the unseen also takes place in conditions approaching those of prophetic inspiration, when intuitions spring up in the mind unconveyed through any sense channel. The more a man purifies himself from carnal passions and concentrates his mind on God (by strictly following the teachings of the Holy Prophet and abiding by the instructions of the Quran), the more conscious will he be of such intuitions. Those who are not conscious of them have no right to deny their reality.

Just as iron, by sufficient polishing, can be made into a mirror, so any heart by due discipline can be rendered receptive of such impressions. But some hearts are like mirrors so contaminated with rust and dirt, that they send back no clear reflections, while those of the Prophets and saints, though they are men born with human passions, are extremely sensitive to all divine impressions. The Holy Quran refers to such contaminated hearts by saying.

"No! indeed their hearts were rusted (contaminated) by their (bad) deeds." (83:14)

The soul of man is capable of holding the first rank among created things, and this not only by reason of knowledge acquired and intuitive, but also by reason of power. Just as angels preside over the elements, so also does the soul rule the members of the body. These souls which attain a special degree of power not only rule their own bodies but those of others also. If they pray for a sick man to recover, he recovers, and so on. These powerful souls differ from common folk in three ways: (1) What others see in dreams they see in their waking moments. (2) While others will only affect their own bodies, these, by God's power, can move bodies extraneous to themselves, (3) The knowledge which others acquire by laborious learning comes to them by intuition.

The Perception of Truth

These three, of course, are not the only marks which differentiate them from common people, but they are the only ones that come within our knowledge. Just as no one knows the real nature of God but God himself, so no one knows the real nature of a saint but a saint. Nor is this to be wondered at, as in everyday matters we see that it is impossible to explain the charm of poetry to one whose ear is insusceptible to cadence and rhythm, or the glories of colour to one who is colour-blind. Besides mere incapacity, there are other hindrances to the attainment of spiritual truth. One of these is externally acquired knowledge. To use an illustration, the heart may be represented as a well, and the five senses as five streams which are continually discharging water into it.

In order to find out the real contents of the heart, these

streams must be stopped for a time, at any rate, and the refuse they have brought with them must be cleared out of the well. In other words, if we are to arrive at pure spiritual truth, we must put away for the time being any knowledge which has been acquired by external processes and which too often hardens into dogmatic prejudices.

According to Islamic spiritual experience, happiness, the ideal of every human being, is necessarily linked with the knowledge of God. Each faculty of ours delights in that for which it is created. Lust delights in accomplishing desire, anger in taking vengeance, the eye in seeing beautiful objects, and the ear in hearing harmonious sounds. The highest function of the soul of men is perception of truth; in this accordingly it finds its special delights. As a matter of course, the higher the subject matter of the knowledge obtained, the greater the delight. A man would be pleased into being admitted into the confidence of a prime minister, but how much more so if an emperor made an intimate of him and disclosed state secrets to him!

Seeing then that nothing is higher than God, how great must be the delight which springs from the knowledge of Him.

A person in whom the desire for this knowledge has disappeared is like one who has lost his appetite for wholesome food; all bodily appetites perish at death with the organs they use, but the soul does not die, and retains what knowledge of God it possesses, nay, increases it.

An important part of our knowledge of God arises from the study and contemplation of our own bodies, which reveal to us the power, wisdom, and love of the Creator. His power is that from a mere drop He has built up the wonderful frame of man; his wisdom is revealed in its intricacies and the mutual adaptability of its parts, and His love is shown by His not only supplying such organs as are absolutely necessary for existence, as the liver, the heart, and the brain, but those which are not absolutely necessary, but are added as ornaments, such as the colour of the hair, the redness of the lips, also the eyelashes, and the curve of the eyebrow, etc.

The Steed and its Rider

Man has been truly termed a "microcosm" or a little world in himself, and the structure of his body should be studied not only by those who wish to become physicians, but by those who wish to attain more intimate knowledge of God, just as a close study of the niceties and shades of language in a great poem reveals to us more and more of the genius of its author.

But, when all is said and done, knowledge of the soul plays a more important part in leading to the knowledge of our body and its functions. The body may be compared to a steed and the soul to its rider: the body was created for the soul, the soul for the body. If a man does not know his own soul, which is the nearest thing to him, how can he lay claim to know other's?

A man who neglects his soul and suffers its capacities to rust or to degenerate, must necessarily be the loser in this world and the next. To this the Holy Quran refers saying:

> "Whoever is blind (in this world), he shall also be
> in the hereafter and in more need of light to guide
> him." (17:72)

In another verse, the faithful, the righteous, and the godly shall have light on that day, while the wicked and the undutiful will have no light as if they were totally blind.

> "On that day you shall see the true believers with
> light streaming before them." (17:13)

The true greatness of man lies in his capacity for eternal progress, otherwise in this temporal sphere he is the weakest of all things, being subject to hunger, thirst, heat, cold and sorrow. The things in which he takes most delight are often the most injurious to him, and the things which benefit him are not to be obtained without toil and trouble. As to his intellect, a slight disarrangement of matter in his brain is sufficient to destroy or madden him; as to his power, the sting of a wasp is sufficient to rob him of ease and sleep; as to his temper, he is upset by the loss of a shilling. In truth, man in this world is extremely weak and contemptible; it is only in the next world that he will be valued, if by means of the Islamic alchemy of happiness he has risen from the ranks of animals to that of angels.

Otherwise his condition will be worse than that of the brutes, which perish and turn to dust. It is necessary for him, at the same time, that he be conscious of his superiority as the climax of created things, and he must learn to know also his helplessness, as that too is one of the keys to the knowledge of God.

2. The Knowledge Of God

He who knows himself knows God, that is by contemplation of his own being and attributes, man arrives at some knowledge of God. But since many who contemplate themselves do not find God, it follows that there must be some special way of doing so. When a man considers himself, he knows that there was a time when he was non-existent, as it is stated in the Quran:

"Does it not occur to man that he was not a thing that could be spoken of ?" (76:1).

Furthermore, he knows that he was made out of a drop of water in which there was neither intellect nor hearing, sight, head, hands, feet, etc. It is obvious that whatever degree of perfection he might have arrived at, he did not make himself, nor could he ever make a single hair. How helpless, then, was his condition when he was a mere drop of water!

Reflection of God's Attributes

Thus, he finds reflected in miniature in his own being so to speak, the power, wisdom, and love of the Creator. If all the scientists of the world were assembled, and their lives prolonged for an indefinite time, they could not effect any improvement in the construction of a single part of the body.

For instance, in the adaptation of the front and side teeth to the mastication of food, and in the construction of the tongue, salivary glands, and throat for swallowing, we never find a single factor which can be improved upon. Similarly, whoever considers his hand, with its five fingers of unequal lengths, four of them with three joints and the thumb with only two, and the way in which it can be used for grasping, or for carrying, or for smiting, will frankly acknowledge that no amount of human wisdom could better it by altering the number and arrangement of the fingers, or in any other way.

When a man further considers how his various wants of food, lodging etc., are amply supplied from the storehouse of creation, he becomes aware that God's mercy is as great as His Power and Wisdom, according to the Prophet's saying:

"God is more tender to His servants than a mother
to her suckling child."

Thus, from his own creation, man comes to know of God's existence; from the wonders of his bodily frame, God's power and wisdom, and from the ample provision made for his various needs, God's love.

In this way, the knowledge of oneself becomes a key to the knowledge of God.

Not only are man's attributes a reflection of God's attributes, but the mode of existence of man's soul affords some insight into God's mode of existence. Both God and the soul are invisible, indivisible, unconfined by space and time, and outside the categories of quantity and quality. Nor can the ideas of shape, colour, or size attach to them. People find it hard to form a conception of such realities as are devoid of quality and quantity, etc. but a similar difficulty attaches to the conception of our everyday feelings, such as anger, pain, pleasure or love. They are thought-concepts, and cannot be recognized by the senses, whereas quality, quantity, etc., are sense-concepts. Just as the ear cannot take cognizance of colour, nor the eye of sound, so in conceiving of the ultimate realities, God and the soul, we find ourselves in a region in which sense-concepts can bear no part. However, we can see that, just as God is the Ruler of the universe, and, being Himself beyond space and time, quantity and quality, He governs things that are so conditioned, so also does the soul, being itself invisible, indivisible, and unlocated in any special part, rule the body and its members. From all this we see how true is the saying of the Prophet:

"God created man in His own likeness."

Man-A King in Miniature

As we arrive at some knowledge of God's essence and attributes from the contemplation of the soul's essence and attributes, so we come to understand God's method of working and government and delegation of power to angelic forces, etc., by observing how each of us governs his own kingdom. To take a simple instance: Suppose a man wishes to write the name of God. First of all the wish is conceived in his heart, it is then conveyed to the brain by the vital spirits, the form of the word "God" takes shape in the thought-chambers of the brain, then it travels by the nerve-channels, and sets in motion the fingers, which in turn set in action the pen, and thus the name of "God" is traced on paper exactly as it had been conceived in the writer's brain. Similarly, when God wills a thing, it appears on the spiritual plane, which is called in the Quran Al-'Arsh or the Throne. From the throne it passes by a spiritual current to a lower current called Al-Kursi or the Chair, then the shape of it appears on "Al-Lawh Al-Mahfuz' or the Reserved Tablet whence by the mediation of the forces called "angels," it assumes actuality and appears on the earth in the form of plants, trees, and animals, representing the will and command of God, just as the written letters represent the wish and thought conceived in the heart, and the shape present in the brain of the writer.

God has made each of us a king in miniature, so to speak, over a kingdom which is an infinitely reduced copy of His own. In the kingdom of man, God's throne is represented by the soul, the "archangel" by the heart, the "chair" by the brain, and the "tablet" by the treasure-chamber of thought. The soul, itself unlocated and indivisible, governs the body, as God governs the universe. In short, each of us is entrusted with a little kingdom, and charged not to be careless in its administration. It is a wonderful trust charged to the care of man. To this the Holy Quran alludes by saying:-

> "We have offered the Trust to the heavens and the earth and the mountains, but they were afraid to become unfaithful to it and feared it, and man accepted it, but he was unfaithful to it. Surely he was unjust and ignorant." (33:72).

As regards the recognition of God's providence, there are several degrees of knowledge. The mere physicist is like an ant—who, crawling on a sheet of paper, and observing black letters being written by a pen, would attribute the cause to the pen alone. The astronomer is like an ant of somewhat wider vision who would catch sight of the fingers moving the pen, *i.e.* he knows that the elements are under the control of the stars, but he does not know that the stars are under the control of angels. Thus owing to the different degrees of perception in men, disputes must arise in tracing effects to causes. Those whose eyes never see beyond the world of phenomena are like those who mistake servants for the master. The laws of phenomena must be constant, or there could be no such thing as science. But it is a great error to mistake the servants for the master.

A Lustrous Pearl

As long as this difference in the perceptive faculty of observers exists, disputes must necessarily continue. It is like the blind men, hearing that an elephant has come to their town, who go and examine it. The only knowledge of it which they can obtain comes through the sense of touch, so one handles the animal's leg, another his tusk, another his ear, and according to their individual perceptions, declare it to be a column, a thick pole, or a quilt, each taking a part for the whole. Similarly, the physicist and astronomer confound the laws they perceive with the lawgiver. A similar mistake is attributed to Prophet Abraham in the Quran, where he turned successively to the stars, the moon and the sun as the objects of his worship. Grown aware of Him who made all these, he exclaimed:

"I love not those that set." (6-76)

We have a common instance of this attribution to second causes which ought to be attributed to the First Cause in the case of so-called illness. For instance, if a man ceases to take any interest in worldly matters, conceives a distaste for common pleasure and appears sunk in depression, the doctor will say: "This is a case of melancholy and requires such and such a prescription." The physicist will say: "This is a dryness of the brain caused by hot weather and cannot be relieved till the air becomes moist." The astrologer will attribute it to some particular conjunction or opposition of planets. *"Thus far their knowledge reaches"*, says the Quran. It does not occur to them that what has really happened is that the Almighty God has a concern for the welfare of that man, and has, therefore, commanded His servants, the planets or the elements to produce such a condition in him that he may turn away from the world to his Maker. The knowledge of this fact, declares the Muslim saint, is a lustrous pearl from the ocean of inspirational knowledge, to which all other forms of knowledge are like islands in the sea.

The doctor, physicist, and astrologer are no doubt right, each in his particular branch of knowledge, but they do not see that sickness is, so to speak, a cord of love by which God draws to Himself the Saints.

Similarly, common folk are right when they exclaim, as they often do, that "God is Great." Most of them, however, understand this exclamation to mean that God is greater than creation. But when we consider that creation is God's manifestation just as light makes manifest the sun, we will see that it is not correct to say that the sun is greater than its own light. So the exclamation "God is Great" rather means that God's Greatness immeasurably transcends our cognitive faculties, and that we can only form a very dim and imperfect idea of it. If a child asks us to explain to him the pleasure which exists in wielding sovereignty, we may say it is like the pleasure he feels in playing bat and ball, though in reality the two have nothing in common except that they both come under the category of pleasure. Moreover, such imperfect knowledge of God as we can attain is not a mere speculative knowledge, but must be accompanied by devotion and worship.

The Seed of Happiness

When a men dies, he has to do with God alone, and if we have to live with a person, our happiness entirely depends upon the degree of affection we feel towards him. Love is the seed of happiness, and love of God is fostered and developed by worship. Such worship and constant remembrance of God imply a certain degree of austerity and curbing of bodily appetites. Not that a man is intended to eradicate these entirely, for then the human race would perish altogether. But strict limits must be set to indulgence in them, and as man is not the best judge in his own case as to what these limits should be, he had better consult some spiritual guide on the subject. Such spiritual guides are the Prophets, and the laws laid down by them under divine inspiration, which prescribe the limits to be strictly observed in these matters. As the Quran puts it:

> "Whoever goes beyond the limits of Allah, indeed
> does injustice to himself." (56:1)

And again we read in the Quran:

> "Those are God's limits and he who does not
> exceed them but obeys God and His Apostle, God
> will cause him to enter Paradise to abide in it."
> (4:13)

Notwithstanding this clear pronouncement of the Quran, there are those who, through their ignorance of God, do transgress these limits, and this ignorance may be due to several different causes. First, there are some persons who, failing to find God by observation, conclude that there is no God, and that this world of wonders has made itself, or has existed from time immemorial. They are like a man who, seeing a beautifully written letter, supposes that it has written itself without a writer, and has always existed.

Some, through ignorance of the real nature of the soul, repudiate the doctrine of a future life, in which man will be called to account and will be rewarded or punished according to his good or bad deeds. They regard themselves as no better than animals or vegetables, and equally perishable. Some, on the other hand, believe in God and a future life, but with a weak belief. They say to themselves that "God is great and independent of us. Our worship or abstinence from worship is a matter of indifference to Him." Their state of mind is like that of a sick man who, having been prescribed a certain treatment by his doctor, says: "Well if I follow it or do not follow it, what does it matter to the doctor." It certainly does not matter to the doctor, but the patient may destroy himself by his disobedience. Just as surely as an unchecked sickness of the body ends in bodily death, so do uncured diseases of the soul end in future misery, according to the Divine message in the Quran:

> Only those shall be saved who come to God with
> a sound heart" (not with a heart contaminated
> with sin).

A fourth kind of unbelievers are those who say: "The law commands us to abstain from anger, lust and bodily passions. This is quite impossible, for man is created with these qualities inherent in him." These people ignore the fact that the law does not require us to uproot these passions altogether but to restrain them within due limits, so that by avoiding the greater sins we may obtain God's forgiveness for the smaller ones. Even the Holy Prophet said in one instance; *"I am a man like you, and I get angry sometimes, but I am apt to subdue my anger."* In the Quran we find that God tells us:

> "He loves those who restrain their anger." (not
> those who have no anger at all) (3:134).

Another kind of people lay stress on the beneficence of God, while they ignore His justice. They say to themselves: "Well, whatever misdeed we commit, God will pardon us because He is Merciful." They do not consider that though God is Merciful, thousands of human beings perish miserably in hunger and disease. They know that whosoever wishes for a livelihood, or learning, would never get it by merely saying: "God is merciful," He must exert himself as well.

Although the Quran states:-

> "Every living creature's sustenance comes from God." (11:6)

> 'Man obtains nothing except by striving." (53:39)

Indeed, it is the devil that spreads his teachings among those people, and really they speak with their lips, and not with their hearts.

It is to be hoped that it has now been made clear how, by contemplation of his own being and attributes, man arrives at some knowledge of God. He who does not master his appetites does not deserve the name of a man, and a true believer in God is he who cheerfully acknowledges the obligations imposed upon him by the law. But he who endeavours on whatever pretext to ignore these obligations, or fails to put them into practice, must not expect to acquire any true knowledge of God.

3. The Knowledge Of This World

This world is a stage or market-place passed through by pilgrims on their way to the next. It is here that they are to supply themselves with provision for the way, or, to put it plainly, it is here that man acquires by the use of his bodily senses some knowledge of the works of God, and, through them, of God Himself, the sight of Whom will determine his future attitude. It is for the acquisition of this knowledge that the spirit of man has descended into this world of water and clay. As long as his senses remain with him, he is said to be "in this world;" when they depart, and when only his essential attributes remain, he is said to have gone to "the next world."

The Soul of the Body

While man is in this world, two things are necessary for him: First, the protection and nurture of his soul; secondly, care and nurture of his body. The proper nourishment of the soul is the knowledge and love of God, and to be absorbed in the love of anything but God is the ruin of the soul. The body, so to speak, is simply the riding-animal of the soul and perishes while the soul endures. The soul should take care of the body, just as a pilgrim on his way to Makkah takes care of his camel; but if the pilgrim spends his whole time in feeding and adorning his camel, the caravan will leave him behind, and he will miss the performance of the pilgrimage. Man's bodily needs are simple, being comprised under three headings, namely food, clothing and a dwelling place; but the bodily desires which are implanted in him with a view to procuring them are apt to rebel against reason, which is of later growth than they. Accordingly, as we have seen in the foregoing, they require to be curbed and restrained by the divine laws promulgated by God's Messengers.

Considering the world with which we have for a time to do, we find it essentially divided into three departments: animal, vegetable and mineral. The products of all three are continually needed by man and have given rise to some principal occupations: those of the cultivators, the weaver, the builder and the worker in metals. These, again, have many subordinate branches, such as tailors, masons, smiths, carpenters, glaziers, etc. None can be quite independent of the others; this gives rise to various business connections and relations, and these all too frequently afford occasions for hatred, envy, jealousy and other maladies of the soul. All these negative tendencies result in quarrels and strife, and then finally there is the need for political and civil government and a knowledge of the law.

The Three Necessities

Thus the occupations and business of the world have become more and more complicated and troublesome, chiefly owing to the fact that men have forgotten that their real necessities are only three:

clothing, food and shelter, and that those exist only with the object of making the body a fit vehicle for the soul in its journey to the next world. They have fallen into the same mistake as the pilgrim to Makkah mentioned above, who, forgetting the object of his pilgrimage and himself, spends his whole time in feeding and adorning his camel. Unless a man maintains the strictest watch, he is certain to be fascinated and entangled by the world.

The deceitful character of the world comes out in the following ways: In the first place, it pretends that it will always remain with you, while, as a matter of fact, it is slipping away from you, moment by moment, and bidding you farewell, like a shadow which seems stationary, but is actually always moving. Again the world presents itself under the guise of a radiant but immoral sorceress; it pretends to be in love with you; it fondles you and then goes off to your enemies, leaving you to die of chagrin and despair.

Those who have indulged themselves without limit in the pleasure of the world, will, at the time of death, be like a man who has gorged himself to repletion on delicious viands and then vomits them up. The deliciousness is gone, but the disgrace remains. The greater the abundance of the possessions which they have enjoyed in the shape of gardens, castles, male and female servants, gold, silver, etc., the more keenly will they feel the bitterness of parting from them. This is a bitterness which will outlast death, for the soul which has contracted covetousness as a *fixed habit* will necessarily in the next world suffer from the pangs of unsatisfied desire.

Another dangerous property of worldly things is that they at first appear as mere trifles, but each of those so-called "trifles" branches out into countless ramifications until they swallow up the whole of a man's time and energy.

It is reported that Jesus Christ (upon whom be peace) said, *"The Lover of the world is like a man drinking sea-water, the more he drinks, the more thirsty he gets, till at last he perishes with thirst unquenched."* Prophet Muhammad (upon whom be peace) said, *"You can no more mix with the lust of the world without being contaminated by it than you can go into water without getting wet."*

Likeness of the World

The world is like a table spread for successive relays of guests who come and go. There are various dishes, abundance of food and perfumes. The wise guest eats as much as is sufficient for him, smells the perfumes, thanks his host and departs. The foolish guest, on the other hand, tries to carry off some of the gold and silver dishes, only to find them wrenched out of his hands and himself thrust forth, disappointed and disgraced.

We may close these illustrations of the deceitfulness of the world with the following short parable: Suppose a ship is to arrive at a certain well-wooded island. The captain of the ship tells the passengers that he will stop a few hours there, and that they can go on shore for a short time, but warns them not to remain there too long. Accordingly, the passengers disembark and stroll in different directions. The wisest, however, return after a short time, and finding the ship empty, choose the most comfortable place in it. A second band of passengers spend a somewhat longer time on the island, admiring the foliage of the trees and listening to the songs of the birds. Coming back on board, they find the best places in the ship already occupied, and have therefore to content themselves with the less comfortable ones. A third party wander still farther, and finding some brilliantly coloured stones, carry them back to the ship. Their lateness in coming on board compels them to stow themselves away in the lower parts of the ship, where they find their loads of stones, which by this time have lost all their brilliance and are very much in their way. The last group go so far in their wanderings that they get quite out of reach of the captain's voice calling them to come on board, so at last he has to sail away without them. They wander about in a hopeless condition and finally either perish with hunger or fall a prey to wild beasts.

The first group represents the faithful who keep aloof from the fascination of the world altogether, and the last group the infidels who care only for this world and nothing for the next. The two intermediate classes are those who preserve their faith, but entangle themselves more or less with the vanities of things present.

Although we have said so much against the world, it must be remembered that there are certain things in the world which are not really of it, such as knowledge and good deeds. A man carries what knowledge he possesses with him into the next world, and, though his good deeds have passed, the effect of them remains in his character. This is especially true of acts of devotion, which result in the perpetual remembrance and love of God. These are among "those good things" which, the Quran contrasts with the transitory:

> "What is with you passes away and what is with God is enduring; and We will most surely give to those who were patient and will reward them according to the best of what they earned." (16:96).

There are other good things in the world, such as marriage, food, clothing, etc., which a wise man uses only in proportion as they help him to attain in safety to the next world. Other things which engross the mind, causing it to cleave to this world and to be careless of the next, are purely evil and were alluded to by the Holy Prophet Muhammad when he said: "The *world is but a vanity fair and all occupations in it are mere vanity except when they do not hinder a man from remembering God and worshipping Him, and doing good deeds.*"

4. The Knowledge Of The Next World

All believers in the scriptures of God are sufficiently informed as to the joys of heaven and the pains of hell which will follow this life. But according to the Saints there is also a spiritual heaven and hell. They believe that in the heart of the righteous or the enlightened man there is a window opening on the realities of the spiritual world through which he may come to know, not by hearsay or traditional belief, but by actual experience, what produces wretchedness or happiness in the soul, just as clearly and decidedly as the physician knows what produces sickness or health in the body.

The effect of death on the composite nature of man is

illustrated by the Muslim saints as follows: Man has two souls, an animal soul and a spiritual soul, the latter being more or less of an angelic nature. The seat of the animal soul is the heart, from which this soul issues like a subtle vapour and pervades all the members of the body, giving the power of sight to the eye, the power of hearing to the ear, and every member the faculty of performing its own appropriate functions. It may be compared to a lamp, carried about within a cottage, the light of which falls upon the walls wherever it goes. The heart is the wick of this lamp, and when the supply of oil is cut off for any reason, the lamp is sure to die. Such is the death of the animal soul. With the spiritual or human soul, the case is different. It is indivisible and by it man knows God. As it were, it is the rider of the animal soul, and when that perishes it still remains but like a horseman who has dismounted, or like a hunter who has lost his weapons. That steed and those weapons were granted to the human soul so that by means of them it might pursue and capture the Phoenix of love and knowledge of God. If it has effected that capture, it is not a grief but rather a relief to be able to lay those weapons aside, and to dismount from that weary steed. Therefore, all saints consider death as a welcome gift of God to His lovers. But as for that soul which loses its steed and hunting-weapons before it has captured the prize its misery and regret will be indescribable.

Further consideration will show how clearly distinct the human soul is from the body and its members. Limb after limb may be paralysed and cease working, but the individuality of the soul is unimpaired. Again, the body which we have now is no longer the body which we had when young, but entirely different, yet our personality now is identical with our personality then. It is, therefore, easy to conceive of it as persisting when the body is done with altogether along with its essential attributes which were independent of the body, such as the knowledge and love of God. But if, instead of carrying away with us knowledge and love, we depart in ignorance of God, this ignorance is also an essential and will abide as darkness of the soul and the seed of misery. Therefore, the Quran teaches the godly Muslims that "He who is blind in this life will be blind in the next life and will be still more astray from the path of happiness. (17:72)

The reason for the human spirit seeking to return to the upper world is that its origin was from thence, that it is of celestial origin. It was sent down into this lower sphere against its will to experience devotion of God and acquire divine love through worshipping Him; and to do good deeds and avoid evil ones before departing to receive its reward with the righteous. This is clearly taught by the Quranic verse which may be rendered as follows:

> "Go down (Adam and Eve) from hence, all of you (your posterity); and when comes to you true guidance, whoever followers need not fear, nor shall they be grieved." (2:38).

The mystic conception is that just as the health of the animal soul consists in the equilibrium of its component parts, and this equilibrium is restored, when impaired, by appropriate medicine, so the health of the human soul consists in a moral equilibrium which is maintained and repaired when necessary, by ethical instructions and moral precepts.

As already pointed out, the human soul is essentially independent of the body. It has been supposed by some, however, that the human soul is annihilated after death and then restored, but this is contrary both to reason and to the word of God as revealed in the Holy Book. The former shows us that death does not destroy the essential individuality of men, and the Quran teaches us that "those who are killed while defending the religion of God are not dead, but still alive, rejoicing in the presence of their Lord and in the grace bestowed on them." Not a word is said in the law about any of the dead, good or bad, being annihilated. Nay, the Prophet is said to have questioned the spirits of those who were killed among the infidels in battle against the early Muslims, as to whether they had found the punishments with which God had threatened them, real or not. When the followers of the Holy Prophet asked him what was the good of his

237

questioning them who were dead, he replied, *"They hear my words better than you do."*

Some Sufis have had the unseen world of heaven and hell revealed to them when in a state of death-like trance. On their recovering consciousness, their faces betrayed the nature of the revelations they had by marks of joy or terror. But no visions are necessary to prove what will occur to every thinking man, i.e. that when death has stripped him of his bodily senses and has left him nothing but his bare personality, if while on earth he has too closely attached himself to lust and vanities, he must necessarily suffer when bereft of such things. Whereas, on the contrary, if he has as far as possible turned his back on all earthly allurements and concentrated his supreme affection upon God, and acted in accordance with His ordinance, he will welcome death as a means of escape from worldly entanglements, so that he may be united with Him whom he loved and obeyed. In this connection the Holy Prophet has taught us that *"death is a bridge which unites friend to friend. And the world is a paradise to the infidel, but a prison to the faithful."*

On the other hand, the pains which souls suffer after death have their source in excessive love of the world. The Messengers of God warned that sinners, after death, will be tormented by so many snakes; some simple-minded men have examined the graves of the sinners and wondered at failing to see these snakes. They do not understand that the tormenting snakes have their abode within the unbeliever's spirit, and that they existed in him even before he died, for they were but his own evil qualities symbolized, such as jealousy, hatred, hypocrisy, pride, deceit, etc., every one of which springs, directly or indirectly, from excessive love of the world.

Every sinner thus carries with him into the world beyond death the instruments of his own punishment, and in the Quran it is stated that *"Hell surely surrounds the infidels."*

Some may object and say, "If such is the case, then who can escape hell, and who is not more or less bound to the world by various ties of affection and interest?" To this we answer that the verse simply refers to the state of the infidels who have no faith in God and who disregarded His injunctions, giving themselves up entirely to the fascination of the world. As to the faithful and doers of good, the Quran says to the Prophet:

> "Give good tidings to the faithful who do what is
> right that they shall inherit gardens beneath which
> rivers flow." (2:25)

Many people profess to love God, but a man can easily test himself by watching which way the balance of his affection inclines when the commands of God come into collision with some of his ambitions and desires. Any profession of love for God which is not confirmed by obedience to Him is simply false.

Kinds of Spiritual Hell

We have seen above that one kind of spiritual hell is the forcible separation by death from worldly things to which the heart cleaved too fondly. Another kind is that of shame, when a man wakes up to see the nature of the bad actions he committed in their naked reality.

A third spiritual hell is that of disappointment and failure to reach the real objects of existence. Man was intended to mirror forth the light of the knowledge of God, but if he arrives in the next world with his soul thickly coated with the rust of sensual indulgence he will entirely fail to acquire the object for which he was created. His disappointment may be illustrated the by an allegory:

Suppose a man is passing with some friends through a dark wood. Here and there, glimmering on the ground, lie various coloured stones. His friends collect and carry these and advise him to do the same, "for," say they, "we have heard that these stones will fetch a high price in the place where we are going." He, on the other hand, laughs at them and calls them fools for loading themselves in the vain hope of gain, while he walks free and unencumbered. Presently they emerge into broad daylight and find that these coloured stones are rubles, emeralds and other jewels of priceless value. The man's disappointment and chagrin at not having gathered some when they were so easily within his reach may be more easily imagined than described. Such will be the remorse of those, in the hereafter, who, while passing through this world to the next, have been at no pains to acquire the jewels of virtue and the treasures of good deeds.

Many people, however, having no fixed convictions about the future world, are slaves to their sensual appetites, and deny it altogether. They say that hell is merely an invention of theologians to frighten people, and they regard theologians themselves with thinly veiled contempt. To argue with men who indulge in this kind of thinking is of very little use. This much, however, may be said to such a man with the possible result of making him pause and reflect: Suppose you are about to eat food and someone tells you a serpent has spat venom on it, you would probably refrain from eating it and rather endure the pangs of hunger, though your informant may have spoken in jest or be lying. Or suppose you are ill and a charm-writer says: "Give me a shilling and I will write a charm which you can tie round your neck and which will cure you." You would probably give the shilling on the chance of deriving benefit from the charm. Or if an astrologer tells you, when the moon has entered a certain constellation, drink such and such a medicine, and you will recover, though you may have very little faith in astrology, you would very likely try the experiment on the chance that he might be right. And do you not think that reliance is better placed on the words of all the Prophets, saints and holy men and hundreds of millions of wise men, convinced as they were of a future life, than on the promise of a charm-writer or an astrologer? If people can make perilous voyages in ships merely for the sake of probable profit, will you not suffer a little pain of abstinence now for the sake of eternal joy hereafter?

A certain saint[1] in arguing with an unbeliever said, "If you are right, then neither of us will be any the worse in the future, but if we are right, then we shall escape and you will suffer." This he said not because he himself was in doubt, but merely to make an impression on the unbeliever.

From all that we have said, it follows that man's chief business in this world is to prepare for the next. Even if he is doubtful about a future existence, reason suggests that he should act as if there were one, considering the tremendous issues at stake. Peace be on those who follow the true guidance.

5. The Three Stages of Man's Development

The Holy Quran has dealt fully with three conditions of man, namely the physical, the moral and the spiritual. It observes this division, fixing three respective sources for this threefold condition of man. It mentions three springs termed *"An-Nafsil-ammara,"* which signifies the uncontrollable soul or the soul prone to lust and evil. Thus the Quran says: *"The soul is prone to evil."* (12:53) i.e. it is the characteristic of the (primitive) soul that it inclines man to evil doings or tends to lead him along iniquitous and immoral paths. In short, man's primitive nature is prone to transgression at a certain age in his development, and so long as he is devoid of high moral qualities, the evil nature is predominant in him. He is subject to this state so long as he does not walk in the light of true wisdom and knowledge, but acts in obedience to his natural inclination, like the lower animals.

As soon, however, as he frees himself from the control of animal passions and is guided by wisdom and knowledge, he holds the reins of his natural desires and governs them instead of being governed by them; when a transformation is worked in his soul from grossness to virtue, he then passes from the physical stage and becomes a moral being in the strict sense of the word. The source of the moral conditions of man is called *"An Nafsil-Lawwama"* or the self-accusing soul (conscience), in the terminology of the Quran. In the Quranic Chapter entitled "Al-Qiyama" or "the Resurrection," we read:

> "And I swear by the soul that blames itself" (on every dereliction of duty, being conscious of having offended) (75:2).

This is the spring from which flows a highly moral life and, on reaching this stage, man is freed from bestiality. The swearing by the self-accusing soul indicates the regard in which it is held.

For the change from the disobedient to the self-accusing soul, being a sure sign of its improvement and purification, makes it deserving of approbation in the sight of God. "*An-Nafsil-lawwama*" or the self-accusing soul is so called because it upbraids a man for the doing of an evil deed and expresses intense hatred of unbridled passions and bestial appetites. Its tendency, on the other hand, is to generate noble qualities and a virtuous disposition, to transform life so as to bring the whole course and conduct of it to moderation and to restrain the carnal passions and sensual desires so as to keep them within due bounds. Although the self-accusing soul upbraids itself for its faults and frailties, it is not the master of its passions, nor is it powerful enough to practice virtue exclusively. The weakness of the flesh has the upper hand sometimes and then it stumbles and falls down. Its weakness then resembles that of a child who does not like to fall, but whose infirm legs are sometimes unable to support him. But it does not persist in its fault, every failure bringing only fresh reproach the mind. In short, at this stage the soul is anxious to attain to moral excellence and revolts against disobedience which is the characteristic of the first or the animal stage, but does, notwithstanding its yearning for virtue, sometimes deviate from the straight path, the path of God.

The third or the last stage in the outward movement of the soul is reached on attaining to the source of all spiritual qualities. The soul at this stage is in the word of the Holy Quran: "*An-Nafsil-Mutma'inna*" or the soul at rest.

> "O you soul who are at rest! Return to Your Lord,
> joyful and pleasing in His sight. So enter among
> my beloved servants; and enter into My paradise."
> (89:9-10).

At this stage, the soul is freed from all weaknesses and frailties and is braced with spiritual power. The guidance of the soul at rest with its Lord is in the Quran's teaching:

> "He who purifies his soul (of the carnal passions)
> is entitled to success, while he who indulges in a
> degrading passion is entitled to failure." (91:9-10)

In short, these three stages of the soul may be called the physical, the moral and the spiritual. Of these, it is the physical state in which man's passions run wild, dealing a death-blow to the moral and spiritual states of man, and hence this state has been described in the words of God as that attended with failure.

Teachings of the Quran on the Physical State of Man

According to the Muslim Scriptures, the physical condition of man is closely connected with his moral and spiritual qualities. If, therefore, his natural desires are subjected to the directions of the law, they take the form of moral qualities and deeply affect the spiritual state of the soul. It is for this reason that in all forms of devotion and prayer and in all the injunctions relating to internal purity and moral rectitude, the greatest stress has been laid upon external purity and cleanliness and on the proper attitudes of the body. The relation between the physical and spiritual natures of man would become evident on a careful consideration of the actions of the outward organs and the effect they produce upon the internal nature of man. Weeping, even if articifial, at once saddens the heart, while an artificial laugh makes it cheerful. Likewise a prostration of the body, as is done in Muslim prayer, causes the soul to humble itself and adore the Creator; whereas strutting produces vanity and vainglory. These examples sufficiently illustrate the effect of bodily postures, as enjoined upon Muslims when fulfilling their fixed daily prayers upon the spiritual state of man. On the other hand, there is not the least doubt that food plays an important part in the formation of character. It is with this great law in view that the Holy Quran says:

> "Eat (meat or other food) and drink, but do not
> give way to excess" (in any particular form of diet
> so that your character and health may not suffer
> from it) (7:31).

The physical side of man's life being of such great importance even to the soul, the true word of God cannot be silent on this point. The Holy Quran has, therefore, applied itself sedulously to the reformation of the physical state of man's life. It gives us the most valuable and precise directions on all matters of importance with which man is concerned. All his movements, the manner of the satisfaction of all his requirements, his family, social and general connections, health and sickness, are all regulated by rules, and it is shown how external order and purity have their effect upon the spiritual state of man.

A close study of the Quranic injunctions and directions relating to the reformation of the external life of man and his gradual advancement from savageness to civilization until he reaches the highest pinnacle of a spiritual life, reveals following all-wise method. In the first place, Almighty God has been pleased to lead him out of darkness and raise him up from the savage state by teaching him the rules relating to his ordinary daily actions and modes of social life. Thus, it begins at the lowest point of man's development and, first of all drawing a line of distinction between man and the lower animals, teaches him the rules of morality, which may go by the name of sociality. Next, it undertakes to improve upon the low degree of morality, already acquired, by bringing the habits of man to moderation, thus turning them into sublime morals.

We pass now to the third stage of advancement when man forgets himself in the love of God and in doing His will, and when his whole life is only for the sake of his Master. It is to this stage that the name Islam alludes, for it signifies total resignation to the commands and service of God and total forgetfulness of selfishness. Thus says the Holy Quran:

> "Nay! whoever submits himself entirely to God and is the doer of good, will get his reward with his Lord, for such there is no fear, nor shall they grieve." (2:112).

> "Say: 'My prayers and my devoutness and my life and my death, all are devoted to Allah, the Lord of the Universe who has no partner. Thus I am

commanded and I am the .....first to submit to His commandment.'" (6:162)

"This is my way, leading straight: Follow it and do not follow other ways, lest they should scatter you about from straight Path." (6:63).

"Say (to them): 'If you love Allah, come and follow me; then God will love you and forgive you your former sins, and He is surely Forgiving and Merciful.'" (3:31)

Now we shall deal with the three states of life one after another. As already stated, there are three sources which give rise to the threefold nature of man, viz. the disobedient soul, the self-accusing soul and the soul at rest or the contented soul.

Our Holy Prophet Muhammad was raised at a time when the whole world had sunk to the lowest depths of degradation. The threefold reformation of man was, therefore, destined to be brought about at this period by means of the Holy Quran. It is for this reason that the Holy Book claims to be perfect guidance to mankind, as to it alone was given the opportunity to work a reformation complete on all sides. The Quran was, therefore, sent to bring life to the dead as it says:-

"Both land and water have become corrupt." (30:41)

"Know it for certain that God restores life to the earth which had been dead."(57:17)

Utter darkness and barbarism at that time prevailed over the whole of Arabia. No social laws were observed; and the most despicable deeds were openly committed. An unlimited number of wives was taken, and all prohibited attitudes were made lawful. Raping and incest raged supreme and not infrequently mothers were taken for wives.

Now the Quran had a grand aim before it. It had to reclaim mankind from savagery and to make human beings men: then to teach them simple morals and make them good men, and last of all, to take them to the highest pinnacles of advancement and make them godly. The Holy Book gives excellent instructions on these three aspects. It does not inculcate doctrines which are against the reason of man, and which, therefore, one has to follow against one's better judgment.

The whole drift of the Holy Book and the substance of its teachings are the threefold reformation of man and all other directions are simply means to that end. All its moral teachings, precepts and doctrines have an all-pervading purpose beneath them which consists in transforming men by raising them from the physical state imbued with a tinge of savageness to the moral state, and from the moral to the boundless deep of the spiritual state.

To attain the desired end of the highest spiritual advancement, the Holy Quran has taught us two means, *viz.* complete submission to the will of God, which is known by the name of Islam, by leading a life guided and fostered by the injunctions and ordinances of God and the Traditions of the Holy Prophet; and striving our best to recollect and love our Creator and Sustainer, Almighty God. In the meantime, we must engage in constant self-examination in order to find out if we are treading on the right path or not.

6. Self-Examination the Recollection and Love of God

The saints have always conceived that men have come into this world to carry on a spiritual traffic, the resulting gain or loss of which is heaven or hell. They have always kept a jealous eye upon the flesh which, like a treacherous partner in business, may cause them great loss. He is, therefore, really a wise man who, after his morning prayers, spends a whole hour in making a spiritual reckoning, and says to himself, "O my soul, you have only one life, no single moment that has passed can be recovered, for in the counsel of God the number of breaths allotted to you is fixed, and cannot be increased. When life is over, no further spiritual traffic is possible for you, therefore what you do, do now, just treat this day as if the life had been already spent, and this were an extra day granted to you by the special favour of the Almighty. What can be greater folly than to lose it?"

It was a saying of Khalifa 'Omar, "Call yourselves to account before you be called to account."

The saints relate that on the day of resurrection a man will find all the hours of his life arranged like a long series of treasure chests. The door of one will be opened, and it will be seen to be full of light. It represents an hour which he spent in doing good. The door of a second will be opened; it is pitch dark within. It represents an hour which he spent in doing evil. The door of a third treasure-chest will be opened, it will be seen to be empty and neither light nor dark within; this represents the hour in which he did neither good nor evil. Then he will feel remorse and confusion like that of a man who has been the possessor of a great treasure and wasted it, or let it slip from his grasp. Thus the whole series of the hours of his life will be displayed, one by one, to his gaze. Therefore, a man should say to his soul every morning: "God has given you twenty-four treasures. Take heed lest you should lose any one of them, for you will not be able to endure the regret that will follow such a loss."

Muslim saints have said, "Even suppose that God should forgive you after a wasted life, you will not attain to the ranks of the righteous and must deplore your loss." Thus, keep a strict watch over your tongue, your eyes, and each of your various organs for each of these is, as it were, a possible gate to misery in the hereafter. Say to the flesh, "If you are rebellious, I will indeed punish you." For, though the flesh is headstrong, it is capable or receiving instruction, and can be tamed by austerity.

Such, then, is the aim of self-examination, and the Arabian Prophet has taught: *"Happy is he who does now that which will benefit his human soul after death."*

The Recollection of God

We come now to the recollection of God. This consists in a man's remembering that God observes all his acts and thoughts. People only see the outward, while God sees both the outer and the inner man. He who really believes this will have both his outer and inner being well disciplined. If he disbelieves it, he is an infidel, and if while believing it, he acts contrary to that belief, he is guilty of the grossest presumption.

A certain Muslim guide had a disciple whom he favoured above his other disciples, thus incurring their envy. One day the guide gave each of them a fowl and told him to go and kill it in a place where no one could see him. Accordingly, each killed his fowl in some retired spot and brought it back, with the exception of the guide's favourite disciple, who brought his fowl back alive, saying, "I have found no place, for God sees everywhere." The guide said to the others, "You see now this youth's rank, He has attained to the constant remembrance of God."

In Muslim spiritual literature, we read the following story told by 'Abdullah Ibn Dinar, one of the most intelligent disciples of the Arabian Prophet. He said, "Once I was walking with Khalifa 'Omar near Makkah when we met a shepherd's slave-boy driving his flock. 'Omar said to him, 'Sell me a sheep.' The boy answered. 'They are not mine, but my master's.' Then to try him, 'Omar said, 'Well, you can tell him that a wolf carried one off, and he will know nothing about it.' 'No, he won't, said the boy, 'but God will.' Omar was so pleased with the boy's remark that he sent for the boy's master, purchased him and set him free, exclaiming, 'For so saying you are free in this world and shall be saved in the next."

Therefore, he is a wise man who keeps a constant watch not only over his own actions but also over his own thoughts which are likely to end in action. Rightly to discriminate among such thoughts is rather a difficult and delicate matter, and requires a special training, and he who is not capable of it should attach himself to some spiritual guide, intercourse with whom may illuminate his heart.

The Holy Prophet Muhammad said: "*God loves that man who is keen to discern in doubtful things, and who does not allow his reason to be swayed by the assaults of passion.*" Reason and discrimination are closely connected, and he in whom reason does not rule passion will not be keen to discriminate.

Besides such cautious discrimination before acting, a man

should call himself strictly to account for his past actions. Every evening he should examine his heart as to what he has done to see whether he has gained or lost in his spiritual capital. This is more necessary as the heart is sometimes like a treacherous business partner, always ready to cajole and deceive, sometimes presenting its own selfishness under the guise of obedience to God, so that a man supposes he has gained, whereas he has really lost.

The Love of God

The love of God is the highest of all topics, and is the final aim which this work has striven to achieve. Human perfection consists in the love of God conquering a man's heart and possessing it wholly, and even if it does not possess it wholly, it should predominate in the heart over the love of all other things. Nevertheless, rightly to understand the love of God is so difficult a matter that one sect of philosophers have altogether denied that man can love a being who is not of his own species, and they have defined the love of God as consisting merely in obedience to Him. But this is not true. All Muslims are agreed that the love of God is a duty. In Muslim literature, it is related that when the angel of death came to take the soul of Prophet Abraham, the latter said, "Have you ever seen a friend unwilling to see his friend?" Then Abraham said to the angel, "Come and be quick to take my soul." The following prayer was taught by the Arabian Prophet to his followers: "O God, grant that I may love You and love those who love You, and whatsoever brings me nearer to Your love, and make Your love dearer to me than cold water to the thirsty traveller in the desert." A Muslim saint guide used to say, "He who knows God naturally loves Him and he who knows the deceitful world certainly hates it."

We come now to treat love of its essential nature, according to the spiritual Muslim conception. Love may be defined as an inclination to that which is pleasant. This is apparent in the case of the five senses, each of which may be said to love that which gives it delight; thus the eye loves beautiful forms, the ear music, etc. This is a kind of love we share with the animals. But there is a sixth sense, or faculty of perception, implanted in the heart, which lower animals do not possess, through which we become aware of spiritual beauty and excellence. Thus a man who is only acquainted with sensuous delights cannot understand what the Holy Prophet meant when he declared that *"he loved prayer more than any pleasant and beautiful thing."* But he whose inner eye is opened to behold the beauty and perfection of God will despise all outward sights in comparison, however fair and excellent they may be.

Man will say that beauty resides in a red and white complexion, well-proportioned limbs, and so forth, but he will be blind to moral quality, such as men refer to when they speak of such and such a man as possessing a beautiful character.

It is for this reason that we love the righteous, saints and the godly, because the love of such men really means the love of God.

The causes of love are several. One of them is that man loves himself and the perfection of his own nature. This leads him directly to the love of God, for man's very existence and man's attributes are nothing other than the gift of God, but for whose grace and kindness man would never have emerged from behind the curtain of non-existence into the visible world. Man's preservation and eventual attainment to perfection are also entirely dependent upon the grace of God. It would be a wonder if one should take refuge from the heat of the sun under the shadow of a tree and not be grateful to the tree, without which there would be no shadow at all. Precisely in the same way, were it not for God, man would have no existence, nor any attributes at all; why then, should he not love God, unless he be ignorant of Him? Doubtless fools cannot love Him, for the love of Him springs directly from the knowledge of Him, and whence should a fool have knowledge?

A second cause of this love is that man loves his benefactor, and in truth his only benefactor is God, for whatever kindness he receives from any fellow creature is due to the immediate instigation of God. Whatever motive may have prompted the kindness he receives from another, God is the Agent who sets that motive to work.

The third cause is the love that is aroused by contemplation

THE TREASURES OF HAPPINESS

of the attributes of God, His power and wisdom, of which human power and wisdom are but the feeblest reflections. This love is akin to the love we feel towards the great and wise men of the past, though we never expect to derive personal benefit from them, and is, therefore, a more disinterested kind of love.

God said to the Prophet David, "that servant is dearest to Me who does not seek Me for fear of punishment or hope of reward, but to pay the debt due to My being the Deity." And in the Psalms it is written, "Who is more selfish than he who worships Me from fear of hell or hope of heaven? If I had created neither, should I not then have deserved to be worshipped?"

The fourth cause of this love is the affinity which exists between God and man as referred to in the saying of the Holy Prophet: *Truly God created man in his likeness.*" This is a somewhat dangerous topic to dwell upon, as it is beyond the conception of common people, and even intelligent men have stumbled in treating it, and have come to believe in incarnation and union with God. Still, the affinity which does exist between man and God disposes of the objection of those philosophers mentioned above, who maintain that man cannot love a being who is not of his own species. However great this distance between them, man can love God because of that affinity indicated in the saying of the Holy Prophet that *"God created man in His own likeness."*

The Vision of God

All believers in God profess to believe that the vision of Him is the summit of human felicity, though with many this is a mere lip-profession which arouses no emotion in their hearts. But with the godly the matter is quite different. To these, the vision of God is really the greatest happiness that a man can attain. Every one of man's faculties has its appropriate function which it delights to fulfil. This holds good of them all, from the lowest bodily appetite to the highest form of intellectual apprehension. But even a comparatively low level of mental exertion affords greater pleasure than the satisfaction of bodily appetites. Thus, if a man happens to be absorbed in a game of chess, he will not come to his meal, though repeatedly summoned. And the higher the subject-matter of our knowledge, the greater is our delight in it; for instance, we would take more pleasure in knowing the secrets of a king than the secrets of a minister. Seeing then that God is the highest possible object of knowledge, the knowledge of Him must afford more delight than of any other.

But the delight of knowledge still falls short of the delight of vision, just as our pleasure in thinking of those we love is much less than the pleasure afforded by the actual sight of them. Our imprisonment in bodies of clay and water, and our entanglement in the things of the senses constitute a veil which hides the Vision of God from us, although it does not prevent our attaining to some knowledge of Him. For this reason, God is reported to have said to Moses on Mount Sinai: *"Thou shalt not see Me."* (that is, so long as Moses was imprisoned in his bodily form).

The truth of the matter is that, just as the seed of man becomes a man, and a buried date-stone becomes a palm-tree, so the knowledge of God acquired in this world will in the next world change into the vision of God, and he who has never learnt the knowledge will never have the vision. This vision will not be shared alike by all who know, but their discernment of it will vary with the extent of their knowledge. God is one, but He will be seen in many different ways, just as one object is reflected in different forms by different mirrors, some showing it straight and some distorted, some clearly and some dimly. A mirror may be so crooked as to make even a beautiful form appeared misshapen, and a man entering into the next world may have a heart so dark and distorted that the sight of it, which would be a source of peace and joy to others, would be to him a source of misery. He in whose heart the love of God has prevailed over all else will certainly derive more joy from this vision than he in whose heart it has not so prevailed. It is like two men with equally powerful eyesight, gazing on a beautiful face, He who already loves the possessor of the face will rejoice in beholding it more than he who does not. For perfect happiness, mere knowledge unaccompanied by love is not enough, and the love of God cannot take possession of a man's heart till it be purified of the love of the world, which purification can be effected only by abstinence, righteousness, austerity and obedience to the Law.

The Signs of the Love of God

Many claim to love God, but each should examine himself as to the genuineness of the love which he professes. The first test is this: He should not dislike the thought of death, for no lover shrinks from going to see his own beloved. The Holy Prophet said, *"Whoever wishes to see God, God wishes to see him."* It is true that a sincere lover of God may shrink from the thought of death coming before he has finished his preparation for the next world, but if he is really sincere, he will be diligent in making such preparation.

The second test of sincerity is that a man should be willing to sacrifice his will to God's, should cleave to what brings him nearer to God. The fact of a man's sinning is no proof that he does not love Him with his whole heart. A saint said to a certain man, "If anyone asks you whether you love God, keep silent, for if you say, `I do not love Him,' you are an infidel; and if you say, `I do,' your evil deeds contradict you."

A third test is that the remembrance of God should always remain fresh in a man's heart without effort; for what a man loves he constantly remembers, and if his love is perfect, he never forgets it. It is possible, however, that while the love of God does not take the first place in a man's heart, the love of the *love of God* may, for love is one thing and the love of the love is another.

A fourth test is that he will love all men who love God and who obey Him; if his love is really very strong, he will be merciful and kind to every human being without distinction, nay, love will embrace the whole creation, it being the direct work of his beloved. With regard to the unjust, the sinners, the unbelievers, who are nonetheless the of creation of God, the lover of Him will ever be anxious to see them turn righteous, just, obedient and faithful. Although he may dislike them, such dislike will not extend to their persons but will be directed towards their evil actions and irreligious deeds. Because among the tests of the love of God is that the lovers of God will love those who obey Him.

Now let us end our illustrations of the spiritual guide's views of the treasure of happiness by quoting the author's own saint guide:

"The next world is the world of spirit and of the manifestation of the beauty of God. Happy is that man who has aimed at and acquired affinity with it. All abstinence, devotions, worship and true knowledge have the acquisition of that affinity for their aim, and that affinity is love, while sins and lusts oppose that affinity." The Quran—the saints' main Scripture of God—says:

"Happy is he who has purified his soul; and miserable is he who has corrupted it." (91:9-10)

Those who are gifted with spiritual insight have really grasped this truth as a fact of experience, and not merely a traditional maxim. Their clear perception of it leads them to the conviction that he by whom it is revealed is a Prophet indeed, just as a man who has studied medicine knows when he is listening to a true physician. This is the kind of certainty which requires no support from miracles, such as the conversion of a rod into a snake, the credit of which may be shaken by apparently equally extraordinary miracles performed by magicians.

References

1.   Abu-Dawud: Standard Collection of Traditions.
2.   Al-Ashbah wan-Naza'ir: A Standard Work on Hanafi Theology.
3.   Al-Quran.
4.   Imam Isma'il Al-Ash'ari: *Al-Maqalatul-Islamiya*
5.   Al-Imam Ali: *Nahjul Blaghah*
6.   Al-Tabari's History, Vol. II.
7.   Shah Abdul Aziz : *Al-Ugalan-Nafia*
8.   Alfred Guillaume : *Tradition of Islam*
9.   *As-Sira Al-Halabiya* : A Standard Book on the Life of the Prophet.
10. Book of *Sahih Muslim*
11. Bosworth Smith: *Mohammed and Mohammedanism*
12. Bukhari : *Standard Collection of Traditions*
13. Muhammad Ibn Yusuf : *Commentary of Bahrul-Muhit*
14. Denison: *Emotion as the Basis of Civilisation*
15. Dr. Imam Abu-Hanif's School of Jurisprudence.
16. Dr. Klein's article on Jihad.
17. Draper's *History of the Intellectual Development of Europe*, Vol. II.
18. *Durratul-Mukhtar* Book.
19. *Encyclopoedia of Islam*, printed by E. Brill, Leyden.
20. *Fat-hul-Bayan fi Maqasidul-Quran*, by Ibn Ali Al-Bukhari.
21. *Golden Cleaning,Thoughts of General Gordon.*
22. Hamilton's *Hidaya*.
23. *History of the Khalifas*, by Al-Sayuti,

24. Holland's Jurisprudence.
25. Hughes' *Dictionary of Islam*.
26. Ibn Al-Gawzi's *Fat-hul-Mughith*.
27. Ibn Hisham's History.
28. *Irshadul Sari*, by Al-Khatibul-Qastallani.
29. *Jamieus-Saghir*, by Imam Al-Sayuti.
30. *Kashful-Asrar*, by Abdul-Aziz Al-Bukhari.
31. *Mitahus-Sa'ada*, by Maulana Ahmed ibn Mustafa.
32. Mishkatul-Masabih.
33. Muhammad Zaid's book on Jurisprudence.
34. Muir's *Caliphate*.
35. Mulla Ali Al-Qari' Mawdut Book.
36. *Muwatta*, a Standard Book on the Prophet's Traditions, by Imam Malik.
37. *Nuzhatul-Absar*, by Ibu Hajar.
38. *Outlines of Islamic Culture*, by A.M. Shushtery.
39. Palmer's Translation of the Quran.
40. Rev. Sell, *The Faith of Islam.*
41. Review of Religions, 19613.
42. Rodwell's Translation of the Quran.
43. *Sharful-Mawahib Al-Ladunniya*, by Al-Allama Al-Zurqani
44. Sir William Muir's *Life of Mahomet*.
45. St. John's Gospel.
46. St. Matthew's Gospel.
47. Stanley Lane Pool's Book on Islam.
48. *Tabaqatul-Qur'an*, by Ibn Sad.
49. *Tajul-Arus*, Arabic Lexicon, by Al-Husaini.
50. The Caliphate, by Sir. W. Muir.
51. *The Preachings of Islam*, by Sir Thomas Arnold.
52. *The Principles of the Mohammadan Jurisprudence*, by Maulana Abdul-Rasheed.
53. *The Religion of Islam*, by F.A. Klein.
54. *The Religion of Islam*, by Maulana Muhammad Ali.
55. Von Goethe's West Ostlicher Divan.
56. Wherry's Commentary on Islam.
57. *Zadul-M'ad*, by Ibn Al-Qayyim.

Endnotes

1. And saying, the time is fulfilled, and the Kingdom of God is at (ST.Mark, 1-15).
2. Golden Gleaning from the thoughts of General Gordon
3. St, Fohn, XXI-16.
4. One who calls to prayer.
5. Rak'a literally means a bending
6. "Family" also means those believers who are dutiful to God.
7. Imploring God for any help the worshipper is in need of will do.
8. A misqal is equivalent to 4.680 grammes.
9. A qirat equals one-sixteenth of a dirham or 0.195 grammes.
10. A qirat equals one—sixteenth of a dirham or 0.195 grammes.
11. Bounty here stands for trading. What is meant is that there is no harm in seeking an increase of wealth by trading in Makkah in the pilgrimage season. Before the advent of Islam, fairs were held for trading purposes in the pilgrimage season. The Muslims thought it a sin to take part in this, and they are told that trade was not forbidden to them even in these days.
12. In the days of ignorance, i.e. before the advent of Islam, the Arabs used to boast among themselves of the greatness of their fathers or forefathers after they had performed their pilgrimage. They were now bidden to laud God who would make them much greater than their forefathers.
13. But women must always keep their heads covered.
14. The eight day of the pilgrimage is so called because the pilgrims happen to give drinking water to their camels.

15. Vide introduction to Lane's Selections.
16. This exception refers to what had taken place in the time of ignorance previous to the revelation of the Quran.
17. Cp. Review of Religion, April 1913.
18. With Christians the case is different; Whosoever shall put away his wife, save for the cause of fornication, causes her to commit adultery; and whosoever shall marry her that is divorced commits adultery (Matt.V 32).
19. The law of England similarly vested in the husband the right of chastising his wife for levity of conduct (vide Holland's Jurisprudence, 240).
20. *The Review of Religions,* May 1913, states: Evidently J.S. Mill wrote this prior to the present Married Women's Property Act; but the same position of married women as illustrated by him is still prevalent to this day under the usage of the Catholic and other Christian churches.
21. *Al-Sirajiyah* by Sirajud-din Mohammad, based on the Traditions of the Prophet on the subject, as collected by Zaid ibn Thabit, one of the earliest companions.
22. Sahih Muslim, Chapter on Riba (Usury)
23. "Fatawa al-maghiri"
24. Vide Taj-el-Arus Lexicon.
25. Chastity, as a virtue, is not given the first place in modern civilized society, and hence, while fornication is not a criminal offence, even adultery is not considered sufficiently serious to subject the guilty party to any punishment except the payment of damages to the injured husband. This, indeed, is a very low view of sexual morality. Materialism has taken such a strong hold of the civilized mind that even chastity, the most precious jewel in a woman's crown of virtue, can be compensated by a few pounds. Hence Islamic Law seems to be too severe to an easy going Westerner. The breach of the greatest trust which can be imposed in a man or a woman, the breach which ruins families and destroys household peace, is not valued any higher than a few pounds.
26. This is an effectual restraint on slander and gossip, which so often bring disaster upon the heads of innocent women. Unless there is the clearest evidence of adultery against a woman— the evidence of four witnesses— the slanderer himself is to be punished.

27. The ordinance relates to the case of husbands who accuse their wives of adultery and have no evidence. In such a case divorce is effected, the husband not being punishable for the accusation, though he cannot produce witnesses, and the wife not being punishable for adultery, if he denies the charge in the manner stated.

28. *References:* Hidaya, Durrul-Mukhtar, the Fatawa-al-Maghiri, etc.,

29. The exception may apply to the five classes related. The meaning is that if an animal partly eaten by wild beasts is found still alive and is slaughtered in the proper manner, its flesh is allowed.

30. Vide Chapter on Marriage where it is stated that "marriage in Islam is but a 'civil contract.'"

31. There was a custom among some ignorant Bedouins that if children were not born to a man, his wife would secretly go to another man to get children. It was to extirpate this savage custom that the last clause of the above teaching was expressed.

32. According to Dr. Imam Hanifa School of Jurisprudence, if at that are maturityd of mind is not attained, the limit may be extended.

33. As Islam discouraged rigorous practices such as monastic life, it also prohibited asking questions relating to details on many points, which would make this or that practice obligatory, and such was left to individual will or circumstances of the time or place.

34. See chapter on *Jihad* in Religious Defensive Warfare.

35. If we seek God's help, we must first serve God's will *i.e.* dedicate ourselves entirely to Him and without reserve by obeying His ordinances and forbidding what He has declared forbidden.

36. The inspiration by God into the soul of "what is right and what is wrong" is meant that the Almighty God has gifted man with the faculty of distinguishing and the power of choosing between right and wrong; in other words. He pointed out to man the two conspicuous ways. Commentators explain the verse to mean that God has perfected man by making him understand and know both ways—the wrong and the right.

    It should be noted here that Rodwell and Palmer are wrong in translating the verse as meaning: and breathed into it (the soul) its wickedness and its piety (Palmer), for the statement in this form is not only contradicted by the whole of the Koran, but is also self-contradictory and meaningless, because the words would thus imply that when a man left evil and did good it was

God who taught in him to do so, and when a man left good and did evil it was again God who taught him to do so, which is manifestly absurd.

37. cf. Goethe's *West-Ostlicher Divan.* It is worthy of remark that these words of Goethe were placed by Dr. Rodwell by way of motto on the reverse of the title page of his translation of the Quran—*Author.*

38. *of.* on Goeth's West-Ostilicher Divan.

39. Hence the Holy Quran is also spoken of as *hadith* (18; 39; 23) The word *sunna* is used in the Holy Quran in a general sense, meaning a way or rule. Thus *Sunnat-al-Awwalin* (18; 38; 15; 13; 18; 55; 55; 43) means the way or example of the former generations and is frequently used in the Holy Quran as signifying God's way of dealing with people.This is also spoken of as *Sunnat-Allah.*

40. Bukhari reportson *hadith.*

41. *Ibid.*

42. Muir writes in his introduction to The Life of Mohammed : Scarcely was the Prophet buried when his followers resolved to adopt the custom (*sunna*) of Mohammed, that is his sayings and practices as supplementary to the Quran (page 29) And even a recent writer, Guillaume, writes in the *Tradition of Islam*: While, the Prophet was alive he was the sole guide in all matters whether spiritual or secular.The *Hadith or* tradition in the technical sense may be said to have begun at his death (p. 13).

43. It was in this safe custody (memory) that the beautiful poetry of the pre-Islamic days had been kept alive and intact.

44. A woman came to Abu-Bakr, the Khalifa, claiming her share of inheritance from her deceased grandson. The Khalifa said that he could not find either in the Book of God (the Quran) or the *Sunna* of the Prophet that she was entitled to any share. Thereupon, Al-Mughira ibn Shu'ba (a companion) got up to say that he had seen the Prophet granting a one-sixth share to a grandmother. The Khalifa asked for a second witness and Muhammad ibn Musallam supported Al-Mughira and, accordingly, judgment was delivered in favour of the woman. Again Fatima, the Prophet's daughter, claimed that she was entitled to an inheritance of the Holy Prophet. As against this Abu-Bakr cited a saying of the Prophet: *We prophets do not leave an inheritance; whatever we leave is a charity.* The truth of this *hadith*

was not questioned by any one, and Fatima's claim was, therefore, rejected. Such incidents happened daily and became the occasion for establishing, or otherwise, the truth of many sayings of the Holy Prophet.

45. Vide *Sunan of Abu Dawuda*, Book 24, Chapter 1.

46. Vide Bukhari, Book 3, Chapter 34.

47. *Vide Muir's Life of Mohammad*, p. 30. of which he says,it is "a collection of all traditions." Also vide *Fat-hul-Baris*, by Al-Hafiz Shahab-ud-Din Ahmad, Book I, p. 174, Cairo Press edition.

48. Cide "Traditions of Islam," by Alfred Cuillaume (Calendron Press, Oxford), 1942.

49. "Khariji" belongs to an old party of protest against the ascendancy of the Koraishites.

50. "Al-Ugalan-Nafi'a," by `Abdul-`Aziz.

51. Similar rules of criticism are laid down by Mulla 'Ali Al-Cari' in his work entitled *Mawdu'at"*, and by Ibn Al-Gawzi's "Fat-hul-Mughith", as well as by Ibn Hajar in his "Nuzhatul-Absar".

52. Vide: "Mishkat", Book 1. Chapter VI.

53. As regards the introduction of "from", the following gives an example: If *A* says that he had heard from *B* and *B* says he had heard from *C* and leaving out several names in the middle, says that *X* heard from the Prophet. There are, however, exceptions in a narration of this kind. If the narrator was a known companion of the Prophet, his narration, even if the chain was broken, had been accepted by some theologians.

54. Vide "An Essay on Muhammadan Tradition," by the honourable Syed Ahmed Khan of Bahadour. of Nukhbatul. Fagry," by Sheikh Shahab-ed-Din Ahmed.

55. of "Kashful-Asrar," by Abdul Aziz Al-Bukhari.

56. Koran II—171.

57. VII—179

58. VIII—22

59. XXV—44.

60. III—189, 190

61. Ibid IV—83

62. Wide "Tajul-Arabic Lexicon by Imam Murtada Hussaini

63. When asked by the Prophet how he would judge cases if he not find directions either in the Books of God or inthe Sunna, Mu'az who was to be appointed governor of Yemen, replied— to the

satisfaction and consent of the Prophet—"I would then exercises my own judgement."

64. Vide "Tarhul-Khaulfa (History of the Khalifas), by Imam Jalalud-Din Al-Sayuti, Chapter relating to Abu Bakr (see his knowledge).

65. For these conditions, vide pp. 178-179 of this work (author),

66. "Kashjul-Asrar" by Abdul-Aziz Al-Bukhari, Vol. 3

67. "Al Magalatul-Lstamiya," by Isma'il Al-Ashri.

68. "Al-Ashbah wan-Nazair, Book a standard of the Hanafi Theology.

69. Vide *Mishkatul-Masabih,* by Walyid-Din Muhammad ibn Abdulla.

70. Vide *ia mi-es Saghir,* by *Imam* Al-Hafiz Jalalud-Din Al-Sayuti, Cairo Edition.

71. *Kitabut-Tabagat-ek-Kobra,* by Muhammad ibn Sad.

72. References: *Fact-hul-Bayan* fi *Magasidul-Quran,* ibn Ali-Bukhari; *Fatawal-Mughiri; Al-Hidaya,* by Ali ibn Bakr Al-Marghani: *fighul-Akbar,* by Master *Imam* Abu-Hanifa; *Commentary of Bahrul-Muhit,* by Muhammad ibn Yusuf.

73. Vide Wherry's Commentary.

74. *Hidaya* Book of Traditions, Chapter on *Jihads.*

75. Vide *Authentic Collections of Traditions,* by Divine *Imams Al-Bukhari,* Muslim, etc., in Chapter on *Jihad.*

76. Dr. Klein's article on Jihad in the Review of the Religion of Islam.

77. *Draper's* "History of the Intellectual Development of Egypt," Vol. II.

78. Al-Sira Al-Halabiya, a standard book on "The life of the Holy Prophets; Ibn Hisham. Al-Tabari.

79. Vide Encycl. of Islam.

80. Muir's Caliphates, P. 142, The Precahing of Islam by Sir Thomas Arnol.

81. Vide Ibn Hisam History al-Tabari, etc.

82. of Ibn Hisham al-Tabari, etc

83. Vide *Sahih Al-Bukhari,* 40:7.

84. Ibn Jarir, Tabari's History III: op. 132, Cario Edition.

85. Ibn Jarir, Vol. 3, p. 66.

86. Musnad ibn Hanbal, I: 247, *Sharhul-Mmawahib, by Al-Zurgam,* Vol. I:534.

87. Al- Bukhari , 2-22

88. Al-Tabari History vol. 2-287

89. Imam Muslim collection of Hadith vol. 2:32

89. Saint Ali ibn Abu Talib fourth Khalifa and cousin and son-in-law to holy Prophet.

I'm learning about...
Eid-ul-Fitr

LIFE BEGINS
Quran Stories for Little Hearts
Goodword kids

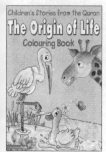

Children's Stories from the Quran
The Origin of Life
Colouring Book

Children's Stories from the Quran
Ark of Nuh and the Animals
COLOURING BOOK

Children's Stories from the Quran
The First Man on the Earth
COLOURING BOOK

Children's Stories from the Quran
The Two Sons of Adam
COLOURING BOOK

Children's Stories from the Quran
The Brave Boy
COLOURING BOOK

Children's Stories from the Quran
Tale of A Fish
COLORING BOOK

Children's Stories from the Quran
The Ant's Panic
COLORING BOOK

Children's Stories from the Quran
The Queen and the Bird
COLORING BOOK

Children's Stories from the Quran
Allah's Best Friend
COLOURING BOOK

Children's Stories from the Quran
The Story of the Prophet Ibrahim
COLOURING BOOK

HONEYBEES
THAT BUILD PERFECT COMBS
HARUN YAHYA

THE WORLD OF OUR LITTLE FRIENDS
THE ANTS
HARUN YAHYA

Printed in India

The Blessings of RAMADAN
Javed Ali

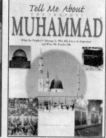

Tell Me About MUHAMMAD
What the Prophet's Message Is, Who His Life Is So Important and What He Teaches Me

Tell Me About MUSA

Tell Me About CREATION

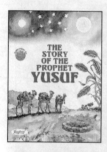

THE STORY OF THE PROPHET YUSUF

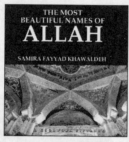

THE MOST BEAUTIFUL NAMES OF ALLAH
SAMIRA FAYYAD KHAWALDEH

The Travels of Ibn Battúta
H.A.R. GIBB

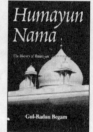

Humayun Nama
The History of Humayun
Gul-Badan Begam

THE STORY OF ISLAMIC SPAIN
SYED AZIZUR RAHMAN

ISLAM AT THE CROSSROADS
MUHAMMAD ASAD

DECISIVE MOMENTS IN THE HISTORY OF ISLAM
MUHAMMAD ABDULLAH ENAN

Islamic Medicine
EDWARD G. BROWNE

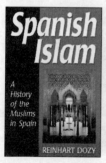

Spanish Islam
A History of the Muslims in Spain
REINHART DOZY

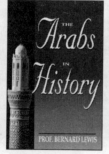

The Arabs in History
PROF. BERNARD LEWIS

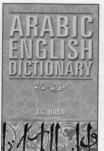

ARABIC ENGLISH DICTIONARY
J.G. HAVA

How Greek Science Passed to the Arabs
De Lacy O'Leary

Printed in India